THE LITERARY IN THEORY

Cultural Memory
in
the
Present

Mieke Bal and Hent de Vries, Editors

THE LITERARY IN THEORY

Jonathan Culler

STANFORD UNIVERSITY PRESS

STANFORD, CALIFORNIA

2007

Stanford University Press
Stanford, California

Printed in the United States of America on acid-free, archival-quality paper

Library of Congress Cataloging-in-Publication Data

Culler, Jonathan D.
    The literary in theory / Jonathan Culler.
        p.   cm.—(Cultural memory in the present)
    Includes bibliographical references and index.
    ISBN-10: 0-8047-5373-3 (cloth : alk. paper)
    ISBN-10: 0-8047-5374-1 (pbk. : alk. paper)
    ISBN-13: 978-0-8047-5373-9 (cloth : alk. paper)
    ISBN-13: 978-0-8047-5374-6 (pbk. : alk. paper)
        1. Literature—History and criticism—Theory, etc.   2. Criticism.
I. Title.

PN441.C85 2006
801'.95—dc22

                                                              2006017967

Contents

Acknowledgments

The arguments and analyses in this book have developed over a number of years. Most of these discussions began, as so often happens, in a lecture or in a conference presentation. Objections and responses prompted further thinking and reworking, as did the comments of journal editors and other readers. In the process I have incurred debts to far more people than I can thank. Let me express my gratitude here to Benedict Anderson, Mieke Bal, Simon Bouquet, Pheng Cheah, Jacques Courcil, Umberto Eco, Jonathan Monroe, James Phelan, and Harry Shaw, while acknowledging that the responses of many others unnamed have also been extremely valuable.

Mieke Bal has for some time urged me to write a book for the Stanford series Cultural Memory in the Present, which she and Hent de Vries edit. I am delighted finally to have done so, and I thank her for her comments on the manuscript, from which I have profited. I want also to thank those who have helped and advised me most recently, as I produced this volume. Kevin Lamb read a great deal of my writing and gave excellent advice about what to include and what to omit. Haun Saussy read and commented on the manuscript with the broad knowledge and acumen for which he is known. Katherine Sharpe provided invaluable assistance in preparing the manuscript for the publisher, Ezra Feldman helped with the proofs, and Cynthia Chase offered telling criticisms at various points in the process, not all of which I could satisfy but which have certainly led to improvements. I heartily thank all of these colleagues, as well as earlier readers and listeners who remain unnamed.

THE LITERARY IN THEORY

Introduction

Theory is dead, we are told. In recent years newspapers and magazines seem to have delighted in announcing the death of theory, and academic publications have joined the chorus. Articles on "the end of high theory" and books with titles such as *After Theory, Life After Theory, What's Left of Theory,* and *Reading After Theory* are endemic, with only the occasional optimistic title: *The Future of Theory* or *Theory Matters.* Declarations of the death of theory have long been attempts by opponents to bring about, performatively, the demise they purport to describe, but such titles do not come only from opponents of theory. Since the activities that have come to answer to the nickname *theory* are no longer the latest thing in the humanities, theorists themselves, not wanting to be left behind defending something thought to belong to the past, have been swift to write about theory after theory, post-theory, and so on. This American penchant— "Everything's up to date in Kansas City"—marked even the heyday of so-called high theory, when no sooner had the arrival of structuralism been noted by American scholars than theorists who had been major representatives of structuralism—Barthes, Lacan, Foucault—were deemed *post*structuralists so that they could represent something newer still.[1]

1. Of course, this renaming also had a good deal to do with the fact that the most visible early event in the introduction of these structuralist thinkers to the United States, the 1966 conference at Johns Hopkins, "The Languages of Criticism and the Sciences of Man," ended up featuring the critique of Lévi-Strauss's conception of structure by the previously unknown Jacques Derrida. Lévi-Strauss, therefore, did not make it into poststructuralism, but Barthes and Lacan (both present at that conference) certainly did.

But anyone who has served on an appointments committee in a literature department recently has confronted all too palpable evidence that theory is not dead. In the very tight academic job market, where any opening can attract hundreds of applications, one can survey the state of literary studies simply by reading through the applications, and the conclusion is inescapable: theory is everywhere. Even fields previously immune or resistant, such as Chinese studies or medieval studies, today produce candidates with great theoretical sophistication—acquainted with a wide range of theoretical discourses and, more important, a penchant for posing questions that these theoretical discourses have helped them formulate, about relations between literature and popular culture, literature and politics, literature and forces of globalization, and so on. Texts are read intensively, with theoretical issues in mind, and symptomatically, in work in cultural studies that explores how they fit into various discursive practices of identity formation or the production of sexuality, the projection of imagined communities, the resistance to globalization, or the dialectics of subversion and containment.

So it is not, I would stress, just that references to figures recognized as theorists—Butler, Derrida, Foucault, Jameson, Lacan, Spivak, Zizek—pop up in dissertations and writing samples. The way questions in dissertation or postdissertation projects are framed is generated or inflected by theoretical investigations, speculations, argument. In that sense literary and cultural studies are very much *in theory* these days, even if theory itself is not seen as the cutting edge, as we used to say, of literary and cultural studies. If theory is not so prominent as a vanguard movement, a set of texts or discourses that challenge insiders and outsiders, it is perhaps because literary and cultural studies take place within a space articulated by theory, or theories, theoretical discourses, theoretical debates.

This is true not only of English, French, German, and literature but also of areas of literary study that had hitherto remained relatively untouched by theoretical discourses and of fields that have themselves frequently been most hostile to so-called high theory, such as cultural studies (as I discuss later in this volume) or the study of American literature, which now finds itself increasingly transformed into the study of the literatures of America, or the Americas, stimulated by theoretical discourses of hybridity, multiculturalism, and subalternity. And publishers display their conviction that theory is a live market by preferring to publish introductions to theory or anthologies of theory rather than critical monographs. Despite its alleged demise, writes Jean-Michel Rabaté, "theory never stops coming back, which is confirmed by the huge numbers of anthologies, guides, companions, and new introductions. If Theory is reduced to the ghost of itself, then this is a very obtrusive ghost that keeps walking and shaking its chains in our old academic castles."[2]

But rather than Theory as a persistent ghost in the castle, I prefer the less dramatic figure of theory as a discursive space within which literary and cultural studies now occur, even if we manage to forget it, as we forget the air we breathe. We are ineluctably in theory. And if things were to change radically in literary and cultural studies, it would not be because we had left theory behind but because theoretical arguments had persuaded us that literary and cultural studies should henceforth proceed, for instance, as a branch of cognitive psychology, or of historical studies in some new, more generous, configuration, or as a version of artistic practice itself.

Although these days books about theory manage to avoid defining it, on the doubtless correct assumption that people interested in a book on theory already have an idea about what it is, it is worth briefly addressing the question, if only because a lack of definition has permitted attacks on theory to define the object for themselves. In "Against Theory" Steven Knapp and Walter Benn Michaels treat theory as a set of axioms supposed to control interpretative practice through a general account of interpretation. This would exclude from the realm of theory almost every work, from Agamben to Zizek, usually taken to belong to it. But it is this definition that enables Knapp and Michaels to argue that theory should just cease because it has no useful work to do, no effects.[3]

One might argue that, on the contrary, theory consists precisely of those discourses that do have effects on literary and cultural studies. In the past I have defined *theory* as work that succeeds in challenging and reorienting thinking in fields other than those in which it originates.[4] We use

2. Jean-Michel Rabaté, *The Future of Theory* (Oxford, UK: Blackwell, 2002), 10.

3. For discussion see Chapter 3.

4. See Jonathan Culler, *On Deconstruction* (Ithaca, NY: Cornell University Press, 1982), 8–10. See also "What Is Theory?" in Jonathan Culler, *Literary Theory: A Very Short Introduction* (Oxford: Oxford University Press, 1997), 1–17.

the term *theory* to designate discourses that come to exercise influence outside their apparent disciplinary realm because they offer new and persuasive characterizations of problems or phenomena of general interest: language, consciousness, meaning, nature and culture, the functioning of the
psyche, the relations of individual experience to larger structures, and so
on. Theory in this sense is inescapably interdisciplinary: works of philosophy, linguistics, anthropology, political or social theory, history, psychoanalysis, gender studies, film theory, and so on are taken up by people in
literary and cultural studies because their accounts of matters relevant to
the functioning of texts have made strange the familiar and enabled people
to conceive the matters with which they are dealing in new ways.[5] Works
of theory characteristically function not as demonstration but as speculation—ideas whose range of applicability is not known in advance. Theory
is analytical, speculative, reflexive, interdisciplinary, and a counter to com-
monsense views. And this interdisciplinary character of theory helps to explain why "literary theory"—in the sense of analyses of the nature of literature or the functioning of particular literary modes or genres—has played a
less prominent role in "theory" in literary studies recently than one would
have been led to expect. Insofar as the theory of literature functions resolutely within the discipline of literary studies, it has not seemed really to *be*
theory and so has been relatively neglected by theorists. What we call *theory* for short is manifestly not theory of literature, despite the fact that *theory*
has served as the nickname for "literary and cultural theory."

One of the complaints against theory, in fact, has been that it takes
students away from literature and literary values. Since time is always limited, and those reading Foucault, Derrida, Lacan, and Butler have less time
to read Ashbery and Zukovsky, not to mention Dickens and Thackeray,
there is some justice to the complaint; but of course most schools of criticism have recommended immersion in various sorts of nonliterary materials, from philological language study to biographies and works of history.
If Americanists are reading Foucault rather than Puritan sermons, it is not
that they have less time to devote to literature—Americanists used to be
compelled to read vast amounts of "background" material. The complaint

5. For a lively account of the interdisciplinarity of theory in the humanities see Mieke Bal, *Traveling Concepts in the Humanities: A Rough Guide* (Toronto:
University of Toronto Press, 2002).

derives, rather, from the sense that since theory consists primarily of works originating in other, nonliterary areas of endeavor, whether philosophy, linguistics, psychoanalysis, or intellectual history, theory must therefore inculcate nonliterary values.

The essays collected here contest that view, arguing that the apparent eclipse of the literary is something of an illusion. Wherever the discourses of theory originate, they generally work to alert us to versions of literariness at work in discourses of all sorts and thus reaffirm, in their way, the centrality of the literary. It is true, however, that work on language, desire, power, the body, and so on has led to a neglect of theoretical issues that are particular to literature and the system of the literary. I myself contributed to the neglect of the literary in the article "Literary Theory," for the second edition of the MLA's *Introduction to Scholarship in Modern Languages and Literatures* in 1992.[6] Busy talking about race and gender, identity and agency, distracted by the notoriety of Knapp and Michaels's now largely forgotten antitheory theory, I inadvertently forgot the theory of literature. I think it is essential not to forget it: narrative theory, for example, is crucial for the analysis of texts of all sorts. These days, beginning graduate students often have little acquaintance with basic narratology (they have read Foucault but not Barthes or Genette, much less Wayne Booth). They may not know about identifying narrative point of view or the analysis of implied readers or narratees, despite the centrality of such matters to questions that *do* urgently concern them, such as the analysis of what is taken for granted by a text.[7]

Exploring the role of the literary in theory, I seek to rectify this neglect by bringing theory *to* literature and bringing out the literary in theory—not keeping literature and theory safe from each other.

The eclipse of literature in theory is a very recent phenomenon. In the early days of "theory" the term meant, above all, theory of literature.

6. Jonathan Culler, "Literary Theory," in *Introduction to Scholarship in Modern Languages and Literatures*, ed. Joseph Gibaldi, 2nd ed. (New York: Modern Language Association, 1992), 201–35.

7. Trying to make good my omission of the theory of literature from my MLA account of literary theory, I wrote *Literary Theory: A Very Short Introduction*, which leaves out Knapp and Michaels and puts in not just "what is literature?" but also discussion of narrative and of poetry and poetics. I am eager to help keep the literary in theory.

For the Russian Formalists and some of their successors, the French structuralists, the "literariness" of literature was the object of analysis: what makes discourses literary? how do they function? As one who came to theory in the 1960s, when I undertook a doctoral dissertation on the use of linguistic models in literary studies, I took for granted the centrality of literary theory, even as I followed the exploration of literariness in many other sorts of discourses, from history writing and psychoanalytic case histories to myths and advertising. In *Structuralist Poetics* (which grew out of that doctoral dissertation) I focus on work by French structuralists, particularly Roland Barthes, Gérard Genette, and Tzvetan Todorov, but also draw on articles by Russian Formalists, especially Roman Jakobson and Victor Shklovsky, as well as other members of the Leningrad Opojaz school, Boris Eichenbaum, and Juri Tynianov. Although in retrospect it seems odd to have mingled Russian Formalists with French structuralists, clearly I was treating them as participating in the same enterprise. The immediate impetus came from the fact that although French structuralists had produced a certain number of literary analyses, they had not, with the exceptions of the very systematic work in narratology by Genette and the somewhat fragmentary and self-undermining analyses and indications of Barthes, offered efficient and accessible analyses of aspects of the system of literature, and if one wanted a salient illustration of the functioning of literary devices and techniques, one might find it more easily in the works of Shklovsky or even in suggestive remarks by Jakobson.

What was the common enterprise to which I took the structuralists and Formalists to be contributing? Or, what is the form of the formalism that I took to be at work here, animating two historically diverse intellectual conjunctures? Put simply, it was the development of a systematic poetics. In opposition to the "life and works" approach, which sought to situate literary or cultural objects in the biographically defined experience of a historical author, the formalism of poetics presumed the primacy of a system of conventions that made possible literary production. While literary study might take as its goal the elucidation of individual literary works, or the interpretation of works as products of a historical or biographical situation, the claim of formalism was that forms are neither ornaments to be admired for their embellishment of a thematic content nor the expression of a content that is the burden of the work and whose elucidation is the goal of critical activity but that, on the contrary, the forms are themselves the central elements of the work, and the understanding of form is a condition of other possible critical and historical projects. The work of art is above all a combination of devices or formal structures that defamiliarize and deploy a logic of artistic convention against that of empirical experience or historiography.

This orientation comes out nicely in the slogans of the Russian Formalists' more pugnacious moments: that the device is the true hero of the work, for instance; that theme exists in order to allow the work to come into being; or that form creates for itself its own content. One could also say that at the level of the biographical experience of literary production the formalist orientation is eminently defensible: the poet characteristically is seeking not to represent something but to write a sonnet or an ode or an epic, or to experiment with diction, or to give free rein to a certain rhythm that has been haunting him or her. Very often, it is, shall we say, the form that inspires literary desire. In this sense the Formalists did not cut themselves off from the practice of poets and novelists but, as Jakobson insisted, pursued a line of inquiry that is often consonant with reflections of poets themselves.

The Russian Formalists had special importance in this general project of developing a poetics that would provide the conditions of possibility for literary works because they were more attuned to the idea of a literary system. French structuralists, taking structural linguistics as a model for their enterprise, were often less alert to what I took to be the logic of their enterprise; they often inclined, for instance, to treat the individual work itself, or the corpus of an author's works, as the system to be elucidated. This is frequently the case with Barthes, for example, whose *Sur Racine* undertakes a structural analysis of what he calls the Racinian universe. His *Sade, Fourier, Loyola* also takes each of these writers as the producer of a system, which can be analyzed as a language: they are logothètes, inventers of languages, combinatory systems.

In *Structuralist Poetics* I distinguish between the direct application of linguistic categories to the language of literary works, as in Jakobson's poetics analyses or in A. J. Greimas's attempts at describing the semantic structure of literary works or literary universes, and the indirect application of linguistic terminology, but within this second mode there is a range of possibilities: in addition to poetics, for instance, there is the attempt to treat the author's oeuvre as a system to be elucidated through the deployment of categories or methodological steps derived from linguistics. This orientation—which, strangely, often rejoins thematic criticism of various sorts, including the phenomenological criticism of the Geneva School (what are the elements of the author's fictional world? how do they combine?)—seems to me often to miss the fundamental insight of the Russian Formalists, which I take to be also at work in the most perspicacious moments of French structuralism: that the literary work is dependent for its meaning and effects on a system of possibilities, which need to be described. There are, to be sure, moments when Russian Formalists describe the work of art itself as a system (I take this to be above all the result of the focus on the device, the desire to conceive of the work as mechanism rather than as mimesis or means of expression), but Tynianov, for instance, declares, "Before embarking on any study of literature it is necessary to establish that the literary work constitutes one system and literature itself another, unrelated one. This convention is the only foundation upon which we can build a literary science which is capable of going beyond unsatisfactory collection of heterogeneous material and submitting them to proper study."[8] This splendid, paradoxical insight insists that we have two levels of systematicity: on the one hand, the individual work can be treated as a system and the function of various elements within this system analyzed; but this is not sufficient, for unrelated to the work of art as autotelic whole there is, on the other hand, the system of literary possibilities, which is quite a different matter. Proper literary study involves this second level of systematicity, poetics.

In this powerful essay on literary evolution Tynianov appeals to a linguistic example (the way the function of an element changes) and articulates principles that resemble those of the linguistic model that would later come into prominence: the point of view adopted determines the nature of the object; the function of an element depends on the system to which it belongs; it is wrong to imagine that an element in one system is the same as an element in another. Thus, a rhythm that is new and startling in the literary system of one era will be banal, even nonpoetic, in another.[9]

8. Juri Tynianov, "De l'évolution littéraire," in *Théorie de la littérature*, ed. Tzvetan Todorov (Paris: Seuil, 1965), 122–23.

9. Ibid., 125–26.

The linguistic model offers great methodological clarity here. It teaches that where there is meaning there is system and that just as the utterances of a speaker are made possible by the rules of a language (grammatical, phonological, semantic, and pragmatic), which enable listeners in turn to make sense of them, so literary works are made possible by a system of conventions and expectations, the analysis of which is crucial to an understanding of their functioning. The task of the linguist is to make explicit the grammar that makes possible the production and comprehension of utterances, and the task of the formalist critic or poetician is to try to make explicit the conventions of the literary system that make possible the production and interpretation of literary works. But, ironically, the French structuralists, who were much given to proclaiming the crucial role of linguistics as the pilot discipline for the human sciences, may have been misled by the hope that linguistics, with its terms and categories, would provide a discovery procedure for literary structure; and they often missed the true relevance of the linguistic model (linguistics is to language as poetics is to literature). The Russian Formalists, however, precisely because they were not thinking about taking the linguistics of their day as a methodological model but only hoped to use some of its insights in advancing their own goals, were able to keep in view a clearer sense of the goal of the kind of formal analysis that they were practicing: analyzing the system that makes possible literary events, the "grammar" that governs the production of literary works.[10]

The term *formalism* has become something of a pejorative epithet in our era of historicisms, but formalism does not involve a denial of history, as is sometimes claimed. What it rejects is historical interpretation that makes the work a symptom, whose causes are to be found in historical reality. The Saussurean model can clarify this issue: it is precisely because lan-

10. No doubt I am reading the Russian Formalists selectively and attributing a centrality to the project that I find best expressed, for example, in works such as Tynianov's "De l'évolution littéraire" and Victor Shklovsky's *Theory of Prose* (Elmwood Park, IL: Dalkey Archive Press, 1990). It is also the logic of this project, I would claim, that has determined the historical legacy of Russian Formalism, for instance, in its most important modern incarnation, the Tel Aviv School of Poetics, founded by Benjamin Hrushovski, which has formed several generations of students in the projects of poetics, which persists actively in the journal *Poetics Today*.

guage is historical through and through, always changing, that the distinction between synchronic and diachronic analysis is necessary, that we must relate any linguistic event to the synchronic system from which it emerges. If language were not so radically historical, we would have less need of the distinction. But what might appear to be a particular form or even sign is not the same in two different stages of the language, because what it is depends on what surrounds it.

In the poetics promoted by the Russian Formalists the historical character of the literary system is emphasized, for that is the basis of the dialectic of defamiliarization and automatization: what has become automatic or familiar is defamiliarized by art. Shklovsky writes,

As a general rule I would like to add: a work of art is perceived against a background of, and by means of association with, other works of art. The form of a work of art is determined by the relation to other forms existing before it. The material of a work of art is definitely played with a pedal, i.e. is separated out, voiced. Not only a parody, but also in general any work of art is created as a parallel and a contradiction to some kind of model. A new form appears not in order to express a new content, but in order to replace an old form, which has already lost its artistic value.[11]

Formalism posits a study of literature that focuses on an underlying system always in evolution, since the mechanism of evolution is the functioning of literary works themselves. Today, when we are surrounded by historicisms of all kinds, we could do worse than to insist on the necessity of formalism for understanding the historicity of semiotic systems.

This version of literary theory, poetics, is considerably more difficult than theoretically inflected interpretation, and it therefore is continually being evaded or avoided, especially since poetics is always vulnerable to accusations of trying to systematize an object or practice, literature, that is valued for escaping or evading system. One could say that literary studies in the American academy, precisely because of its commitment to the priority of interpretation as the goal of literary study, was swift to posit a "poststructuralism" based on the impossibility or inappropriateness of the

11. Victor Shklovsky, "The Connection Between Devices of *Sjuzet* Construction and General Stylistic Devices," *Twentieth Century Studies* 7–8 (1972): 53.

systematic projects of structuralism, so that interpretation, albeit of different kinds, might remain the task of literary studies. Not only has the excitement of theory seemed to lie in its interdisciplinarity, which has led to the neglect of, say, theories of genres, of the novel, of the lyric, or of rhythm, but a belief that the systematizing ambitions of structuralism are passé has encouraged theory to focus on broad but unsystematizable issues of language, identity, the body, hybridity, desire, and power rather than on specific literary modes. We are rich in theories about language, discourse, hybridity, identity, sexuality but not in theories of the rules and conventions of particular genres, though such theories are necessary for understanding the ways individual works subvert these conventions—which, after all, is a major point of interest for interpretation. One problem of postcolonial studies, for instance, which otherwise is thriving, is the absence of good accounts of the literary norms against which postcolonial authors are said to be writing. Lacking descriptions of such norms, the discourse of critics either swiftly becomes thematic, focusing on questions of identity and resistance to authority, rather than on artistic innovation; or else it takes theoretical arguments themselves as the norms, so that the literary works are used to challenge Homi Bhabha's account of hybridity or colonial mimicry or the appropriateness of Gayatri Spivak's question, "Can the subaltern speak?" for the case under discussion. These are interesting and productive uses of literature, but one wonders whether a more robust poetics would enable different approaches to the literary works, which might, for instance, explore how the conventions or formal conditions of literary works, rather than their themes, make possible certain kinds of critical engagements with institutions of power.

But if the formalism of the Russian Formalists and French structuralists leads logically to a poetics, this project is not without its difficulties. One of the critics and theorists most likely today to be accused of formalism, Paul de Man, writes,

Literary theory comes into being when the approach to literary texts is no longer based on non-linguistic, that is to say historical and aesthetic considerations, or, to put it somewhat less crudely, when the object of discussion is no longer the meaning or the value but the modalities of production and reception of meaning and value prior to their establishment, the implication being that this establishment is problematic enough to require an autonomous discipline of critical investigation to consider its possibility and its status.[12]

But de Man identifies theory not with the projects of a systematic poetics but with what he calls reading, a hermeneutics attentive to the ways in which the rhetorical structures of the text resist proposed interpretations, and he can be aligned with a resistance to poetics, albeit in a particularly sophisticated mode. In "The Resistance to Theory" and "Semiology and Rhetoric" de Man is critical of the attempt to extend grammatical models beyond the sentence, as in projects that take linguistics as a model for poetics. To attempt to formulate rules and conventions on which literary meaning depends involves for him an obscuring of the rhetorical dimensions of texts, which require interpretation, not decoding by grammarlike models. "The extension of grammar to include para-figural dimensions is in fact the most debatable strategy of contemporary semiology, especially in the study of syntagmatic and narrative structures" (*RT*, 15). The attempt to translate often undecidable rhetorical structures into rules and conventions modeled on grammars is, in de Man's account, a resistance to reading.

In an essay for the *Times Literary Supplement* in 1982 entitled "The Return to Philology," responding to Harvard professor Walter Jackson Bate's call for university administrators and trustees everywhere to stop the destruction of literary studies by denying tenure to dangerous theorists, de Man wrote, "In practice, the turn to theory occurred as a return to philology, to an examination of the structure of language prior to the meaning it produces" (*RT*, 24). De Man traced his own exposure to the subversive force of literary instruction to a course in close reading taught by Bate's Harvard colleague and rival, Reuben Brower. This course, Hum 6, "The Interpretation of Literature," was based not on French theory but on the principle that what counts are "the words on the page": in writing about literature "students were not to make any statements that they could not support by a specific use of language that actually occurred in the text" (*RT*, 23). They were asked to attend to the bafflement that singular turns of phrase and figure produce and to worry their puzzlement rather than, as de Man puts it, "hide their non-understanding behind a screen of received

---

12. Paul de Man, *The Resistance to Theory* (Minneapolis: University of Minnesota Press, 1986), 7; hereafter abbreviated *RT* and cited parenthetically in the text.

ideas" by moving from the language of the text into the realm of history and human experience. "Mere reading," he concludes, "prior to any theory, is able to transform critical discourse in a manner that would appear deeply subversive to those who think of the teaching of literature as a substitute for the teaching of theology, ethics, psychology, or intellectual history" (*RT*, 24).

The impact of this pedagogical practice, de Man argues, was not so different from the impact of recent theory, since both involve the "examination of the structure of language prior to the meaning it produces" (*RT*, 24). At the time, in 1982, this idea of a return to philology seemed a joke. Philologists, after all, were the enemy, the ones who sneered not just at theory but even at interpretation of texts and who wanted students to abandon such matters for required courses in Anglo-Saxon and Old French. De Man's move seemed above all a clever way of turning the tables on Bate: insinuating that the enemy on whom Bate had declared all-out war would prove to be not Jacques Derrida and hordes of Yale deconstructionists spouting foreign theory but a sober Harvard professor, his longtime departmental rival, Reuben Brower.

De Man's late writings, which characterize theory as a resistance to reading and thus a resistance to theory, make such talk of a return to philology something to take more seriously, but de Man's formulation, "mere reading, prior to any theory," should put us on the alert. Insofar as it appears to suggest that there is critical reading unformed by theory, it is belied both by the history of modern reading and by the experience of de Man's own students, who struggled mightily to learn to do something that would indeed qualify as "reading" in his eyes and their own. It did not come naturally, as they could unanimously attest. Reading, in de Man's sense, is not something simple or natural but a strategy informed by considerable knowledge—knowledge about, among other things, the structure and functioning of rhetorical tropes and figures, the intertextual nature of literary discourse, the autonomy of language and its relations to the speaking subject, and the dangers that aesthetic, ethical, and historical views of literature can pose for reading. I discuss de Man's account of reading and of the resistance to theory in Chapter 3.

This book is not a survey or history of theory, though some chapters do contain discussions of the historical vicissitudes of particular concepts or problems. It aims, above all, to articulate the role of the literary in theory and to advance our understanding of the literary through some work in theory, on a range of theoretical concepts. The opening chapters engage the issues I have been discussing: the place of the literary in theory and various forms of resistance to theory, including the resistance of theory itself. Chapter 2, seeking to foreground the role of the literary in theory, takes up Benedict Anderson's celebrated discussion of the nation as an imagined community made possible by novelistic narration and print capitalism, generally, and explores what claims, precisely, are being made for the novel here and how these claims relate to the narrative techniques of novels. Details of narrative technique turn out to be quite important for the postulation of the imagined communities, which are related to the narratees, or narrative audiences implied by novels.

In the past two decades theory has involved the importation and the development within literary and cultural studies of theoretical discourses that do not take literature as their object, but there is evidence of a new centrality of the literary, both in a return to questions of aesthetics, which for a time were regarded as retrograde and elitist, and in the use of literary works to advance and to question theoretical assumptions, as in the work of Derrida on writers such as Celan and the work on poetry of philosophers in whom a new generation is taking an interest, such as Giorgio Agamben. There are also signs of a new theoretical interest in the lyric, but that is the topic of another book.[13] Whether this intensification of interest in the literary will lead to a revival of literary theories of what one might call the middle range—the poetics of particular genres or accounts of concepts of special literary import—it is too early to say, but the second and third sections of this book attempt some steps in that direction, seeking to elucidate a series of theoretical concepts of considerable literary significance and then focusing on philosophy and criticism as writing practices whose conventions we ought to seek to understand.

Text, sign, interpretation, performativity, and *omniscience* are the topics of the following section—a diverse set of concepts with a rich history in theory. The rise of theory itself is associated with the expansion of the concept of text. If for theory everything is a text, what advantages does the concept offer, and what are the variations that it undergoes in mod-

13. See my "Theorizing Lyric," a work in progress.

ern theoretical discourses? *Text* is a notion that arises in literary studies but has proven to be an instrument of considerable power in interdisciplinary studies (anthropology and film theory are two fields where its success was far from obvious), and it has been crucial for cultural studies, linking it to the literary in ways that have often been obscured by an anticanonical rhetoric.

The concept of the arbitrary nature of the sign is another fundamental element of the discursive space of theory. The first principle of Saussurean linguistics, it is foundational for theory, if anything is, linked to the linguistic turn of disciplines of the so-called human sciences, *les sciences humaines*. Saussure's *Course in General Linguistics* calls the arbitrary nature of the sign a principle with "innumerable" consequences, even though all of them are not immediately evident. Among these consequences, fundamental for theory is the idea that language is not a nomenclature: it articulates the world rather than simply representing what is already given; discursive systems and practices produce what they purport to regulate or represent. Another consequence is the conception of theory as demystification, exposure of the arbitrariness or cultural constructedness of forms and structures taken as natural—an idea that does indeed seem to follow from the principle of the arbitrariness of the sign. Fundamental also to the theoretical enterprise of recent years has been Derrida's critique of Saussure, the analysis of Saussure and his theory of the sign as complicitous with logocentrism. This analysis is frequently regarded as one of the pivots that separates structuralism from poststructuralism, separates a Saussurean program of systematic allure from the critique of its possibility. Revisiting this encounter, and drawing on the students' notes used in constructing the *Course*, I find that there is not such a radical difference between Derrida and Saussure, after all. Above all, though, I argue that Saussure's account of the arbitrary nature of the sign needs to be linked to his claim—never previously given its due—that the linguistic system should be analyzed as a *limitation* of arbitrariness. If this claim were taken seriously, what sorts of consequences would it have for the semiology or cultural studies that derives from a determination to explore the arbitrariness of cultural signs?

The performative is a concept that has been extremely important in recent theory, beginning in Austin's speech act theory, articulated anew by Derrida, migrating to literary studies but linking the literary and the political in Derrida and de Man, and providing the basis for rethinking sexuality and identity categories in Judith Butler. Discussion of the fortunes of the performative explores not just the major differences between Austin's and Butler's versions and uses of the concept but also the impact of the implicit reference to theatrical performance. The performative, partly because of the complexity its history gives it, poses important questions for theory and to theory today. Further elaboration of aspects of performativity is likely to be a very active strain of the literary in theory.

The topic of the next chapter, on the other hand, seems wholly traditional—not the cutting edge of theory at all. Chapter 7 takes up in a new context the question of interpretation, which so far in this book has been opposed to poetics. Invited to respond to three lectures by Umberto Eco on the topic of interpretation and overinterpretation, I accepted the task that was obviously expected of me as an expounder of deconstruction: to defend what Eco called "overinterpretation."

Now Eco's is a very interesting case, for this early champion of semiotics, holder of "the first chair of semiotics," as we used to say, not knowing that it might also be one of the last, was strongly committed, as a semiotician, to the elaboration of models of sign systems and to the theorization of the functioning of literature—thus to poetics rather than hermeneutics. His early *L'Opera aperta*, articulating a distinction between open works (which solicit the collaboration of the reader) and closed works (which are more univocal), contributed to such a poetics, and one would expect him to be interested in the structure of interpretive systems rather than in correct interpretation. What should one make, then, of Eco's lectures, which develop a contrast between good and bad interpretation? In fact, he seems more engaged by interpretive practices of "overinterpretation" than by sound, moderate interpretation. And his own celebrated novels, especially *The Name of the Rose* and *Foucault's Pendulum*, show great fascination in chronicling the aberrant, obsessional, passion-driven interpretation of his characters and compel readers to take such an interest. This discrepancy between what Eco preaches and what he practices may carry a lesson about interpretation in general.

Chapter 8 is no doubt the purest venture into literary theory and poetics proper in this book: returning to narratology, once a very active structuralist enterprise, I take up a prenarratological category that has generally escaped scrutiny by narratologists and other analysts of fiction, that of "omniscient" narration. The notion comes, of course, from a comparison of the novelist with God: the novelist stands to his or her work as God does to his creation. It is odd that such a blatantly theological notion should persist in discussions of fiction, despite the so-called hermeneutics of suspicion and critique of ideology that supposedly reigns in literary and cultural studies; odder still that it has scarcely been subjected to critical scrutiny. I argue that "omniscience" is not a useful notion, that it lumps together a number of different effects or strategies, which ought to be discriminated for the better analysis of narrative techniques, and that to make progress here we need to dispense with a concept of omniscience that has in fact misled critics and made certain sorts of novels seem ideologically suspect.

The next section continues the work of poetics but in a different mode. Though theory has contested the presumed priority of speech over writing and argued for the pertinence of writing as a model for signification in general, and though it has been resolutely self-reflexive, interrogating the status of theory, its history, its interests, still, theory has not often explicitly posed the question of its own nature as a practice of writing with its own conventions. Chapter 9 looks at philosophy as a kind of writing, addressing the charge of bad writing often leveled at theorists. Examining the case of Stanley Cavell, a notoriously difficult writer, I attempt to understand the purposes, the strategies, of difficult writing of this kind. Does its provocation of the reader work to philosophical ends, and, if so, how? Seeking to avoid the facile answer that difficult problems require difficult writing, I attempt to understand its functioning.

Chapter 10 takes up this sort of issue in broader terms, sketching the history of criticism over the last fifty years or so as a history of writing practices or discursive strategies, looking at some of the varying assumptions on which critical writing relies and the way in which its goals are manifested in writing techniques.

The last two chapters discuss more institutional questions in the realm of theory. First, there is the issue, inseparable from the contemporary fate of theory, of the nature of cultural studies. Might cultural studies be, in principle, the practice of which what we call "theory" is the theory? I argue that the opposition between cultural studies and literary studies, which has been a major cause of the sense that the literary has been abandoned or neglected by theory and theorists, is based on a dubious though understandable polemic that neglects the literary dimensions of many of cultural studies' most potent concepts. Although some practitioners have sought to introduce the term *cultural analysis* for a cultural studies that would not set itself against literary studies or against analysis of texts and culture of the past, I believe that it is better to retain the name and to recall cultural studies to its underlying literariness, as a space where such concepts as text, sign, and performativity, for instance, can be intensively and productively pursued.

Finally, I turn to the situation of comparative literature, which in the 1960s and 1970s took on an important identity as the home of theory (the conduit for the importation of foreign theory) but which—with the broad dissemination of theory and national literature departments' abandonment of the commitment to the historical study of a national literature—has lost much of its distinctiveness and some of its rationale. At a time when, with the spread of theory, English, French, and even German departments pursue postcolonial theory and cultural studies, teach courses on psychoanalysis and philosophy, when the high and the low, the verbal and the visual, the fictional and the nonfictional are everywhere compared, is this the triumph of comparative literature or its eclipse?

In fact, the chapters in this book seem to identify a common structure in the fate of theory, of literature, and of comparative literature. In each case we find a dissemination that leads to the loss of much of the distinctiveness and salience of the original object. Theory is no longer something distinct and alien that some scholars promote or practice and others combat: it is everywhere, but, no longer seen as new and distinctive, it can be denounced as dead or passé. Literature, as I argue in "The Literary in Theory," has become less a distinct object, fixed in a canon, than a property of discourse of diverse sorts, whose literariness—its narrative, rhetorical, performative qualities—can be studied by what were hitherto methods of literary analysis. And the values that are often taken for granted in literary reading of nonliterary materials are frequently literary values: concreteness, vividness, immediacy, paradoxical complexities. Finally, comparative literature would seem to have won its battles, in that other literature departments now agree that the historical study of the evolution of a national literature is not the only legitimate way to study literature but that there are many sorts of approaches, based on methods and categories that need to be defended theoretically. If such views are widely accepted, this ought to be the triumph of comparative literature, but why does it seem like a crisis? In none of these cases is there pleasure or optimism about the condition of theory, of comparative literature, or of literature "itself." Is the uncertainty about whether to claim victory or a crisis a necessary feature of our cultural condition, or are there other ways in which we might conceive these situations? That is a question to which I hope readers will find some answers.

THEORY

1

The Literary in Theory

When in the 1960s I first became involved with what has come to be called simply "theory," this term—so very odd, theory of what?—made a good deal more sense than it does today. In the structuralist moment there was a growing body of theory—essentially the generalization of the model of structural linguistics—which, it was claimed, would apply everywhere, to all domains of culture. *Theory* meant a particular body of structuralist theory that would elucidate diverse sorts of material and be the key to understanding language, social behavior, literature, popular culture, societies with and without writing, and the structures of the human psyche. *Theory* meant the specific interdisciplinary body of theory that animated structuralist linguistics, anthropology, Marxism, semiotics, psychoanalysis, and literary criticism.

But despite the broad interdisciplinary ambitions of theory in those heady days, the question of literature lay at the heart of the theoretical project: for Russian Formalism, for Prague structuralism, and for French structuralism—especially for Roman Jakobson, who introduced Claude Lévi-Strauss to the phonological model that was decisive for the development of structuralism—the question of the literariness of literature was the animating question. Theory sought to treat the objects and events of culture as elements of so many "languages," so it was concerned above all with the nature of language; and literature was what language was when it was most deliberately and most ludically, most freely and most self-reflectively, being language. Literature was the place where the structures and the functioning of language were most explicitly and revealingly foregrounded. To investigate the crucial aspects of language, you had to think about literature. Thus, amid the array of functions of language defined by Roman Jakobson—the referential, the emotive, the phatic, the conative, the metalingual, and the poetic, which involve, respectively, the foregrounding of or stress on the context, the speaker, the contact, the addressee, the code, and the message itself—it is the poetic function of language that, in Jakobson's famous phrase, brings "the focus on the message for its own sake" (where "message" means the utterance itself).[1] And, in a formula that all of us relics of theory knew by heart, Jakobson declared, "The poetic function of language projects the principle of equivalence from the axis of selection into the axis of combination."[2] The poetic function of language involves the superimposition of the two fundamental axes of language.

Now even at that time, when the nature of the literariness of literature was a question that every good theorist had to address, it was clear that in some sense theory was displacing the literary—clear, at least to all those who attacked theory, accusing us of forswearing literary values and undermining the prestige or the special character of literature. Narratologists studied the narrative structures of James Joyce and James Bond with equal assiduousness. Roman Jakobson, notoriously, took as his key example of the poetic function of language not Baudelaire's sonnet "Les Chats," which he and Lévi-Strauss had exhaustively analyzed, but the political slogan "I like Ike," where the object liked (Ike) and the liking subject (I) are embraced in and contained by the act, *like*, so that the necessity of my liking Ike seems inscribed in the very structure of the language.[3] The special status of literature as privileged object of study was in an important sense undermined, but the effect of this sort of study (and this is important) was to locate a "literariness" in cultural objects of all sorts and thus to retain a certain centrality of the literary.

The attempt to theorize the distinctiveness of literary language or the

1. Roman Jakobson, "Closing Statement: Linguistics and Poetics," in *Style in Language*, ed. Thomas Sebeok (Cambridge, MA: MIT Press, 1960), 352. For a discussion of theory in this structuralist moment see Jonathan Culler, *Structuralist Poetics: Structuralism, Linguistics, and the Study of Literature* (Ithaca, NY: Cornell University Press, 1974).

2. Jakobson, "Closing Statement," 358.

3. Ibid., 357.

distinctiveness of literature was central to theory in those early years, but it hasn't been the focus of theoretical activity for some time. This is not, I should add, because we answered the question of the nature of literature. Neither of the principal lines of thought led to an answer that resolved the question. The first approach was to treat literature as a special kind of language, but each definition of literariness led not to a satisfactory account of literature but to an often extremely productive identification of literariness in other cultural phenomena—from historical narratives and Freudian case histories to advertising slogans. The alternative approach was to posit that literature was not a special kind of language but language treated in special ways. But despite valiant efforts by Stanley Fish, who sought to show, for instance, that a list of names of linguists written on the blackboard could be read as a religious lyric, this never proved very satisfactory either.[4]

There are two morals here. First, just as meaning is both a textual fact and an intentional act and cannot be adequately theorized from either one of these points of view alone or through a synthesis of the two,[5] so, in the case of literature, we must shift back and forth between the two perspectives, neither of which successfully incorporates the other to become the comprehensive framework: we can think of literary works as language with particular properties or features, and we can think of them as language framed in particular ways, but any account of particular properties or of perceptual framing leads us to shift back ultimately into the other mode. The qualities of literature, it seems, can't be reduced either to objective properties or to consequences of ways of framing language.

The second moral, I think, is that questions about the nature of literariness or of literature were not, in fact, attempts to discover criteria by

4. Stanley Fish, "How to Recognize a Poem When You See One," in *Is There a Text in This Class?* (Cambridge, MA: Harvard University Press, 1980), 322–37. For general discussions of the problem of literariness see Terry Eagleton, *Literary Theory: An Introduction* (Minneapolis: University of Minnesota Press, 1983), 1–12; Jonathan Culler, "La littérarité," in *Théorie littéraire*, ed. Marc Angenot, Jean Bessière, Douwe Fokkema, and Eva Kushner (Paris: Presses universitaires de France, 1989), 31–43; and Jonathan Culler, *Literary Theory: A Very Short Introduction* (Oxford, UK: Oxford University Press, 1997), 18–42.

5. See William Ray, *Literary Meaning: From Phenomenology to Deconstruction* (Oxford, UK: Blackwell, 1984), 2.

which we could distinguish literary from nonliterary works and sort them into the right categories. On the contrary, attempts to answer these questions always functioned primarily to direct attention to certain aspects of literature. By saying what literature is, theorists promote the critical methods they deem most pertinent and dismiss those that neglect what are claimed to be the most basic and distinctive aspects of literature—whether literature is conceived as the foregrounding of language, or as the integration of linguistic levels, or as intertextual construction. To ask "what is literature?" is in effect a way of arguing about how literature should be studied. If literature is highly patterned language, for instance, then to study it is to look at the patterns, not to focus on the authorial psyche it might express or the social formation it might reflect. Investigations of the nature of literature seem to have functioned, above all, as moves in arguments about critical method.

One of the few exceptions in the United States to the recent neglect of theory of literature has been a book by Steven Knapp, *Literary Interest: The Limits of Anti-Formalism*. For me it is particularly striking and, I confess, the source of a certain perverse pleasure that the purest example of a traditional project of theory of literature should have been produced by the coauthor of the 1982 article, "Against Theory," which argued that literary theory had no useful work to do and should simply stop.[6] Knapp's book takes up the traditional questions of literary theory: "Is there such a thing as a specifically *literary* discourse, distinguishable from other modes of thought and writing? Is there any way to defend the intuition that a work of literature says something that can't be said in any other way?"[7] Knapp's book surprises by giving positive answers to these questions. Philosophically more rigorous than most such investigations, and, I should say, more doggedly determined not to end up with the patently unsatisfying

6. One might argue that this inconsistency is quite consistent with the 1982 article itself, which manifestly fails to practice what it preaches. I argue in Chapter 3 below that in dealing with other critics Knapp and Michaels decline to obey their own axiom that the meaning of a text is what the author means by it, so perhaps it is scarcely surprising that they should not respect their own claim that theory has no work to do and should simply stop.

7. Steven Knapp, *Literary Interest: The Limits of Anti-Formalism* (Cambridge, MA: Harvard University Press, 1993), flyleaf copy; hereafter abbreviated *LI* and cited parenthetically in the text.

answers that so often end such inquiries—such as that literature is whatever a given society means by literature—Knapp's inquiry concludes that, Yes, there *is* a distinctiveness to literature. Yes, literature does do something special.

Knapp's approach takes up and refines traditional kinds of answers but under a different rubric. Having committed himself in the antitheory article to the position that the meaning of a literary work is simply, by definition, what the author meant by it (and that any other notion is incoherent), he approaches the distinctiveness of literature not through the special kinds of meaning that a literary work might have—there are none—but through what he calls "literary interest."

Since Knapp admits that our interest in literary language exceeds our interest in figuring out what its author might have intended by it, that surplus is available to be called something else and is baptized "literary interest." The distinctiveness of the literary lies not in the specificity of literary language: "I came to see," he writes, "that what could not be defended as an account of literary language could be defended instead as an account of a certain kind of representation that provoked a certain kind of interest" (*LI*, 2). Literature is a "linguistically embodied representation that tends to attract a certain kind of interest to itself; that does so by particularizing the emotive and other values of its referents; and that does *that* by inserting its referents into new 'scenarios' inseparable from the particular linguistic and narrative structures of the representation itself" (*LI*, 3). And crucial to the particular structures of the representation itself are what in other theoretical schemes are called the homologies between levels of structure and the self-referential aspects of literary discourse but that Knapp presents as relations between analogical structures involving different levels of agency: is what the author is doing in writing a poem analogous to what happens in the poem? "This sort of recursion," Knapp writes, "—where a problem of agency located as it were outside the work also shows up inside it—is the kind of effect that turns an interpretive problem into a source of literary interest" (*LI*, 3). We are dealing with literary interest when an interpretive problem becomes not just a source of interest but the source of an interest in the analogical structures whose particularity and complexity give the work its peculiarly literary status.

An example—this is my example, not Knapp's, but it has the virtue of great economy—might be Robert Frost's two-line poem "The Secret Sits":

We dance round in a ring and suppose,
But the Secret sits in the middle and knows.[8]

The interpretive problem, "what is the poet saying or doing here?" becomes a source of distinctively literary interest, one might say, when it is
transformed into a question about the relation between what the speaker
or the poem is doing and what the agents within the poem, "we" and "the
Secret," are doing. The poem contrasts our dancing and supposing with
the Secret's sitting and knowing. We can ask what attitude the poem takes
to the contrasted actions or modes of being. Is the poem a sardonic comment on the futility of human activity, or can we contrast the dancing of
communal supposing to the dour and immobile knowing? But to address
the question of the poem's take on these oppositions, one needs to ask
whether the poem itself is engaged in dancing and supposing or in sitting
and knowing. Is the poem itself in the mode of supposing or knowing?

The answer is somewhat complicated. The poem certainly sounds
knowing, but as a verbal construction, can it be other than an act of human
supposing? And if we ask about the status of knowing in the poem, what
we can discover is that the subject supposed to know, the Secret, is produced by a rhetorical operation or supposition that moves it from the place
of the object of "know" to the place of the subject. A secret is something
one knows or does not know. Here the poem capitalizes and personifies the
Secret and, by metonymy, shifts it from the place of what is known to the
place of the knower. The knower is thus represented as produced by a rhetorical supposing or positing that makes the object of knowledge (a secret)
into its subject (the Secret). The poem says that the secret knows but shows
that this is the performative product of a rhetorical supposition.

Since Knapp wants to locate literary interest in analogies of *agency*,
what would he say here? His claim would be that literary interest inheres in
the relation between the act that Frost is performing in this poem and the
acts represented. Is Frost knowing or supposing, dancing round or sitting
in the middle, and what difference does it make? Are the difficulties of deciding what act Frost is performing illuminated by the difficulties of sorting
out the relation between the acts of the poem's "we" and the acts of the Se-

8. Robert Frost, *The Complete Poems* (New York: Holt, Rinehart, 1958), 495.
First published under the title "Ring Around" in *Poetry*, 1936, this poem acquired
its definitive title in Robert Frost, *A Witness Tree* (New York: Holt, 1942).

cret? This poem would, I think, be a good example for Knapp's approach, though in insisting that we focus on analogies of *authorial* agency, he has us ask what Frost is doing rather than what the poem is doing. I am not convinced that this is helpful, much less necessary. It may be more pertinent and productive to ask what the speaker or the poem is doing, and how that relates to what is done in the poem, than to focus on what Frost is doing and its relation to actions in the poem. But this may well be a separate issue. I do think that the problem of literariness is sharpened and illuminated by Knapp's suggestion that a text has literary interest insofar as our interest in it exceeds our interest in figuring out what the author intends.

Knapp seeks to reinterpret in terms of agency the kind of complexity of structure that has generally been taken to characterize literariness. He then proceeds to argue that although literature does indeed have the distinctiveness that it has recently been denied, often on general political grounds (as an unwarranted, elitist privileging of certain modes of discourse), still, literature does not have the moral and political benefits that those defending literature are wont to claim for it. He thus hopes, as in the antitheory articles he wrote with Walter Benn Michaels, to succeed in provoking everyone, on both sides of the question. But there are probably few of us left in theory who will be surprised or annoyed by the conclusion that literature does not necessarily have moral and political benefits: arguments for the disruptive and emancipatory value of the avant-garde can always be countered by claims about the normalizing and policing functions of literary scenarios. But Knapp's example illustrates—albeit in an unusual traditional mode—what has been the tendency in recent thinking about the theory of literature: to relate the defense of the literary and the specificity thereof not to questions of the distinctiveness of literary language nor to the radical potential of disruptions of meanings but to the staging of agency on the one hand and to engagements with otherness on the other.[9]

9. The range of theoretical writings treating literature's relation to otherness is considerable, from the work of Martha Nussbaum, cited below, which articulates the traditional view that literature is distinctive for its success in enabling us to appreciate the situation of the other, to that of Jacques Derrida, which treats literature as a response to the call of the other. See Derrida, "Psyche: Inventions of the Other," trans. Catherine Porter, in *Reading de Man Reading*, ed. Lindsay Waters and Wlad Godzich (Minneapolis: University of Minnesota Press, 1989); and, for general discussion, Derek Attridge, "Innovation, Literature, Ethics: Relating to the Other," *PMLA* 119 (Jan. 1999); and Derek Attridge, *The Singularity of Literature* (London: Routledge, 2004).

Knapp's argument is that literary representations, which foreground analogically complex representations of agency, do not tell us how to act but help us to discover what our evaluative dispositions are and enhance our awareness of the complex relations—perhaps relations of contradiction—among our evaluative dispositions. An example he offers is Chinua Achebe's *Things Fall Apart*, where the colonial intervention into traditional Ibo culture is presented simultaneously as a cruel act of aggression and as an answer to the often extreme injustices of Ibo custom (the subordination of women; the exposure of twins; the murder, if an oracle so commands, of an adopted child). For readers the novel may set up a clash between sets of values readers hold. Reading the novel, Knapp writes, "a feminist anticolonialist might discover that her negative response to patriarchal customs far outweighed her commitment to preserving indigenous cultures (or the reverse)" (*LI*, 100–101). If literature helps to make us self-conscious agents, it does so by promoting thick description over simplifying principle, so that potential conflicts of value and principle may emerge. Knapp cites Locke's account of freedom of the liberal subject as the possibility of suspending decisions to examine carefully the alternatives and their values, and he concludes that literary interest provides a model for the exercise of liberal agency. "It isn't," he warns, "that literary interest makes someone a better agent." (He is not convinced that self-conscious agency is better agency.) But it "does give an unusually pure experience of what agency, for better or worse, is like" (*LI*, 103).

Agency involves a structure akin to what literary theory has called "the concrete universal," that special combination of particularity and generality that enables Hamlet, for instance, to be more than a merely actual person: Hamlet is embodied in particular details yet nevertheless open and general in ways that actual persons are not. To understand myself as agent is to see myself both in a concrete situation determined by my particular past and yet able to consider alternative courses of action by debating what is appropriate for *someone* in my situation to do and thus to consider choices open to a certain type of agent—a type of which I am only one possible example. Since the ideal of full agency is that of the fusion of particularity and generality—that the determined particular which I am would be able effectively to choose any of the courses open to an agent—it is no surprise that, as Knapp puts it, encountering literary interest "should feel like glimpsing the ideal condition of practical agency itself" (*LI*, 140).

Such arguments go some way toward explaining the common intuition that the experience of literature has a bearing on the act of making judgments. Literature offers, as others have often said, a kind of mental calisthenics, a practice that instructs in exercise of agency. But if Knapp explicitly denies that literary interest makes someone a better agent, other critics and theorists have recently attempted to show why it should. Martha Nussbaum, for instance, has stressed the potential role of literary representations in bringing us to exercise agency in the interests of justice. In *Poetic Justice: The Literary Imagination and Public Life* she presents the literary imagination, or, more specifically, literary representation and the dealings with the kind of representations that characterize the literary imagination, as paradigms for the act of judging, where action should be based on as rich and comprehensive as possible an understanding of the situation and experiences of the people and groups involved in the case.

There are two aspects to this argument, I believe. First, there is a claim that readers are constituted by literary works as judges of a certain sort. The reading of literature instances the model of judicious spectatorship, where what qualifies the spectator to judge is, first, an ability vividly to imagine what it is like to be the persons whose situation confronts the reader engaged with the text and, second, a practice of critical assessment. The techniques of literary narrative in particular work to constitute readers as observers who sympathize but who must in the end judge, deciding how far characters' self-understanding is exemplary or flawed, how far the outcomes of their stories are due to their own choices or to chance or to social influences which they could not overcome.

In this way literature creates a model of what Nussbaum calls "the literary judge," which she contrasts with other models of the judge.[10] Citing some legal opinions where a rich fabric of narrative, reconstructing the experience of the people in question, shows the literary judge at work, she contrasts these with, for instance, Supreme Court opinions in *Bowers v. Hardwick*, the celebrated case that bore on whether privacy rights established by Fourteenth Amendment privacy cases extend protection to consensual homosexual sodomy. (The Court held that they do not.) In Bowers the majority opinions by Justices White and Burger display no interest

---

10. Martha Nussbaum, *Poetic Justice: The Literary Imagination and Public Life* (Boston: Beacon, 1995), 82; hereafter abbreviated *PJ* and cited parenthetically in the text.

in the experience of those whose privacy rights they deny and fail to treat the events as something that might happen to someone one could know or even be. (The police burst into the house of a gay man and into his bedroom, where he and his partner were making love.) The texts of these opinions work to keep the human story at a distance, remarking sardonically on "the claimed constitutional right of homosexuals to engage in acts of sodomy." Nussbaum writes that the model of literary judging would have entailed consideration of a more detailed, empathetic and concrete sort (such as would have been necessary to adjudicating Bowers as an equal protection case). The literary judge, she concludes, "has a better grasp of the totality of the facts than the nonliterary judge. . . . Literary judging is by no means sufficient for good judging, . . . but we should demand it in appropriate circumstances, whatever else we also demand" (*PJ*, 118).

In a second line of argument Nussbaum claims—against Knapp—that literature works toward social justice in one particular sense: it is an equalizer. Whitman writes of the poet:

He is the equalizer of his age and land,

. . .

He judges not as the judge judges but as the sun falling round a helpless thing

. . .

He sees eternity in men and women, he does not see men and women as dreams or dots.[11]

What does it mean to call literature equalizing? The concern for the disadvantaged is built into the structure of the literary experience, Nussbaum claims, as it leads the reader to enter vicariously into the concrete circumstances of other lives (*PJ*, 87). Literature draws attention to misery and focuses our attention on the individual, treating characters not as dreams or dots or statistics but as figures in whose experience and vision it may be possible to participate. The novel-reading stance, she concludes, citing E. M. Forster's *Maurice*, calls out for political and social equality as the necessary condition for full humanity for citizens on both sides of "the line" (*PJ*, 97).

This is no doubt an excessively optimistic reading of literature—of the literary relation—but I cite it as an instance of what seems to me a gen-

11. Walt Whitman, "By Blue Ontario's Shore" (ll. 142, 148, 153), in *The Complete Poems*, ed. Francis Murphy (Harmondsworth: Penguin, 1975), 368–69.

eral tendency in recent theory: to locate the distinctive features of literature not in particular qualities of language or framings of language but in
the staging of agency and in the relation to otherness into which readers of
literature are brought. Nussbaum stresses above all the ways in which literary works bring readers to see characters as individuals, in the sense of individual people one might know, but arguably literature undercuts this concept of the individual. The effects of literature here depend on the special
structure of exemplarity in literature—an issue she does not address.

A literary work, whether *Hamlet* or *Maurice*, is typically the story of
a fictional character, but to read it as literature is to take it as in some way
exemplary. Why else would one read it? It presents itself as exemplary but
simultaneously declines to define the range or scope of that exemplarity. A
literary work is more than an anecdote, a singular example that is offered as
an instance of something (though a detailed and well-told anecdote can accede to the condition of literariness). The literary representation has greater autonomy, so the question of what it exemplifies can be left in abeyance
at the same time that that question subtends the significance of the representation. This is why through the years people have often been led to
speak of the "universality" of literature. The structure of literary works is
such that it is easier to take them as telling us about the human condition
in general than to specify some narrower category they describe or illuminate. Is *Hamlet* just about princes, or men of the Renaissance, or introspec-
tive young men, or people whose fathers have died in obscure circumstances? Since all such answers seem unsatisfactory, it is easier for readers not to
answer, thus implicitly accepting a possibility of universality. Novels, poems, and plays, in their singularity, decline to explore what they are exemplary *of* at the same time that they invite their readers to become involved
in the predicaments and the consciousness of narrators and characters who
are in some sense posited as exemplary. And of course while *readers* have
the option of declining to decide what is exemplified by a particular literary example, what Nussbaum calls "the literary judge" must decide, if he or
she is to profit from the thick description that the literarily described case
offers, for the legal judgment is always typifying in effect. It makes law,
through the particular features it chooses to cite as determining: "when *x*
and *y* occur, a right of privacy should obtain."

This structure of exemplarity has been important to the relationship of literature to the problem of identity, which has been so central to recent theory. Is the self something given or something made, and should it be conceived in individual or in social terms? Literature has always been concerned with such questions, and literary works offer a range of implicit models of how identity is formed. There are narratives where identity is essentially determined by birth: the son of a king raised by shepherds is still fundamentally a king and rightfully becomes king when his identity is discovered. In other narratives characters change according to the changes in their fortunes; they acquire identity through identifications, which may go awry but have powerful effects; or else identity is based on personal qualities that are revealed during the tribulations of a life.

The explosion of recent theorizing about race, gender, and sexuality in the field of literary studies may owe a good deal to the fact that literature provides rich materials for complicating political and sociological accounts of the role of such factors in the construction of identity. (I think, for instance, of Eve Sedgwick's and Judith Butler's discussions of cross-gendered identifications in Willa Cather's novels—accounts undreamt of by sociologists.)[12]

Consider the underlying question of whether the identity of the subject is something given or something constructed. Not only are both options amply represented in literature, but the complications or entanglements are frequently laid out for us, as in the common plot where characters, we say, "discover" who they are, not by learning something about their past but by acting in such a way that they *become* what then turns out, in some sense, to have been their "nature."

This structure, where you have to *become* what you supposedly already were, has emerged as a paradox or aporia for recent theory, but it can be considered a defining feature of narratives. Western novels reinforce the notion of an essential self by suggesting that the self which emerges from trying encounters with the world was in some sense there all along, as the basis for the actions that, from the perspective of readers, bring this self into being. The fundamental identity of character emerges as the result of

12. See Eve Kosovsky Sedgwick, "Across Gender, Across Sexuality: Willa Cather and Others," *South Atlantic Quarterly* 88, no. 1 (winter 1989): 53–72; and Judith Butler, "Dangerous Crossing: Willa Cather's Masculine Names," in *Bodies That Matter: On the Discursive Limits of "Sex"* (New York: Routledge, 1993), 143–66.

actions, of struggles with the world, but then this identity is posited as the basis, even the cause of those actions. Isn't that what we are struggling with in theory's debates about essentialism—whether certain aspects of identity are essential, necessary, or whether all are constructed and in that sense contingent?[13]

A good deal of recent theory can be seen as an attempt to sort out the paradoxes that often inform the treatment of identity in literature. Literary works characteristically represent individuals, so struggles about identity are struggles within the individual and between individual and group: characters struggle against or comply with social norms and expectations. In theoretical writings, though, arguments about social identity tend to focus on group identities: what is it to be a woman? to be Black? to be gay? to be a man? Thus there are tensions between literary explorations and critical or theoretical claims. Here we arrive at a crux of the literary in theory—a tension between the literary and theory. The power of literary representations depends on their special combination of singularity and exemplarity: readers encounter concrete portrayals of Prince Hamlet or Jane Eyre or Huckleberry Finn and with them the presumption that these characters' problems are exemplary. But exemplary of what? The novels don't tell. It is as critics or theorists that readers take up the question of exemplarity, in such a way as to decide and tell us what group or class of people the character instantiates: is Hamlet's condition "universal"? Is Jane Eyre's the predicament of women in general? Even when such a decision is not explicit, it can provide the critical account with pathos or intensity, a sense of important stakes, mitigating the effects of abstractness or distance.

Theoretical treatments of identity can seem reductive in comparison with the subtle explorations in novels, which are able to finesse the problem of general claims by presenting singular cases while relying on a generalizing force that is left implicit—perhaps we are all Oedipus, or Hamlet, or Emma Bovary, or Janie Starks. And it is for this reason that theoretical reflection on the structures of exemplarity of literature are crucial to both the kinds of uses theory is making of literature these days, in its reflections

13. See, e.g., Diana Fuss, *Essentially Speaking* (New York: Routledge, 1989). The most powerful and influential exploration of this aporia, through the theorization of a performative notion of identity, comes in Judith Butler, *Gender Trouble: Feminism and the Subversion of Identity* (New York: Routledge, 1990); and Butler, *Bodies That Matter.*

on identity and agency, and to any attempt, as in Nussbaum and Knapp, to link the distinctiveness of literature to its bearing on questions of agency.

But if the literary can function as exemplary representation of agency for theory, it can also be a source *of* agency in theory, as literary works provide leverage for theoretical argument. One impressive case where the role of literature is complex and overdetermined (and hence hard to define) is Judith Butler's *Antigone's Claim*. Antigone, notoriously, makes a claim in Sophocles' play (precisely what sort of claim is the major issue in the history of the play's reception) and thus functions as a potentially exemplary literary representation of agency. Luce Irigaray has suggested, for instance, that Antigone can offer an identification for many girls and women living today.[14] But the terseness of Butler's title suggests that Antigone—representation or text—has a claim on us. If Butler can use the words and deeds of Antigone and the text of Sophocles' play *Antigone* in a sustained argument about the relations between psychoanalysis and politics, focused on the problem of ways of theorizing kinship relations and family structures, it is not just because Antigone the agent is in some ways exemplary but rather because the figure of Antigone has given rise to a powerful tradition of interpretation—from Hegel to Lacan and Irigaray—which has had effects on our conceptions of kinship and of the possible relations between the family and the state.

We can ask, foregrounding the question of exemplarity, what would have happened if psychoanalysis had taken Antigone rather than Oedipus as its point of departure. Butler writes that

> it is perhaps interesting to note that Antigone, who concludes the Oedipal drama, fails to produce the heterosexual closure for that drama, and that this may intimate the direction for a psychoanalytic theory that takes Antigone as its point of departure. . . . She does seem to deinstitute heterosexuality by refusing to do what is necessary to stay alive for Haemon, by refusing to become a mother and wife, by scandalizing the public with her wavering gender, and by embracing death as her bridal chamber.[15]

Her case offers alternatives to the conceptual routes that Western culture

14. Luce Irigaray, *Speculum of the Other Woman* (Ithaca, NY: Cornell University Press, 1985), 70.

15. Judith Butler, *Antigone's Claim: Kinship Between Life and Death* (New York: Columbia University Press, 2000), 76.

has taken. But, more important, the interpretation of Antigone has undergirded a discourse about kinship and its relation to political structures that continues to exercise its effects today. "In her act, she transgresses both gender and kinship norms, and though the Hegelian tradition reads her fate as a sure sign that this transgression is necessarily failed and fatal, another reading is possible in which she exposes the socially contingent character of kinship, only to become the repeated occasion for a rewriting of that contingency as immutable necessity."[16] That is, Butler has given a kind of agency to Antigone that problematizes the agency of theory or criticism. Butler's intervention does not simply cite the figure of Antigone as an agent exercising certain choices or making claims. It undertakes detailed readings of Sophocles' text, *Antigone*, to expose the reductive simplifications in the readings by theorists, which have set kinship (as a configuration of "natural relations") against the state, have idealized kinship as a structural field of intelligibility, and have thus established certain forms of kinship as intelligible and legitimate. This idealization, which legitimates a certain form of family structure as supposedly prior to and outside of politics, has drawn on the story of Antigone but, in so doing, has denied the challenge that Sophocles' text offers to its peremptory inscription of intelligibility. If Hegel attends to Antigone's acts but not her speech, studying that language today reveals the instability of the conceptual apparatus erected on her example. It is by appealing to the complexities and indeterminacies of this literary work that Butler intervenes, in the name of those who today are attempting to work out alternative family structures—where two men or two women may parent a child, for instance—and whose practice encounters the stigmatizing idealization in psychoanalytic, cultural, and political theory of the supposedly primordial, symbolic positions of Father and Mother. Claude Lévi-Strauss in his structuralist studies of myth and totemism maintained that myths are central to culture because they are "good to think with." Butler's use of *Antigone* in an argument about the legitimacy of models of kinship and politics shows that literature is better to think with—in that its language provides powerful resources for a critique of constructions that it has been used to sustain and thus of the institutional arrangements it has helped to support.

16. Ibid., 6.

So far I have approached my subject by discussing some forms that the theorization of the literary has taken in recent theoretical discourses. But one could also argue that what has happened to the literary in theory is that it has migrated from being the object of theory to being the quality of theory itself: what we in America call "theory"—after all, an American invention—is elsewhere the broad movement of modern thought that takes as its "other" instrumental reason and empirical science (some other names for this other are the restricted economy of utility, the logic of enframing, the logic of reification and reifying rationality, the totalizing logic of technological efficiency, the binary logic of the metaphysics of presence, and so on).[17] What if theory is the exfoliation, in the sphere of thought in general, of the literary? Freud, notoriously, said that the poets had been there before him; he tried to found a science on literary insights, and his critics have in our day tried with some success to beat him back into the position of failed scientist and successful storyteller. More generally, one could say that insofar as thought seeks to find passages beyond the familiar, the known, the countable, it is cognate with the literature, or at least the literary efforts, of romanticism and modernism.

One striking signal of this is that philosophical texts have become literary in the classic sense that, like poems, they are not supposed to be paraphrased. To paraphrase is to miss what is essential. People often say this of Derrida, of course, but here is Adorno, a philosopher not usually identified with the literary: In *Negative Dialectics* Adorno writes,

Instead of reducing philosophy to categories, one would in a sense have to compose it first. Its course must be a ceaseless self-renewal, by its own strength as well as in friction with whatever standard it may have. The crux is what happened in it, not a thesis or a position, the texture, not the deductive or inductive course of one-track minds. Essentially, therefore, philosophy is not expoundable. If it were, it would be superfluous; the fact that most of it can be expounded speaks against it.[18]

17. I am indebted for some of these formulations, as for the quotations from Adorno below, to a remarkable doctoral dissertation by Robert Baker, "Poetic Form, Poetic Fiction, and the Way of Extravagance: Twentieth-Century Inventions" (Cornell University, 1997). A radically revised version of this dissertation was published as *The Extravagant: Crossings of Modern Poetry and Modern Philosophy* (Notre Dame: University of Notre Dame Press, 2005), see esp. 33–38.

18. Theodor Adorno, *Negative Dialectics*, trans. E. B. Ashton (New York: Continuum, 1973), 33.

This is a literary way of conceiving philosophy—philosophy as writing that achieves literary effects.[19] This is not to imply that exposition of such texts is not necessary or desirable—only that such texts also require the kind of rhetorical readings and the contextual analysis as acts, as performances, that we take for granted when engaging literary works and, thus, that the literary has migrated into theory.

Insofar as theory is the discourse that seeks the opening of the subject to the nonidentical, to alterity, the other, the indeterminate, or some other site or event beyond instrumental reason, it inscribes itself in the literary lineage of post-Enlightenment poetry. An eloquent passage in *Minima Moralia: Reflections from Damaged Life* evokes the task of thought in a way that brings together possible goals of literature and of theory, though they seek these goals without appealing to the messianic perspective that Adorno adduces here:

Perspectives must be fashioned that displace and estrange the world, reveal it to be, with its rifts and crevices, as indigent and distorted as it will appear one day in the messianic light. To gain such perspectives without velleity or violence, entirely from felt contact with its objects—this alone is the task of thought. It is the simplest of all things, because the situation calls imperatively for such knowledge, indeed because consummate negativity, once squarely faced, delineates the mirror-image of its opposite. But it is also the utterly impossible thing, because it presupposes a standpoint removed, even though by a hair's breadth, from the scope of existence, whereas we well know that any possible knowledge must not only be first wrested from what is, if it shall hold good, but is also marked, for this very reason, by the same distortion and indigence which it seeks to escape. The more passionately thought denies its conditionality for the sake of the unconditional, the more unconsciously, and so calamitously, it is delivered up to the world. Even its own impossibility it must at last comprehend for the sake of the possible. But beside the demand thus placed on thought, the question of the reality or unreality of redemption itself hardly matters.[20]

The literary nature of this project emerges in that difficult concluding sentence: beside the demand thus placed on thought, the question of the reality or unreality of redemption itself hardly matters. Redemption,

19. See my discussion of Stanley Cavell in Chapter 9 below.
20. Theodor Adorno, *Minima Moralia: Reflections from Damaged Life*, trans. E. F. N. Jephcott (London: Verso, 1974), 247.

like the messianic, can be thought of as a figure that enables such discourse. But, as in literature—this is Adorno's point—it is the demand of
otherness placed on thought that counts.

Let me conclude by addressing another form of the pervasiveness of
the literary. In the course of his discussion of literary interest Steve Knapp
remarks that the New Historicism involves the transfer of literary interest from the literary work itself to the literary work grasped in a historical
context: as a result, the new construct that is the object of literary interest is in fact the complex interrelations between text and context (context,
which is of course more text). Literary interest comes no longer from the
complex relations between form and meaning or between what the work
says and what it does but, for instance, from the dialectic of subversion and
containment that it provokes and in which it participates. The explanatory
vagueness of much New Historicism comes from the fact that the goal is
not to decide whether, say, "the theater in a particular era is an effect or a
cause of a certain monarchical ideology" but to illuminate a complex interdependent structure, like that of a literary work. "The point," Knapp
writes, "is to see how the theater, as it exists in its hard-to-define relation
to the state becomes (to someone who notices the right affinities) the theater as suggesting, and suggested by, the state" (*LI*, 104). The object of literary interest—approached as a complex literary structure—is the work
in a posited context. The historical investigations of the New Historicism
take as their object not historical explanation but elucidation as a historical object that displays the structures of literary interest.

A similar point is taken further in David Simpson's *The Academic
Postmodern and the Rule of Literature*, which argues, in a mode of critique
and complaint, I should make clear, that literature, far from being ignored
or relegated to the margins in the university, as conservative critics claim,
has conquered: in the academy literature rules, even though that rule is
disguised as something else. Simpson seeks to show that a range of scholars and disciplines have been willing to accept, for the description of the
world, terms that come from the realm of literary studies. He surveys various dimensions of this phenomenon: the return of storytelling to centrality in history (Simpson speaks of the "epidemic of story-telling"), which
had thought itself rid of that sort of humanistic, literary issue; the general
recourse to anecdote or autobiography, the celebration of "thick descrip-

tion" and "local knowledge," and the use of the figure of "conversation" in the fields of history, philosophy, feminism, anthropology. Such is the transformation of the humanities that knowledge now takes literary forms. The calls for concreteness and historical specificity are, Simpson explains, not part of a renewed empiricism but versions of an appeal to the values of literary singularity, to that presence of the general in the particular that distinguishes literary discourse. Clifford Geertz's *local knowledge*, for instance, brings not empirical mastery but the incompleteness and instability of all knowledge claims and the appeal, instead, to vividness of realization as the substitute for claims to mastery. The literary reigns.

But "how," Simpson asks, "can I make this claim at a time when some of the most astute commentators on our contemporary condition"— he cites Fredric Jameson and John Guillory—"are describing a move *away from* the literary as most urgently definitive of the postmodern condition?"[21] (Jameson says that the replacement of literature by video is the signature of the postmodern condition, and John Guillory describes the flight of cultural capital from literature as the most characteristic element in the evolving state of the humanities.) Since these thinkers are Simpson's friends and co-religionists, he answers, politely, that "culture is not a monolith" (they are looking at different phenomena in the panoply of culture); but fundamentally he thinks that he is right and they are wrong. Literature may have lost its centrality as a specific object of study, but its modes have conquered: in the humanities and the humanistic social sciences everything is literary. Indeed, if literature is, as we used to say, that mode of discourse which knows its own fictionality, then, insofar as the effect of theory has been to inform disciplines of both the fictionality and the performative efficacy of their constructions, there seems a good deal to be said in favor of Simpson's account of the situation of disciplines. Insofar as disciplinary discourses have come to engage with the problem of their positionality, their situatedness, and the constructedness of their schemes, they participate in the literary.

If the literary has triumphed, as Simpson claims (and for him the postmodern is the name of the triumph of the literary), then perhaps it is time to reground the literary in literature: to go back to actual literary

21. David Simpson, *The Academic Postmodern and the Rule of Literature: A Report on Half-Knowledge* (Chicago: University of Chicago Press, 1995), 38.

works to see in what sense a postmodern condition is indeed what should be inferred from the operations of literature. It seems to me quite possible that a return to ground the literary in literature might have a critical edge, since one of the things we know about literary works is that they have the ability to resist or to outplay what they are supposed to be saying. David Simpson's book claims quite explicitly that what's left of theory is the literary. If so, this is all the more reason to return to literary works for the critique of the literary that has historically been one of the tasks of literature.

The Novel and the Nation

I

If theory is work that migrates out of the field in which it originates and is used in other fields as a framework for rethinking broad questions, Benedict Anderson's writing about nationalism is a prime example and a splendid case for thinking about the literary in theory, for notions of the novel and narrative technique play a key role in Anderson's account of the conditions of possibility of the nation. A political scientist specializing in Southeast Asia, Anderson wrote *Imagined Communities: Reflections on the Origins and Spread of Nationalism*, which, since its publication in 1983, has become a classic of the humanities and social sciences. Any theoretically savvy discussion of nations or of societies of any sort must cite it for its fundamental insight that nations and, as Anderson points out, "all communities larger than primordial villages of face-to-face contact (and perhaps even these) are imagined."[1] In retrospect, it seems obvious that nationality, "nation-ness," and nationalism "are cultural artifacts of a particular kind" (*IC*, 4), but this had previously been obscured by intellectuals' sense that nationalism was above all an atavistic passion, an often noxious prejudice of the unenlightened. *Imagined Communities* both argued that we had better seek to understand it, since "nation-ness is the most

1. Benedict Anderson, *Imagined Communities: Reflections on the Origins and Spread of Nationalism* [1983], rev. ed. (London: Verso, 1991), 6. All references are to the 1991 edition; hereafter abbreviated *IC* and cited parenthetically in the text.

universally legitimate value in the political life of our time" (*IC*, 3), and gave us a constructivist way of thinking about the phenomenon of nationalism, which becomes more interesting and intellectually more acceptable when we ask how it is created, what discursive, imaginative activities bring particular nationalisms into being and give them their distinctive form. If nationalism is seen as a vulgar passion provoked by empirically occurring nations, it is vulnerable to the objection implicitly or explicitly mounted against it: why should I feel more affinity with people who happen to inhabit the country I live in than with others, more like-minded, who happen to have been born in other nations? Anderson neatly turned the tables on intellectuals by taking this as a serious question. Why indeed do we feel such affinities? How to explain the fact that people are more willing to make great sacrifices for others of the same nation whom they have never met (and whom they might dislike if they did) than for worthy and unfortunate people elsewhere?

Read today, the introduction to *Imagined Communities* has the rightness and efficiency of a classic ("why hadn't anyone realized this before?") as it guides us into the paradoxes of the modern world of nationalism: nations are objectively recent but subjectively antique, even eternal; nations may be messianic, but no nation's citizens imagine that everyone should eventually join their nation. Already here Anderson displays what I take to be the key to his appeal to the nonspecialist: his ability concretely to show us the strangeness of the familiar by judicious comparisons. Try to imagine a "Tomb of the Unknown Marxist or a Cenotaph for fallen Liberals," he suggests. But a Tomb of the Unknown Soldier does not seem risible. Why? "Many different nations have such tombs without feeling any need to specify the nationality of their absent occupants. What else could they be *but* Germans, Americans, Armenians?" (*IC*, 10). In a sentence or two, wit and comparison bring readers to appreciate the necessity of accounting for a social and cultural phenomenon.

The second edition of *Imagined Communities* demonstrates, in a compelling if serendipitous way, just how much we need Anderson to provide such insights, as it takes up what he and his readers had failed to notice in the first edition. There he had quoted Ernest Renan remarking "in his suavely backhanded way," "Or l'essence d'une nation est que tous les individus aient beaucoup de choses en commun, et aussi que tous aient oubliés bien des choses" [In fact the essence of a nation is that all the individuals have many things in common and also that they have all forgotten many things], with a footnote continuing the quotation: "Tout citoyen français doit avoir oublié la Saint-Barthélemy, les massacres du Midi au XIIIe siècle" [Every French citizen must have forgotten Saint Bartholomew's, the Provence massacres in the 13th century] (*IC*, 6). In the preface to the second edition Anderson notes, "I had quoted Renan without the slightest understanding of what he had actually said: I had taken as something easily ironical what was in fact utterly bizarre" (*IC*, xiv). He calls this a "humiliating recognition," which led him to write the (superb) essay for the second edition, "Memory and Forgetting." This is humbling, if not humiliating, for readers as well as for Anderson himself, for Anderson's readers, too, I dare say, had taken Renan's observation as a version of an amusing, ironical insight: we could say that what Americans share is that they have all forgotten *The Federalist Papers*, for instance.

But now Anderson puts it in a more estranging perspective: "At first sight," he writes in the second edition, "these two sentences may seem straightforward. Yet a few moments' reflection reveals how bizarre they actually are." First, Renan feels no need to tell his readers what these to-have-been forgotten things are. "Yet who but 'Frenchmen,' as it were, would have at once understood" these elliptical references (*IC*, 200). Frenchmen are identified by their recognition of things they are required to forget. But second and most important, the expression, "*la* Saint-Barthélemy" conceals both the killers and those killed in this religious pogrom, whose participants "did not think of themselves cosily together as 'Frenchmen'" but who (like the Albigensians of the thirteenth century and the followers of Pope Innocent III, who slaughtered them in the other massacre cited) are now constructed, by the forgotten "memories" of today's nationals, as fratricidal fellow Frenchmen. The peremptory syntax of *doit avoir oublié* [is obliged to have forgotten] casts this forgetting as a civic duty. "Having to 'have already forgotten' tragedies of which one needs unceasingly to be 'reminded' turns out to be a characteristic device in the later construction of national genealogies" (*IC*, 201). On second encounter Anderson exposes in Renan's ironic remark the strange processes by which national communities are constructed as ancient, despite their modernity, and are thus imagined and sustained in a way that forges links with both the dead and the yet unborn.[2]

Anderson's chapter "Cultural Roots" is another tour de force, succinctly outlining nationalism's links and contrasts with the fundamental modes of organizing experience: with religions and dynasties, which preceded nationalism, but, above all, with a new conception of time that made the imagining of nations possible, a conception of simultaneity "marked not by prefiguring and fulfillment, but by temporal coincidence, and measured by clock and calendar" (*IC*, 24). "So deep lying is this new idea that one could argue that every essential modern conception is based upon a conception of 'meanwhile'" (*IC*, 24n34). The imagined community of a nation involves the simultaneous existence of large numbers of individuals, and the most vivid figure "for the secular, historically clocked, imagined community" is the daily ceremony of the simultaneous consumption of the newspaper: "each communicant is well aware that the ceremony he performs is being replicated simultaneously by thousands (or millions) of others of whose existence he is confident, yet of whose identity he has not the slightest notion" (*IC*, 35). Moreover the newspaper itself is constructed on the principle of simultaneity: the only link between the items that appear in it is calendrical coincidence.

The other aspect of "print-capitalism"—to use Anderson's key phrase—that "made it possible for rapidly growing numbers of people to think about themselves, and to relate to others, in profoundly new ways"

2. Homi Bhabha, in his critique of Anderson in *Nation and Narration*, uses Renan's quote as a primary piece of evidence for Anderson's neglect of "the alienating and iterative time of the sign." Bhabha, "DissemiNation: Time, Narrative, and the Margins of the Modern Nation," in *Nation and Narration*, ed. Homi Bhabha (London: Routledge, 1990), 309. Renan shows us that forgetting constitutes the beginning, writes Bhabha: "Listen to the complexity of this form of forgetting which is the moment in which the national will is articulated. . . . To be obliged to forget—in the construction of the national present—is not a question of historical memory; it is the construction of a discourse on society that performs the problematic totalization of the national will" (310–11). Bhabha's reading of Renan depends on Anderson's new account of Renan's obligatory forgetting, published as "Narrating the Nation," in the *Times Literary Supplement* [*TLS*] of June 13, 1986, before being taken up in the revised edition of *Imagined Communities*.

was the novel (*IC*, 36). The old-fashioned novel, Anderson writes, "is clear-ly a device for the presentation of simultaneity in 'homogeneous, empty time,' or a complex gloss upon the word 'meanwhile'" (*IC*, 25). The nar-rative voice, taking a quasi-omniscient view that helps to constitute some-thing like a "society," tells us what different characters—who may never encounter one another—are doing at the same time. This imagined world, "conjured up by the author in his readers' minds," "a sociological organ-ism moving calendrically through homogeneous, empty time, is a precise analogue of the idea of a nation" (*IC*, 26). Through the basic structures of address of novels and newspapers, "fiction seeps quietly and continuous-ly into reality, creating that remarkable confidence of community in ano-nymity which is the hallmark of modern nations" (*IC*, 36).

Anderson's deft analysis of novels as a force for imagining the com-munities that are nations is doubtless one reason for the great appeal of his work for people in literary and cultural studies, who have a stake in the cultural and political significance of the literary objects they study. But despite the frequency with which Anderson's general claims are cited and deployed, there has been surprisingly little discussion of his claims about the novel and of the possible ramifications of its characteristic structures of narration. Yet his later collection, *The Spectre of Comparisons*, makes clear the continuing importance of the novel for his theory of nations.[3] Ander-son devotes several essays to José Rizal's novel *Noli me tangere*, a crucial founding text for Filipino nationalism; and he develops his line of thought about novels and the nation further in another essay, "El malhadado país," which takes Mario Vargas Llosa's *El hablador* as an instance of imagining the nation in the novel of the postwar, postcolonial era, where the issues of the nature of the national community and of the novelist's role in imagin-ing it have acquired new complications.

I want to focus on three elements or aspects of the novel that are par-ticularly relevant to claims about their relation to the imagined communi-ties of nations: the formal structure of narrative point of view, the national content of the fictions (which may include both the plot and the particular

3. Benedict Anderson, *The Spectre of Comparisons: Nationalism, Southeast Asia, and the World* (London: Verso, 1998); hereafter cited parenthetically in the text as *Spectre*. One might also note the place of novels—Cooper's *The Pathfinder*, Melville's *Moby Dick*, and Twain's *Huckleberry Finn*—in the new chapter of *Imag-ined Communities* (1991), "Memory and Forgetting" (202–3).

nature of the world of the novel), and finally the construction of the reader. If Anderson's insights are to have the value they should in literary studies, we need to be more precise about what we are claiming when we cite his authority to discuss the role of fiction in the construction of nations. I propose to raise questions about several of these possible claims.

II

The most important feature of the novel for Anderson's claim seems to be a narrative technique that, through its presentation of simultaneous events, creates a world "embedded in the minds of the omniscient readers. Only they, like God, watch A telephoning C, B shopping, and D playing pool all *at once*" (*IC*, 26). The novel represents to readers a bounded community. What sort of narrative does this? Our narratological terminology is not especially helpful here. The effect is achieved by a broad range of narratives in which the narrator is not limited to what an empirical individual might know or perceive. So-called omniscient narrative certainly fits the bill, but the narrative need not be omniscient, for the narrator need not be privy to the thoughts and feelings of the different characters.[4] All that is necessary is that the narrative provide a point of view exterior to and superior to that of any particular character, with access to what is happening in different places at the same time. Interestingly, Anderson speaks not of an omniscient narrator but of an "omniscient reader," a concept hitherto unattested in narratology. The reader is positioned by the narrative as knowing what happens in several places at once. This set of novels, then, it would seem, consists of narratives where the narrator is not a character in the story, not confined to what a character might know, but provides information about simultaneous and possibly unrelated happenings. Most significant (and this is why Anderson speaks of the "old-fashioned novel"), the narrative is not filtered through the consciousness or position of a single observer. What is excluded is the limited point of view that developed in the novel during the course of the nineteenth century.

4. See Chapter 8 for discussion of the problem of omniscience. The fact that access to the minds of multiple characters is not required in this case is yet another piece of evidence that the concept of omniscience misses crucial discriminations.

Though many novels represent a society conceived as national, in Anderson's account what is crucial to the role of fiction in the imagining of nations is not this representation but that the world evoked by the novel include events happening simultaneously, extend beyond the experience of particular individuals, and be conceived as geographically situated or bounded. This involves "homogeneous empty time"—so called to highlight its difference from an earlier experience of time, the conception of events as instantiating a divine order that is not itself historical. But for thinking about novels (and about which novels do this and which do not), it might be more pertinent to speak of novels that present "the space of a community." There is some ambiguity in Anderson's discussions about whether it is important that the space or community evoked by the novel be that of a nation: does it simply present an *analogue* to the nation, or does it characteristically represent this nation in particular? There is a tension between the explicit claim about the novel as analogue of the nation and Anderson's remarks about the novels he presents in chapter 2 of *Imagined Communities*. He suggests that what is new and striking about Rizal's *Noli me tangere* (from the Philippines), José Joaquin Fernandez de Lizardi's *El periquillo sarniento* (Mexico), and Mas Marco Kartodikromo's *Semkarang hitam* (Indonesia) is that "the national imagination" fuses the world inside the novel with a world outside that is bounded by the potential nation that is the particular colony. The plurals of shops, offices, and prisons "conjure up a social space full of *comparable* prisons," shops, and offices (*IC*, 30). In other words this is not an analogue of the nation but a representation of its social space. But Anderson's explicit claims about the role of the novel and homogeneous empty time treat the world of the novel as in principle an *analogue* of the nation—one that would not therefore need to be a representation of that particular nation in order to contribute to the imagining of the nation.

Since Anderson rests his claim on formal structures, some critiques of his views seem misdirected. An instance is David Lloyd's claim that the absence of consensus about the meaning of Irish history makes the Irish novel an instrument of imposition rather than a vehicle for imagining a nation. Anderson's emphasis on the anti-imperial thrust of the novel, Lloyd writes, "precludes his acknowledging that the dialogism of the novel is not confined to its production of an anti-imperial national culture but also involves, as the Irish example makes evident, the subordination of alternative narratives within a multi-voiced national culture. For the novel not only gives voice to formerly voiceless national elites, but also disenfranchises other possible voices." Lloyd continues: "Like Bakhtin, Anderson omits the crucial regulative function of the novel that puts in place a developmental narrative through which the nation apes empire and through which it orders internally a certain hierarchy of belonging, of identity within the nation. Far from being simply an intrinsically benign and democratic form, the novel enacts the violence that underlies the constitution of identity, diffusing it in the eliciting of identification."[5]

One might reply that Anderson's chapter in *Imagined Communities* on what he calls "official nationalism" provides ample acknowledgment of the ways in which "nation apes empire" and that in "Census, Map, Museum" (a chapter of the second edition) Anderson writes shrewdly about the ways in which minorities are constructed as minorities—more by means of such things as the census than by novels. But, above all, Anderson's account does not treat the novel as "an intrinsically benign and democratic form." The novel offers a particular formal structure, involving what can be called "the space of a community," embracing what an individual cannot in fact perceive, but by no means is this intrinsically benign or democratic. Timothy Brennan, in an article that appeals to Anderson's authority, extends Anderson's formal argument by suggesting, "It was the *novel* that historically accompanied the rise of nations by objectifying the 'one, yet many' of national life, and by mimicking the structure of the nation, a clearly bordered jumble of languages and styles."[6] That is, the novel's formal encompassing of different kinds of speech or discourse enacts the possibility of a community larger than any one individual can know: "objectifying the nation's *composite* nature: a hotch potch of the ostensible separate 'levels of style' corresponding to class."[7] This is relevant to Anderson's analysis of Vargas Llosa discussed below.

5. David Lloyd, *Anomalous States: Irish Writing and the Post-Colonial Movement* (Durham, NC: Duke University Press, 1993), 154.

6. Timothy Brennan, "The National Longing for Form," in *Nation and Narration*, ed. Homi Bhabha (London: Routledge, 1990), 49.

7. Ibid., 51. Franco Moretti argues, on the contrary, "In general, the novel has not stimulated social polyphony [as Bakhtin would have it], but rather reduced it (as I have tried to show here and there in *The Way of the World* and *Modern Epic*). The undeniable polyphony of the Russian novel of ideas is in this

Some novels, of course, are national narratives with plots that are especially pertinent to the imagining of a nation.[8] The two studies of the novel that, to my knowledge, do most to flesh out Anderson's insight about the novel as a precondition for the nation both focus on novels whose plots symbolically represent the resolution of national differences. Such, for instance, are the "foundational fictions" of Latin America that Doris Sommer has studied in her book of that title. These are historical romances that "became national novels in their respective countries," potboilers that "cooked up the desire for authoritative government from the apparently raw material of erotic love."[9] These romances, which illustrate "the inextricability of politics from fiction in the history of nation-building," are "inevitably stories of star-crossed lovers who represent particular regions, races, parties, or economic interests, which should naturally come together."[10] Erotic and political desires reinforce one another: "one libidinal investment ups the ante for the other. And every obstacle that the lovers encounter heightens more than their mutual desire to (be a) couple, more than

---

respect the exception, not the rule, of novelistic evolution: not by chance generated . . . by a European, not a national frame." State building requires streamlining, as various jargons and dialects are reduced to a national language. See Franco Moretti, *Atlas of the European Novel, 1800–1900* (London: Verso, 1998), 45n; hereafter abbreviated *Atlas* and cited parenthetically in the text.

In fact, Brennan might not disagree with Moretti. The question may be how far the novel represents the social polyphony that by its embrace or containment it in effect works to reduce. Critics' eagerness to espouse the Bakhtinian thesis of the dialogic nature of the novel may lead them to neglect the novel's contribution to national homogenization.

8. Fredric Jameson notoriously claims, "All third-world texts are necessarily, I want to argue, allegorical in a very specific way: they are to be read as what I will call national allegories." The relation of this claim about all third-world texts to claims about the "old-fashioned novel" in general is scarcely clear. See Fredric Jameson, "Third-World Literature in the Era of Multi-National Capitalism," *Social Text* 15 (fall 1986): 69.

9. Doris Sommer, *Foundational Fictions: The National Romances of Latin America* (Berkeley: University of California Press, 1991), 51.

10. Doris Sommer, "Irresistible Romance: The Foundational Fictions of Latin America," in *Nation and Narration*, ed. Homi Bhabha (London: Routledge, 1990), 81. The central argument of *Foundational Fictions* is nicely summarized in "Irresistible Romance."

our voyeuristic but keenly felt passion; it also heightens their/our love for the possible nation in which the affair could be consummated."[11] These novels are very different, but they share the project of national reconciliation: the coherence of this special genre comes "from their common need to reconcile and amalgamate national constituencies, and from the strategy to cast the previously unreconciled parties, races, classes, or regions as lovers who are 'naturally' attracted and right for each other."[12]

In Franco Moretti's *Atlas of the European Novel, 1800–1900*, emphasis falls on ways in which "the novel functions as the symbolic form of the nation state. . . . [I]t's a form that (unlike an anthem or a monument) not only does not conceal the nation's internal differences but *manages to turn them into a story*" (*Atlas*, 20). Abstract and enigmatic, the new nation-state was a problem. Readers "needed a symbolic form capable of making sense of the nation-state," but before Jane Austen "no one had really come up with it" (*Atlas*, 20). "Well, the nation-state found the novel. And vice-versa: the novel found the nation-state. And being the only form that could represent it, it became an essential component of our modern culture" (*Atlas*, 17). Jane Austen's novels narrate a national marriage market, taking local gentry and joining them to a national elite; historical novels, with their concern for boundaries and differences that are subjects of contention, represent internal unevenness in nations and its erasure; picaresque novels, with their roads and inns where strangers meet, drink, and tell stories of their adventures, "define the nation as the new space of 'familiarity,' where human beings re-cognize each other as members of the same wide group"; and the *Bildungsroman* provides a new articulation of national space, stressing the contrast between the provinces and the metropolis (old versus young, unfashionable versus fashionable) and the lure of the metropolis for the young of the provinces.[13] In exploring these different relations, Moretti argues that the meeting of the novel and the nation-state "was far from inevitable. The novel didn't simply find the nation as an obvious, pre-formed fictional space: it had to wrest it from other geographical matrices that were just as capable of generating narrative—and that indeed clashed with each other throughout the eighteenth century" (*Atlas*, 53).

11. Sommer, *Foundational Fictions*, 48.
12. Sommer, "Irresistible Romance," 81.
13. Moretti, *Atlas*, 18, 40, 51, 64–65.

The novel of the nation had to wrest supremacy from *supra*national genres such as the *Robinsonade* and the *conte philosophique*, for example.

While pursuing Anderson's insight, Moretti thus ends up with a different claim. What we seem to find is that the more interested one becomes in the ways particular sorts of novels, with their plots and their imagined worlds, might advance, sustain, or legitimate the operations of nation building, the richer and more detailed become one's arguments about novel and nation, but at the cost of losing that general claim about the novelistic organization of time that was alleged to be the condition of possibility of imagining a nation. The more detailed the critical accounts of novels and their possible effects, the less powerful and encompassing the general theory of the novel. I return to this problem below.

III

After the presentation of the space of a community and the representation of the world of a nation, the third aspect of the novel pertinent to Anderson's claim is its address to the reader. His discussion of print capitalism links novels and newspapers in a way that is not obvious but that is fleshed out somewhat by Roddey Reid. Describing a new public discourse, whose effects were feared at the time, Reid declares, "prose fiction had a particularly powerful role to play as a social actor in constructing a discourse that rewrote the social body and cast social relations of post-revolutionary France into a language of family and sexuality. Moreover, I argue that it was this language that was to serve as the foundation for what Benedict Anderson has termed modern, discursively based 'imagined communities of national identity.'"[14] In France in the 1840s "the new public sphere produced by the commercial print media granted the laboring classes a

14. Roddey Reid, *Families in Jeopardy: Regulating the Social Body in France, 1750–1910* (Stanford, CA: Stanford University Press, 1993), 3. Especially piquant evidence for the "invention of a national community based on new norms for the family" comes from a contemporary complaint (by Alfred Nettement) that journalism had created "an invisible man seated in the home, between husband and wife, who returns every morning with the newspaper, seizes hold of the thoughts of a young woman, and creates for her a new ideal" (Reid, *Families in Jeopardy*, 145). Even more frequently, though, the ideas disturbing young women were attributed to novels.

droit de cité that they had not enjoyed before." "The reading of best-sellers and the daily consumption of newspapers by the middle class and workers alike amounted to identical rituals of 'imagining' a national community, however internally differentiated or divided it may be."[15] This is especially true of serial novels, such as Eugene Sue's *Les mystères de Paris* of 1842–43 and *Le Juif errant* of 1844, which were initially consumed in newspapers. (The latter helped raise the circulation of *Le Constitutionnel* to twenty-five thousand readers.)[16]

But as we start to think about audiences for novels and newspapers, and especially about empirical examples in which the media are conjoined, such as serialized novels, it is easy to miss what is most striking and original about Anderson's claim: that is, "the profound *fictiveness* of the newspaper," insofar as it depends on the literary convention of novelistic time, of an imagined world where characters go about their business independently of one another. The newspaper represents what is happening in different arenas, and when, say, events in Mali disappear from its pages, "the novelistic format of the newspaper assures [readers] that somewhere out there the character 'Mali' moves along quietly, awaiting his next appearance in the plot" (*IC*, 33). Newspapers may be thought of as "one-day best-sellers." Through them and novels, joined by the formal structure of a way of representing the space-time of a community, "fiction seeps quietly and continuously into reality, creating that remarkable confidence of community in anonymity which is the hallmark of modern nations" (*IC*, 35–36).

What is not clear, once we try to take this claim further, beyond the formal *analogy* between the space-time presumed by novels and newspapers to the idea of a national community imagined by readers of novels, as by readers of newspapers, is how far novels or newspapers do indeed lead to imagining a national community of readers. Few newspapers in the period of nation building are sufficiently dominant to serve by themselves as a national voice or to constitute their readers as a national community, and few are genuinely national in their readership. What of provincial newspapers? In nineteenth-century France, for instance, none of the many Parisian papers was dominant. Do readers of *La Presse* imagine a national

15. Ibid., 140, 139.

16. Peter McPhee, *A Social History of France, 1780–1880* (London: Routledge, 1992), 127.

community composed of readers of this journal or of all journals?[17] What is the evidence that readers of a Parisian newspaper imagine a French community of readers performing together the daily ritual? None of this matters if the argument depends on the fact that the community of readers of a novel or newspaper is the *model* for the imagined community of a nation or if the readers of one newspaper are imagining a community that can be equated with the communities imagined by readers of the other, but it does matter if the national community is supposed to be that imagined by those simultaneously reading a given newspaper.

But, while it is easy to imagine (though hard to demonstrate) that readers of newspapers are brought together as a community (whether regional or national) by the shared daily ritual of reading the same text at the same time, what about readers of novels? For novel readers the notion of a community of readers who together are consuming the best-seller of the day is accompanied by another possibility: the potential community of all those addressed by the novel, wherever and whenever they should pick it up. Since newspapers are read on the day of publication and thrown away, whereas novels are characteristically readable at any time, not tied, as newspapers are, to a particular time and place of origination, we cannot assume that they generate the same kind of community of readers, created in the ritual of reading.

We should, therefore, ask about the audience of novels. This is not only a question of who actually reads them but of whom they address; indeed, we need to distinguish their address—the readerly role they construct—and their actual audiences. Novels (and of course not only novels) construct a role for readers by positing a reader who knows some things but not everything, needs to have some things explained but not others. But let us look at Anderson's first example of the nation-imagining novel, José Rizal's *Noli me tangere*. Here is the beginning:

A fines de octubre, don Santiago de los Santos, conocido popularmente bajo el nombre de Capitán Tiago, daba una cena, que, sin embargo de haberlo anunciado aquella tarde tan sólo, contra su costumbre, era ya el tema de todas las conversaciones en Binondo, en otros arrabales y hasta en Intramuros. Capitán Tiago pasaba

17. For discussion see ibid.; and Claude Bellanger, Jacques Godechot, Pierre Guiral, and Fernand Terrou, eds., *Histoire générale de la presse française* (Paris: Presses universitaires de France, 1969).

entonces por el hombre más ramboso y sabíase que su casa, como su país, no cerraba las puertas a nadie, como no sea al comercio o a toda idea nueva o atrevia.

Como una sacudida eléctrica corrió la noticia en el mundo de los parásitos, moscas, o colados, que Dios crió en su infinita bondad, y tan cariñosamente multiplica en Manila. . . .

Dábase esta cena en una casa de la calle de Anloague, y, ya que no recordamos su número, la describiremos de manera que se la reconozca aún, si esque los temblores no la han arruinado.[18]

Towards the end of October, Don Santiago de los Santos, popularly known as Capitan Tiago, was giving a dinner party. Although, contrary to his usual practice, he had announced it only that afternoon, it was already the subject of every conversation in Binondo, in other quarters of the city, and even in Intramuros. In those days Capitan Tiago had the reputation of a lavish host. It was known that his house, like his country, closed its doors to nothing, except to commerce and to any new or daring idea.

So the news coursed like an electric shock through the community of parasites, spongers, and gatecrashers whom God, in His infinite goodness, created and so tenderly multiplies in Manila. . . .

The dinner was being given at a house on Anloague Street. Since we do not recall the street number, we shall describe it in such a way that it may still be recognized—that is, if earthquakes have not yet destroyed it. (*IC*, 26–27)[19]

Anderson comments:

[T]he image (wholly new to Filipino writing) of a dinner-party being discussed by hundreds of unnamed people, who do not know each other, in quite different parts of Manila, . . . immediately conjures up the imagined community. And in the phrase "a house on Anloague Street" which "we shall describe in such a way that it may still be recognized," the would-be recognizers are we-Filipino-readers. The casual progression of this house from the "interior" time of the novel to the "exterior" time of the [Manila] reader's everyday life gives a hypnotic confirmation of the solidity of a single community, embracing characters, author and readers, moving onward through calendrical time. (*IC*, 27)

18. José Rizal, *Noli me tangere* (1887; repr., Madrid: Ediciones de Cultural Hispánica, 1992), 49–50.

19. Since Anderson convincingly analyzes the inadequacies of the English translation, I quote the English from Anderson's version, where he provides it. I have also consulted the excellent French translation: José Rizal, *N'y touchez pas!* trans. Jovita Ventura Castro (Paris: Gallimard, 1980).

A community within the novel is evoked, and it is subtly extended to the community of those addressed, who might still recognize the house. But the fact that Anderson puts "Manila" in brackets—"the [Manila] reader"— indicates that there is a difficulty here. One cannot simply say that the community addressed is the residents of Manila in Rizal's day, nor its residents since Rizal's day, nor simply "we-Filipino-readers." Even the Westerner reading this in translation is drawn in by the narrative address, which assures him or her that if one were there, one could recognize the house, that there is a continuity between the world of the novel and the reader's own. Indeed, the parenthetical stipulation "if earthquakes have not yet destroyed it," evoking a time extending beyond the moment of narration (as well as an ironic take on the consequence of the islands' geology), posits a future audience of those who might arrive on the scene. Although the novel is replete with place-names from Manila (Binondo, Intramuros), presented as if they needed no explanation and thus presuming a reader who knows Manila, this is a technique by which realistic fiction posits the reality and independence of the world it describes—asserts by presupposing.

In fact, the mode of address of *Noli me tangere* often suggests that the reader is not a Manileño but someone who needs to be told how things are done there—a stranger, even. The house on Anloague Street, we are told, "[e]s un edificio bastante grande, al estilo de muchos del país, situado hacia la parte que da a un brazo des Pásig, llamado por algunos ría de Binondo, y que desempeña, como todos los ríos de Manila, el múltiple papel de baño, alcantarilla, lavadero, pesquería, medio de transporte y comunicación y hasta fuente de aqua potabile, si lo tiene por conveniente el chino aguador"[20] [is a sizable building in the style of many houses of the country, situated in a spot that gave onto an arm of the Pasig, which some call the river of Binondo, and which, like all the rivers in Manila, plays the multiple role of bath, sewer, washing place, fishing spot, means of transport, and even source of drinking water, if the seller of Chinese water finds it convenient].

The explanations "like all the rivers in Manila" and "in the style of many buildings of the country" have a quasi-anthropological air, as if telling others about a land not theirs. And there are many similar passages in the novel: "we will immediately find ourselves in a large room, called *caí-*

20. Rizal, *Noli me tangere*, 50.

da in these parts, I don't know why" [nos encontraremos de golpe en una espaciosa estancia llamada allí *caída*, no sé por qué (51)]; a beautiful girl "dressed in the picturesque costume of women of the Philippines" [vestida con el pintoresco traje de las hijas de Filipinas (81–82)]; the door "leads to a little chapel or oratory, which no Filipino house should be without" [que non debe faltar en ninguna casa filipina (88)]. The effect here is similar to Balzac: offering a veritable anthropology of Manila and its ways, with references that would not have been necessary for Manila readers, who don't need to be told what things are called in their country or that someone is dressed like a Filipino or what every Filipino house must have. While it could be argued that this last phrase, for instance, works to satirize, for Manila readers, the empty piety of the land that makes chapels obligatory, whatever the faith of their owners, one can reply that it is by speaking anthropologically, as if to an outsider to whom these things need to be explained, that the narrator achieves this effect.

Another distinctive passage to which Anderson draws our attention contains a direct address to the reader: "Pues no hay porteros ni criados que pidan o pregunten por el billete de invitación, subiremos, ¡oh tú que me lees, amigo o enemigo! si es que te atraen a ti los acordes de la orquesta, la luz o el significativo *clin-clan* de la vajilla y de los cubiertos, y quieres ver cómo son las reuniones allá en la Perla del Oriente" (50–51) [Since there are no porters or servants requesting or asking to see invitation cards, let us proceed upstairs, O reader mine, be you enemy or friend, if you are drawn to the strains of the orchestra, the light(s) or the suggestive clinking of dishes and trays, and if you wish to see how parties are given in the Pearl of the Orient] (*Spectre*, 240). Anderson's translation of "allá en la Perla del Oriente" as simply "in the Pearl of the Orient" rather than, say, "*over there* in the Pearl of the Orient" attenuates the implication of the Spanish original that the readers addressed are not necessarily themselves in Manila (the French renders this "*là-bas* au pays de la Perle d'Orient").[21] But the main point here is the address, "O you who read me, be you enemy or friend." In *Imagined Communities* Anderson spoke of these opening pages being addressed to "we-Filipino-readers" (27), but in *The Spectre of Comparisons* he notes that the text "makes its readership marvelously problematic: *amigo ó enemigo?* Who are these *enemigos*? Surely not other Filipinos?

21. See Rizal, *N'y touchez pas!* 44.

Surely not Spaniards? After all, the *Noli* was written to inspire the nationalism of Filipino youth, and for the Filipino people! What on earth would Spanish readers be doing 'inside it'?" (*Spectre*, 240). But inside it they are, as addressees. A footnote allows that "Rizal certainly expected copies of his novels to fall into the hands of the colonial regime and the hated friars, and doubtless enjoyed the prospect of their squirming at his biting barbs" (*Spectre*, 240n), and earlier, contrasting Rizal with Tagore, Anderson notes that only 3 percent of Rizal's countrymen understood Spanish (*Spectre*, 232). The audience for a novel in Spanish necessarily included many who were not potential Filipinos—whence "you who read me, friend or enemy." "He wrote as much for the enemy as the friend," Anderson concludes here. This is indeed the implication of the structures of presupposition and address adopted in the novel.

One might add, further, that in his address to readers Rizal evokes the antagonism, the opposition between friend and enemy, that will prove crucial for building a nationalist movement and a nation, as for politics in general. Far from assuming that the community he addresses consists of like-minded friends, he recognizes that they can band together as friends only against the enemies, whom his work helps to constitute as enemies of the national project.[22] I will return to this problem later.

In Balzac, whose national situation is quite different, we find a similarity in the structures of presupposition and the role created for the reader. What is common is the novelistic address, which creates a community of those who pick up the book and accept the readerly role that it offers. Thus Balzac purveys ethnological information about Parisian habits and types, as if for readers who view them from a distance, but at the same

22. For the constitutive role of "antagonism" in the construction of hegemony, and in politics generally, see Ernesto Laclau and Chantal Mouffe, *Hegemony and Socialist Strategy: Toward a Radical Democratic Politics* (London: New Left Books, 1985). For the crucial role of the distinction between friend and enemy see Jacques Derrida's discussion of Blake, Nietzsche, and especially Carl Schmitt in *Politiques de l'amitié* (Paris: Galilée, 1994), 91–157, 272–80. Schmitt's *Der Begriff des Politischen* (1932) treats the discrimination of friend from enemy as constitutive for politics; and the essence of a people's political existence is its determining for itself who is friend and who enemy (quoted in Derrida, *Politiques de l'amitié*, 276). Derrida stresses that in this distinction "one concept bears the ghost of the other: the enemy the friend and the friend the enemy" (92).

time evokes a community of readers through the presupposition of shared knowledge: "he was one of those Parisians who always manages to look inordinately pleased with himself," for instance, presupposes familiarity with the type, and thus an insider's view, at the same time that it gives us, French or not, the information we need to position ourselves as insider. The phrase "one of those" marks this as a category that readers are presumed already to possess, as if they were already initiated into the mysteries of Paris, but in fact gives them what they need to know, in the Balzacian ethnology of Paris. And, more important perhaps, it makes this sort of "insider information" into an object of readerly desire. For readers of Rizal's novel, who may have never before taken any interest in the inhabitants of Manila, much less in its inhabitants of the late nineteenth century, it becomes desirable to be such an insider, to know about the types that constitute this nation. The presentation of "the Pearl of the Orient" as an object of interest, as something people might or might not know about, gives it a position in the world and makes it something to which one might feel allegiance. In short, novels such as Rizal's and Balzac's, in their evocation of a world of diverse characters, adventures, and national or regional ways of being, may do much to encourage the imagining of those communities that are or become nations, but they do not do so, I submit, by addressing readers *as nationals*. One might say, rather, that the posited audience is those who could recognize that the community being described is, if not a nation, one about which it is an issue whether it is a nation. At the very least, the relation between national community and the community presupposed by novelistic address is a question that needs to be examined more closely for a range of cases.

IV

Anderson's essay on Mario Vargas Llosa's *El hablador* [The Story-teller] in *The Spectre of Comparisons* offers an opportunity to pursue further the problem of the community of readers addressed. First, though, we need to consider its credentials as a novel of the nation. Anderson notes that "our century's hard times have made some at least of the utopian elements of nineteenth-century nationalism, for which universal progress was the foundation, decreasingly plausible," so that novelists today are "faced with aporiae with which the great novelists of the last century did not feel compelled to contend" (*Spectre*, 335).[23] If nineteenth-century novels of the nation enacted the overcoming of national divisions or inequalities, readers today are more prepared to appreciate the obduracy of the problems and obstacles. In the Americas, as elsewhere, we are today all too aware that the triumph of the nation involves the conquest or oppression of indigenous peoples; but dramatizing their situation in a novel of the nation is a matter of some difficulty, since "we are living in a time when ventriloquizing persecuted and oppressed minorities has become (and not only ethically) intolerable" (*Spectre*, 335).

Vargas Llosa's novel might be said to take as an implied point of reference San Martin's 1821 proclamation that "in the future the aborigines shall not be called Indians or natives; they are children and citizens of Peru and they shall be known as Peruvians" (*Spectre*, 193). It has not yet happened, but could it, and if so, at what cost? In dramatizing debates about the future of the Indians of Peru and the impossibility of satisfactory solutions, this novel does not pretend to resolve national differences, as earlier novels did. Yet, Anderson writes, "that *El Hablador* is a nationalist novel is beyond doubt, but the interesting question is how its nationalism is 'performed'" (*Spectre*, 356).

The narrator of *El hablador* is a cosmopolitan Peruvian writer, living in Italy, trying to escape his "malhadado país"—his "unfortunate" or "accursed" nation. He comes upon an exhibition of photographs of a tribe of Amazonian Indians of Peru, the Machiguenga, who had obsessed a friend from his student days, Saúl Zuratas. He and Saúl had debated the moral and political issues concerning the status of the Indians, and he himself had come to be haunted by the idea of this tribe. The narrator speaks of his past and of exchanges with Saúl in chapters that alternate with chapters presenting the world of the Machiguenga in the voice of a tribal storyteller who is not identified but whom readers eventually come to take as Saúl Zuratas himself.

The novel does not account for the presence of these Machiguenga

23. For discussion of the novels of nationalist projects by two contemporary writers, the Indonesian Pramoedya Ananta Toer, to whom Anderson alludes (*Spectre*, 337–38), and the Kenyan Ngugi wa Thiong'o, see Pheng Cheah, *Spectral Nationality: Passages of Freedom from Kant to Postcolonial Literatures of Liberation* (New York: Columbia University Press, 2003).

chapters in any way: the narrator has not seen Saúl for two decades, and while he himself had tried to write about the Machiguenga, each time he was blocked by

the difficulty of inventing, in Spanish and within a logically consistent intellectual framework, a literary form that would suggest, with any reasonable degree of credibility, how a primitive man with a magico-religious mentality would go about telling a story. All my attempts led each time to the impasse of a style that struck me as glaringly false, as implausible as the various ways in which philosophers and novelists of the Enlightenment had put words into the mouths of their exotic characters in the eighteenth century when the theme of the "noble savage" was fashionable in Europe.[24]

The narrator's chapters tell of his debates with Saúl about the Indians, his own investigations, his failure to write about them, and his growing conviction that his friend Saúl had, in a process he claims to be unable to imagine, become the storyteller he is convinced he sees in a photograph of the tribe, displayed with others at the spot in Florence where Dante first glimpsed Beatrice. The other chapters—in a language whose grammar suggests a different way of thinking, a different perception of time, space, and individuals—present the lore of the Machiguengas and, at the end, tales recognizable in their links to Kafka or the history of the Jews (Saúl was "an ex-Jew" who knew much of Kafka by heart). The novel presents no warrant for these chapters. As Anderson remarks, Vargas Llosa has set himself the arduous task of "inventing a persuasive voice for the hablador which is as remote as possible from that of any self-imagined Peruvian, yet which at the same time radically undermines its own authenticity" (*Spectre*, 355). The storyteller is supposed to be the voice of the community, the source of its knowledge and its traditions, whose storytelling is "[s]omething primordial, something that the very existence of a people may depend on."[25] Yet in the Americas tales of indigenous communities have had to emerge through translations of the missionaries, anthropologists, or other contaminating intermediaries, and the novel implicitly comments on this fact by inventing this figure of Saúl Zuratas, who is a conspicuously dubious imagined intermediary. One of the distinctive devices of the Machiguenga

24. Mario Vargas Llosa, *The Storyteller*, trans. Helen Lane (New York: Penguin, 1990), 175–78.
25. Ibid., 94.

chapters—the way tales usually conclude with "That, at any rate, is what I have learned" [Eso es, al menos, lo que yo he sabido]—works to undermine any narrative authority, if we think of the storyteller as an individual, such as Saúl; but it works also, or alternatively, to situate this discourse as a repetition of other discourses.[26]

As is clear from the way the novel boldly does what the narrator finds impossible—invents a language for a people with a radically different worldview—this is a novel that takes risks in approaching the problem of the nation and of those who, it seems, cannot be included without losing their identity. The impossible relation between the novel's parts dramatizes the unsolvable problem of the position of the Indians in Peru, where inclusion means assimilation, transformation, and destruction of their world, just as surely as exclusion will bring their destruction. In his debates with Saúl, the narrator argues for integrating and modernizing, but the story puts his position in doubt (shouldn't they, on the contrary, be left alone in their own world?), and his research obsession, which seems disinterested by comparison with that of missionaries, makes more plausible Saúl's position. Yet if the *hablador* is Saúl and not just a fantasy of the narrator's, this implies, on the one hand, a critique of the notion of the Indian community's purity and, on the other hand, the view that preservation occurs through the intervention of an outsider. Culture is preserved through imitation, repetition, and adulteration (for instance, the assimilation to Machiguenga culture of tales from Kafka and from the history of the Jews). Moreover, and this is especially pertinent to the novel's performance, from the point of view of the reader, it is precisely the "dubious," "compromised" representation, in Spanish, of the Machiguenga world that earns support for the idea of preserving this world in its supposed purity and autonomy.

26. In addition, assertions frequently close with *perhaps* [*quizá*, or *tal vez*] ("Everything was going very well, perhaps")—another device that is likely to strike the reader as undermining narrative authority, as traditionally conceived. Efrain Kristal, discussing the language of these chapters, writes that "the most salient feature of this stylized language for the reader is a recursive pattern of ungrammatical conventions, suggestive of a different way of thinking" (Efrain Kristal, *Temptation of the Word: The Novels of Mario Vargas Llosa* [Nashville, TN: Vanderbilt University Press, 1988], 165).

In juxtaposing these two sets of chapters (as if to fulfill Bakhtin's dubious claim that the novel is a dialogic form that cites all forms of discourse without any one dominating) and in offering no explanation or claim about the authenticity of the Machiguenga lore, the novel stages the national project articulated by San Martin, in his claim, before the existence of Peru, that the Indians were "children of Peru." Or rather, as Anderson claims, citing Walter Benjamin's paradox that every document of civilization is at the same time a document of barbarism, *El hablador* "considers the truth of Benjamin's paradox, taking all its terms together. One could say that it 'performs' the impossibility of transcending it, as well as of escaping from it. This is, perhaps, the only way in our time in which the national novel, the narrative of the nation, can be written, and rewritten, and rewritten" (*Spectre*, 359).

Unlike what Anderson calls the "old-fashioned novel," whose narrative voice easily encompasses characters unknown to each other and creates "in the mind of the omniscient reader" the community to which they could belong, which is or is like that of the nation, here there is no all-encompassing narrator, no possibility of inventing a voice that can include all those who might be claimed by the nation. That impossibility may be read—so Anderson does—as bringing "the timbre of tragedy as well as the semantics of shame" to the nation (*Spectre*, 359), but it may also be read as an attempt to imagine a community without unity, or what Jean-Luc Nancy calls a "communauté désoeuvrée": community as spacing rather than fusion, sublation, or transcendence. The community is a "communauté *désoeuvrée*" because it is based on the fact that "there can be no singular being without another singular being"[27] and that what beings share "is not a common work that exceeds them but the differential experience of the other as finite being."[28] One does not recognize the Other

27. Jean-Luc Nancy, *La communauté désoeuvrée* (Paris: Christian Bourgeois, 1986), 71.

28. Natalie Melas, *All the Difference in the World: Postcoloniality and the Ends of Comparison* (Stanford, CA: Stanford University Press, 2007), chap. 3. I am indebted to Melas's discussion of the usefulness of Nancy's concept for conceiving community in the postcolonial world and breaking away from the Hegelian model of mutual recognition as a dialectical model of community based on identity. She herself develops a notion of *dissimilation* to set against the model of assimilation.

but "éprouve son semblable" [experiences one's counterpart], who is similar in being singular.[29]

Anderson reads *El hablador* in the register of tragedy and shame in part because he reads it not just as a novel of Peru but as a novel *for* Peruvians about the problem of their nation; he speaks of "the Peruvian Spanish-reading public which is the writer's first audience" (*Spectre*, 355). But one might wonder. Vargas Llosa is a novelist of international fame, whose non-Peruvian Spanish readers far outnumber his Peruvian ones. In "The National Longing for Form" Timothy Brennan describes the way in which—especially for a group of eminent writers from the third world—the novel functions today above all in an international market. Today the novel is "the form through which a thin foreign-educated stratum (however sensitive or committed to domestic political interests) has communicated to metropolitan reading publics, often in translation. It has been, in short, a naturally cosmopolitan form that empire has *allowed to play a national role, as it were, only in an international arena.*"[30] In particular, there has emerged an important strain of third-world writing: "the lament for the necessary and regrettable insistence of nation-forming, in which the writer proclaims his identity with a country whose artificiality and exclusiveness have driven him into a kind of exile—a simultaneous recognition of nationhood and alienation from it."[31]

Though this is not exactly true of Vargas Llosa (Brennan is thinking of writers such as Rushdie and Naipaul), it helps prevent us from taking it for granted that the community of readers addressed by *El hablador* is a national one. Read again its opening lines:

I came to Firenze to escape Peru and Peruvians for a while, and suddenly my unfortunate country [malhadado país] forced itself on me this morning in an unexpected way. I had visited Dante's restored house, the little Church of San Martino del Véscovo, and the lane where, so legend has it, he first saw Beatrice, when in the little Via Santa Margherita, a window display stopped me short: bows, arrows, a carved oar, a pot with a geometric design, a mannequin bundled into a wild cotton cushma.[32]

29. Nancy, *La communauté désoeuvrée*, 82.
30. Brennan, "The National Longing for Form," 56 (my italics).
31. Ibid., 63.
32. Vargas Llosa, *The Storyteller*, 3.

What sort of narrative audience is addressed here? It is first of all one that does not need explanation of the easy references to Firenze and to Dante's glimpse of Beatrice. Proper names, taken for granted, delineate the European scene, but when the narrator turns to the materials from the jungle in the window display and then to the photographs that "suddenly brought back for me the flavor of the Peruvian jungle," he uses terms accessible to the European reader—"bows, arrows, a carved oar"—and only the mild exoticism of the "cotton cushma." If one had to describe the reader whom this opening page appears to imagine and address, it would not be the Peruvian national so much as an international cosmopolitan reader, one likely to be struck by the unexpected contrast between the archetypal literary site and reminders of the unmarked scene identified with Peru: "The wide rivers, the enormous trees, the fragile canoes, the frail huts raised on pilings, and the knots of men and women, naked to the waist and daubed with paint, looking at me unblinkingly from the glossy print."[33]

El hablador may not be addressed to Peruvians, and indeed Peruvian readers may be precisely the wrong audience for this novel. Doris Sommer, whose "About-Face: The Talker Turns" is a brilliant, conflicted critical study of the novel, reports that educated Peruvians dislike it: "One simplified version of the impatience Vargas Llosa's novel, along with his fiction in general, elicits among educated Peruvian readers, is presented by Mirko Lauer. . . . His fundamental objection, it seems, is that the novelist fails to maintain an ethical and coherent position."[34] Peruvians may be in a particularly bad position to read it as a novel, for as inhabitants of a country where the status of the Indians has been a burning political question for some time and where Vargas Llosa is also a political figure with a record of actions, pronouncements, and essays on political and cultural topics, they

33. Ibid. Of course, many Peruvians have had a cosmopolitan education and can certainly join this audience without difficulty, but I do not believe that the audience is a national one.

34. Doris Sommer, "About-Face: The Talker Turns," *boundary 2* 23, no. 1 (spring 1996): 129n. See also the fine treatment by Lucille Kerr, *Reclaiming the Author: Figures and Fictions from Spanish America* (Durham, NC: Duke University Press, 1992); and the discussion by Efrain Kristal in *Temptation of the Word*. Jane O'Bryan-Knight, in *The Story of the Storyteller* (Amsterdam: Rodopoi, 1995), maintains, wrongly in my view, that this is a novel about the novelist writing this novel. I think that the narrator's *inability* to write the part of the storyteller is crucial.

are likely to take the novel, as Sommer herself does for most of her essay, as primarily a political statement, which can then be faulted for quietism or evasiveness. Sommer herself, as a critic responsible to the cultural context, interprets the novel in the light of Vargas Llosa's essays and political activities, where she finds insensitivity to the Indians, "readiness to sacrifice the Indian cultures, since they interfere with modernity's fight against hunger and need."[35] In a passage early in her essay she suggests that the novel is his attempt to give himself an alibi. Vargas Llosa, she argues, does not see himself as internally divided, does not presume to contain the two sides of Peru:

Either this reluctance to contain Peru is a facile admission of limits, based on rigid notions of difference between Indian tradition and modern projects, or the lack of presumption can be an ethical caution against containment and control of the incommensurable cultures in a multifarious nation. On the one hand, Vargas Llosa could be absolving himself from the moral obligation of inclusiveness and tolerance, a likely hand, given his impatient prescriptions for neutralizing and nationalizing specifically Indian cultures. But on the other hand, more promisingly, the refusal could be read against his politics, as a defense of difference.[36]

She makes it clear that his countrymen take the first, "more likely" view, which she resourcefully pursues for most of her essay. The duality that the novel presents "can lead to dismissing indigenous otherness as inassimilable and inessential to the Peruvian body politic, a dismissal that countrymen read in Vargas Llosa's consistent carelessness about Indian cultures and lives."[37] But in the end, putting Peruvian contexts behind her, Som-

---

35. Sommer, "About-Face," 126. In what might be a key point, Sommer suggests that in constructing the Machiguenga chapters Vargas Llosa has been influenced by the better-known native language, Quechua, spoken in the mountains of Peru, and that he there deploys what she calls "Quechua-inflected Spanish": "The Andean sounds are so improbable in the jungle that the effect is to suggest the writer's indifference to Indians" (97). If this were true, it would be a pertinent critique of the artistic realization of these chapters and their failure to imagine a plausible language of otherness. I myself am not competent to judge this point and can note only that other critics I have consulted do not see the Machiguenga chapters in this way, including Efrain Kristal, who has the most convincing discussion of the style of these chapters and especially of the grammatical and other devices by which Vargas Llosa has created the effect of a non-Western mode of thinking.

36. Sommer, "About-Face," 94.

37. Ibid., 128.

mer turns to Emmanuel Levinas, who provides warrant for the second, unlikely possibility that the novel is a defense of difference, a defense of the view that presuming to contain or "to understand the Other willfully ignores the mystery of his Saying." The structure of the novel, by allowing that saying, "holds out a hope: the possibility of recognition—on a reading from this geographic remove—even if the promise is betrayed by the man called Vargas Llosa."[38]

How striking that to permit a reading of this book as a novel with political implications rather than the political statement of the man Vargas Llosa, Doris Sommer requires what she suddenly names as a "geographic remove," the move with which the novel begins! All the more reason to think, as the opening of the novel itself suggests, that the reader the book addresses is not, perhaps, the educated Peruvian intent on evaluating the political statement or reading it like a newspaper but the reader at some geographic remove, who picks up a new novel by a well-known novelist.

V

In the chapter on Vargas Llosa in *The Spectre of Comparisons* Anderson summarizes his original hypothesis about the historic role of the novel:

In *Imagined Communities* I argued that the historical appearance of the novel-as-popular-commodity and the rise of nation-ness were intimately related. Both nation and novel were spawned by the simultaneity made possible by clock-derived, man-made "homogeneous empty time," and thereafter, of Society understood as a bounded intrahistorical entity. All this opened the way for the human beings to imagine large, cross-generational, sharply delineated communities, composed of people mostly unknown to one another, and to understand these communities as gliding endlessly towards a limitless future. The novelty of the novel as a literary form lay in its capacity to represent synchronically this bounded, intrahistorical society-with-a-future (*Spectre*, 334).

His basic claim, he reminds us, was based on the form of the novel. But this linking of novel and nation led to the assumption "that the novel would always be capable of representing, at different levels, the reality and truth of the nation"—an easy assumption since, for instance, "Balzac's *La Comédie humaine* (which is really, if the expression be excused, *La Comédie*

38. Ibid., 130.

française), the huge oeuvre of Zola, and even that of Proust, provide us with incomparable accounts of the France of their time" (*Spectre*, 334). He then lists various reasons why, in the second half of the twentieth century, the affinities between novel and nation become strained, including the division of the novel into subgenres—gothic, crime novel, etc.—"each with its own conventions and audiences which are by no means necessarily the fellow nationals of the author" (*Spectre,* 335). Anderson is scrupulous in distinguishing between the formal argument about the formal representation of time and space in the novel and the fact that, at "different levels," *particular* traditional novels provide a convincing representation of the society of a nation. But his own choice of examples, Rizal and Balzac, with their national *content*, has encouraged critics to assume that the decisive factor is the novel's representation of the nation.

Anderson's own remark about subgenres and national audiences shows how easy it is to pass without noticing it from one sort of argument to another—to a different argument that may be highly contestable. It is only from the vantage point of a twentieth- or twenty-first-century reader that the nineteenth-century novel looks "unified" in a national way, without subgenres and without international audiences. Just by way of indication—this is a subject that would require much fuller discussion and documentation—Franco Moretti's lively brief chapter on "Narrative Markets" notes the dominance in nineteenth-century Europe of the subgenres of the historical novel, the sensation novel, and the sentimental novel, whose audiences were international:

the great successes of the nineteenth century: Scott, Bulwer-Lytton, most of Dickens, and sensation novels from the British sample; sentimental novels, Dumas, Sue and Hugo from the French one. It is a regular and monotonous pattern: all of Europe reading the same books, with the same enthusiasm, and roughly in the same years (when not months). All of Europe unified by a desire, not for "realism" (the mediocre fortune of Stendhal and Balzac leaves no doubts on this point)—not for realism but for . . . "the melodramatic imagination": a rhetoric of stark contrasts that is present a bit everywhere and is perfected by Dumas and Sue, (and Verdi), who are the most popular writers of the day.[39]

39. Moretti, *Atlas of the European Novel*, 176–77. In fact, this quotation ("all of Europe reading the same books") exaggerates what Moretti's data show, for he goes on to describe the uneven diffusion of British and French novels, for example. But the central points remain: niche markets are not a twentieth-century invention, and the audiences are international, not simply national.

When we are discussing the audience for novels, we need to avoid unwarranted presumptions about both the novels' address—the readerly role they construct—and their actual audiences. It seems to me very likely that in both cases the link between novel and nation will prove weaker than those who cite Anderson's authority are inclined to assume.

The power of Anderson's thesis about the novel is to make the form of the novel—in particular its construction of a narrative audience—a condition of imagining the nation: a structural condition of possibility. Critics, who are interested in the plots, themes, and imaginative worlds of particular novels, have tended to transform that thesis into a claim about the way some novels, by their contents, help to encourage, shape, justify, or legitimate the nation—a different claim, though one of considerable interest. The fact that Anderson's own examples involve some slippage from one claim to the other helps to explain the critical reception but does not excuse it. Literary critics in particular ought to be skilled at distinguishing an argument about the implications and consequences of a literary form from claims about the effects of particular sorts of plots and thematic representations.

The distinction between the novel as condition of possibility of imagining the nation (the form of the novel as condition of possibility of the imagined communities that are nations) and the role of novels in shaping or legitimating the nation needs to be maintained, not only for greater theoretical rigor and perspicacity but also for the force of the argument. When there is slippage from an argument about conditions of possibility to one about the effects of certain novelistic representations, the argument may become richer and more specific in some respects but also considerably weaker, vastly more dubious.

If, for instance, we ask what made Britons "Britons," it is more plausible to answer "war with France" than "Jane Austen." The historian Linda Colley writes that "we can plausibly regard Great Britain as an invented nation. . . . It was an invention forged above all by war."[40] "Imagining the French as their vile opposites," Britons "defined themselves against the French as they imagined them to be, superstitious, militarist, decadent and unfree."[41] The differential construction of identity makes the oppositions Protestant versus Catholic and British versus French into the princi-

40. Linda Colley, *Britons: Forging the Nation, 1701–1831* (New Haven, CT: Yale University Press, 1992), 5.

41. Ibid., 368, 5.

pal generators of this identity, even though Austen's marriage plots, it can be argued, helped shape a nation in showing that there is a large space in southern England where heroines can be at home. In a similar vein Gopal Balakrishnan argues in "The National Imagination" that "the cultural affinities shaped by print-capitalism do not themselves seem sufficiently resonant to generate the colossal sacrifices that modern peoples are at times willing to make for their nation."[42] It is in wartime and in relation to enemies that the culture of sacrifice takes over and feeds national feeling. The contribution of the plots and themes of novels is likely to be considerably smaller, but their form may be the condition of possibility of the imagined communities that are energized by discourses of war.

In brief, if we try to argue that the novel, through its representations of nationhood, made the nation, we are on shaky ground, but if we argue that the novel was a condition of possibility for imagining something like a nation, for imagining a community that could be opposed to another, as friend to foe, and thus a condition of possibility of a community organized around a political distinction between friend and enemy, the case is markedly stronger. We have considerable warrant for maintaining the novel's importance in the face of the historian's insistence on socioeconomic and political factors, from markets to wars. Note that the work of novels envisioned here is not that of propagandistically opposing the wicked and decadent French to the stalwart Britons (though some novels do this). On the contrary, the novel can be a condition of possibility of imagining communities that may become nations because it addresses readers in a distinctively open way, offering the possibility of adhering to a community, as an insider, without laying down particular criteria that have to be met. If a national community is to come into being, there must be the possibility for large numbers of people to come to feel a part of it, and in offering the insider's view to those who might have been deemed outsiders, the novel creates that possibility. When José Rizal's *Noli me tangere* addresses the reader, "O you who read me, be you friend or enemy," the distinction between friend and enemy, on which the political events that make the nation will come to depend, is exposed as not external to the novel but rather as a possibility that arises within it. The community of readers that aris-

42. Gopal Balakrishnan, "The National Imagination," in *Mapping the Nation*, ed. Gopal Balakrishnan (London: Verso, 1996), 198.

es from a novel is one in which readers may be both friend and enemy, at once insider and outsider. If politics depends on the distinction between friend and enemy, deciding who is which or ranging oneself on one side or the other, the novel provides a space within which the distinction can arise, prior to those decisions.

This is a complex matter because there are radically different ways in which readers of the novel may be both insiders and outsiders. In colonies or former colonies in particular, readers' ideas of a national identity may arise from a vision from outside, when they see how they are placed on the map. In the case of Rizal's *Noli me tangere* the readers as insiders/outsiders might be European-educated Filipinos who observe the inhabitants of the colony through the book's anthropological gaze and who thus come to see themselves as Filipinos through this vision. The insider/outsider might also be the nineteenth-century Spaniard or the twentieth-century cosmopolitan reader who comes to share the narrative's commitment to a Filipino community. Anderson calls this double or comparative vision, with its oscillation between inside and outside, "the spectre of comparisons," and it is a spectre that haunts the novel, that makes it possible.

Anderson's work can lead us to realize that what is distinctive about the novel, about its formal adumbration of the space of a community, is its open invitation to readers of different conditions to become insiders, even while the novel raises as a possibility the distinction between insider and outsider, friend and foe, that becomes the basis of political developments.[43] This is what gives the novel so potent a role as condition of possibility for the nation: the form of the novel as condition of possibility for imagining the nation, not the content of novels as representations of the nation.

43. I am grateful to Pheng Cheah for incisive comments on a draft of this chapter and especially on the point developed here.

3

Resisting Theory

The resistance to theory is varied and endemic. It may emanate from those who believe that theory in the form of general propositions and principles "gets in the way" of their encounter with works of art or from those who develop theoretical arguments not just against particular theoretical orientations but against theory in general. In a celebrated essay, "The Resistance to Theory," which also provides the title for his collection of essays on theory and theorists, Paul de Man explores some forms of resistance to theory, particularly that resistance emanating from traditional literary studies, but for him the only intellectually challenging form of resistance to theory is that summed up in his closing apothegm: "Nothing can overcome the resistance to theory since theory is itself this resistance."[1] Before discussing aspects of de Man's work in the light of this paradox—theory as the resistance to theory—one should consider some forms of what de Man calls "the shared resistance to theory" of extremely diverse trends in criticism.

Opposition to theory may be widely attractive, but books and articles that oppose it by criticizing its difficulty, its obscurity, and its many nefarious effects, such as its politicizing of teaching and research or its alleged critique of literary values, have not fared very well, perhaps because all such approaches concede the power of theory as they complain about

1. Paul de Man, *The Resistance to Theory* (Minneapolis: University of Minnesota Press, 1986), 19; hereafter abbreviated *RT* and cited parenthetically in the text.

it, so that theorists have often felt no need to respond but let these attacks peter out in the void. Steven Knapp and Walter Benn Michaels, in their attack on theory, had the clever and perverse idea of taking the opposite tack, declaring that theory has no consequences, is wholly otiose, and should thus be abandoned. Avoiding the fate of previous attacks, they attracted a good deal of attention with their article "Against Theory" and the sequel, "Against Theory 2," which followed when, like Hollywood producers, they saw that they could profit from a box-office hit. Starting with a strangely narrow definition of theory, as a discourse that attempts to control interpretive practice by constructing a general account of interpretation, Michaels and Knapp claim that theory in this sense takes the form of epistemological arguments about the relationship between authorial intention and textual meaning.[2] Such arguments are misguided or incoherent or simply wrong, they maintain, for they fail to see or recognize or "realize" (a favorite word here), "that the meaning of a text is simply identical to the author's intended meaning."[3] Michaels and Knapp insist that they are not taking a particular position in the argument about the relation of intention to meaning: they are simply claiming that intention and meaning are by definition the same. To construe something as language rather than as meaningless marks is to take it as having been produced by someone, and to inquire about its meaning is simply to ask what its author meant. Understandably, it has seemed to both their supporters and their critics that by asserting that the meaning of a text is what its author meant by it and that it is impossible for a text to mean more than what its author meant, they are championing the view that only evidence about the author's intention is relevant to the determination of the text's meaning. They insist,

2. Most discussions which count as theory do not offer such arguments. Many are not about interpretation at all: Michel Foucault does not tell us how to interpret texts but offers surprising histories that critics use to generate new ideas about the implications of texts they study. The work of Benedict Anderson, to return to the discussion of chapter 2, leads us to think about novels in relation to the projects of nation building and influences interpretation in that way, but it offers no stipulations to control interpretive practice.

3. Steven Knapp and Walter Benn Michaels, "Against Theory," *Critical Inquiry* 8 (1982): 724. See also Knapp and Michaels, "Against Theory 2: Hermeneutics and Deconstruction," *Critical Inquiry* 14 (1987); and Knapp and Michaels, "A Reply to Our Critics," *Critical Inquiry* 9 (1983).

in their response to their critics, that to identify meaning with intention is not to say anything at all about how to find out the meaning of a text, because however you go about construing meaning (by consulting contemporary documents, by looking words up in a dictionary, by free-associating, by seeking to imagine God's will), what you are doing (according to their definition) is construing what its author meant. "Nothing in the claim that authorial intention is the necessary object of interpretation tells us anything at all about what should count as evidence for determining the content of any particular intention."[4] The whole question of what evidence is relevant to the determination of the meaning of a work, then, is not affected at all by their argument.

What, then, should count as evidence for determining the content of any particular intention? If their claim about meaning and intention tells us nothing about this, it might seem that theory still has a good deal of work to do, even if we need to call the discourses doing such work by another name. Theoretical argument that has been concerned with principles of interpretation has sought to champion or to adjudicate among various factors thought to come into play in thinking about the meaning of a text, such as linguistic habits and conventions, contemporaneous historical practices and discourses, the lives and declarations of authors, possible relations between consciousness and unconscious drives or between base and superstructure.

Knapp and Michaels have left these problems aside. Their strangely tautological argument boils down to saying "whatever you think meaning is, it is by definition the same thing as the author's intention, so there is no problem here, no work for theory to do, and it should just stop." But even if we were to accept their equation and henceforth substitute the phrase "what the author intended" for "meaning" wherever it appears, we would need reflection on the relations between this entity (however named) and such things as the kinds of information available to us about authors, historical circumstances, discursive practices, conventions of language and of genres, the work of reading, the structures of the unconscious, and the history of reception—in short, some theory.

Many people have noted that Knapp and Michaels's argument against theory is itself theoretical and, far from stopping theory, generates more

4. Knapp and Michaels, "Reply," 796.

theoretical writing. I would emphasize a different point. There is considerable evidence that Knapp and Michaels themselves do not take meaning and intention to be identical, for one of the moves they characteristically make is to accuse their opponents (who include just about everybody) of failing to understand their own arguments—that is, failing to understand the meaning of their own texts. E. D. Hirsch, they write, has "failed to understand the force of his own formulation."[5] He thinks his formulation means one thing, but he has failed to understand implications inherent to it—a perfectly plausible situation but one that is hard to explain if one accepts the impossibility of a text meaning something other than what the author intended.

The claim that others fail to understand their own arguments becomes central to Walter Benn Michaels's later book, *The Shape of the Signifier*, which claims that anyone who does not recognize that the meaning of a text is just what the author meant by it is abandoning the possibility of there being anything for critics to be right or wrong about and thus implicitly embracing the conclusion that it is the identity or subject position of the reader that is crucial: "if you don't think of texts as meaning what their authors intended, you will end up required to think of them as meaning what they mean to you, which is to say as not really meaning at all but just as producing some effect on their readers."[6]

Knapp and Michaels write in the conclusion of "Against Theory 2": "We have argued that conventions play no role in determining meaning. We have denied that they can give a text an autonomous identity that will allow it to mean more than its author intends."[7] But in their disagreements with other theorists they seek to show that others' arguments mean more or something other than their authors claim they mean. In effect, they seek to identify what they take to be autonomous structures of meaning that function, whether or not the theorist in question intended them. Michaels's project in *The Shape of the Signifier* consists of arguing that all the theorists who reject his view that the meaning of a text is just what the author intended, in fact end up meaning something quite different from

5. Knapp and Michaels, "Against Theory," 725.

6. Walter Benn Michaels, *The Shape of the Signifier* (Princeton, NJ: Princeton University Press, 2004), 73–74.

7. Knapp and Michaels, "Against Theory 2," 68.

what they intended. Of Derrida, he writes, for instance, "What's really asserted by the claim that there is nothing outside the text is that there is no such thing as a text."[8] This is apparently not a claim about what Derrida's assertion means to me or what effect it produces on readers but about what it means according to a principle or logic that Derrida himself has failed to grasp. Indeed, the appeal of *The Shape of the Signifier* lies in its bold attempt to demonstrate that by the logic Michaels seeks to identify, the texts of theorists end up meaning something radically different from—indeed often diametrically opposed to—what they intended and from what others have taken these texts to mean. Such thinkers as de Man and Derrida, who have no interest in identity politics, are said to end up in fact supporting it because their claims about language mean something quite different from what they intend.

It would be possible for Michaels and Knapp to reply that they are distinguishing between the meaning of a text and its force or significance, but this opens precisely the sort of gap they have been at pains to deny—between what an author intends and what the text can be claimed to mean (now called "force" or "significance"). And in any event, they are usually not content to distinguish meaning from force when criticizing others. Michaels speaks of "what is really asserted" by Derrida's claim, not what force or effect it has for people occupying certain subject positions. Knapp and Michaels themselves cannot, it seems, adhere to the equation of meaning and intention by which they seek to dismiss a certain sort of theory. Unintended meaning is such a crucial object of critical investigation and theoretical debate that they cannot do without it. One could argue that even though we cannot determine what an author intended, the conduct of analysis requires an operation of positing and opposing meaning that an author controls to meaning that he or she does not control. Knapp's and Michael's practice bears this out, against the claims of their theory.

The other main move in their antitheory theory (and this is characteristic of the work of Stanley Fish as well) is to seek to shift attention from theory to beliefs, for if theory vanishes, as they say it should, what takes its place are beliefs. We have beliefs that determine what is relevant, what to look for, how to proceed. They want to shift the focus from theories to beliefs, I would argue, because it is easier to maintain that beliefs do not

8. Michaels, *Shape of the Signifier*, 128.

have grounds, do not have to be justified; they are just what we believe, and when we change our beliefs, it is just because we have come to believe something different. "Beliefs," they write, "cannot be grounded in some deeper condition of knowledge."[9] Now of course this may be true for such things as religious beliefs, but if we are talking about the various beliefs that might be described as the principles, criteria, and premises at work in people's discussions of literature or other texts, these are precisely the sort of beliefs that are based on knowledge, for which we can give reasons, and about which we can argue: for example, the "belief" that unity is a principal criterion of the excellence of a work of art, or that the history of the reception of a work is a key to its significance, or that one should attend to the representation or nonrepresentation of gender or of race in any discourse one is studying. Such beliefs or theoretical views are not grounded in demonstrable truths, but they are not ungrounded either—they are connected with a great deal of knowledge and reflection, which is precisely the realm of theory.

If we were to shift focus from theory to beliefs, we would have to ask how beliefs are connected with each other and to these various bodies of thought we now call theory. We would need to ask what in the realm of criticism leads us to change our beliefs (or theoretical perspectives), and the answer doubtless would often be theoretical arguments and the illustrative examples that buttress them. In short the antitheory theory has no consequences, as Knapp and Michaels repeatedly claim, not because abandoning theory as they demand would have no effect but because the acceptance of their conclusions would leave all the work of theory still to be done, albeit in more awkward conditions and under different names. This kind of resistance to theory seems to me a dead end, whose notoriety is explained only by the attractions of the idea of an end to theory.

More widespread is a different sort of resistance, which sees theory as an elaborate, elitist imposition, an intimidating mass of difficult material which, people are told, they must master before they can presume to speak about literature. "What! You haven't read Lacan! How can you talk about the lyric without taking account of the specular constitution of the speaking subject?" Or, "How can you write about the Victorian novel without using Foucault's account of the hysterization of women's bodies and de-

9. Knapp and Michaels, "Against Theory," 738.

ployment of sexuality and Spivak's demonstration of the role of colonialism in the formation of the metropolitan subject?" The worst thing about theory these days is that it is endless. In the days of Wellek and Warren one had to know that a literary work was a set of norms—not the experience of the author, not the experience of the reader, nor an object given once and for all—and a few other things as well. But today—this is the leading characteristic of modern theory—theory is not a circumscribed body of knowledge that one could master, even if one wished to. Theory presents itself as a diabolical assignment of difficult readings from fields one knows little about, where even the completion of an assignment will bring not respite but further more difficult assignments. ("Ah, but have you read Žižek on Lacan and Hitchcock?") There are no limits to what thinkers, from various fields, may be constituted as theorists, and there are always new theorists being invented or promoted by the young and the restless, along with the old chestnuts, so we can't be sure whether we "have to" read Jean Baudrillard or Julia Kristeva or Slavoj Žižek or Giorgio Agamben or Alain Badiou—the last two 2005's candidates for important theorist.

But the point is a serious one; one may resist theory because of the fear that to admit the importance of theory would be to make an open-ended commitment, to leave oneself in a position one could never master, whose very nature is simultaneously to present mastery as a goal (you hope that the theoretical reading will give you the concepts, the metalanguage, to order and understand the phenomena that concern you) and to make mastery impossible, since theory is itself the questioning of presumed results and of the assumptions on which they are based.

Of course, this unmasterability of the domain is true in literature these days as well; one can no longer be quite sure what it is acceptable not to have read. It used to be reasonable for teachers of English in the United States to have no interest in or knowledge of Canadian literature, for example, but now—at least in some places—our students suggest that this is very provincial of us and that an English department has to cover world writing in English. The convenient thing about the canon, one might say, was that you knew what to feel guilty about not having read—that you had never finished *The Fairie Queene*, or *Finnegans Wake*, or *War and Peace*— but you didn't have to worry about *The Wide Wide World* or *The Man in the High Castle*.

It has been said that the New Criticism, with its restriction of attention to structures of literary works alone, was a theory suited to the pedagogical situation of the American academy after the Second World War, with its influx of large numbers of students who did not share cultural experiences or reference points. (This is the well-known move of holding the students responsible for the teachers' shortcomings.) But such a theory is convenient for teachers as well, who need not worry about their ignorance of psychoanalysis, the history of philosophy, the history of the body, and so on. It produces its own anxieties, of course: one must be smart and subtle, and there is no body of knowledge to be acquired that can guarantee this; but for teachers it has the great advantage of circumscribing what they can be expected to know, and the most general effect of theory—especially in its recent unbounded forms—is to destroy this security.

Resistance to theory for such motives makes a good deal of sense. In its most benign form it is a matter of priorities and does not seek to prevent others from doing theory. Moreover, just as the resistance of objects is a necessary condition of the possibility of knowledge—we could not claim knowledge of something that offered no resistance to whatever we attempted to do with it—so resistance to theory may be seen as a necessary force, which calls theory to account.

Although theory today can no longer be seen as simply principles of critical method but must rather be conceived as a broad field of interdisciplinary study—philosophy, history, psychoanalysis, and so on—which includes literary discourses along with many others, when we do bring theory into literary studies, this sort of resistance to theory, which fears it as an excessive intellectual commitment, can have positive effects. It compels the advocates of theory or theories to attempt to show what difference a particular theoretical discourse or orientation can make: at what level does it make a difference? What if, to take Foucault as our example, we pursue his critique of the repressive hypothesis and take up his claim that in fact the nineteenth century witnesses not a repression of sexuality but, on the contrary, an incitement to discourse about sexuality, an increasing propensity to constitute sexuality as the secret of individuality of the self, defined in terms of sexual practice or sexual desire? How does this account of the deployment of sexuality function? What sort of reconceptualizations does it promote? Foucault himself is an opponent of hermeneutics, but does such an account stimulate new interpretations of novels, or is it, on the contrary, a hypothesis about an underlying discursive reality that could be confirmed or falsified by the evidence novels provide?

A certain resistance to theory can make one ask of this, or other theoretical discourses, whether it serves to produce new interpretations by focusing attention on different issues or by providing a new understanding of some central element of the literary and discursive situation. Does it, on the contrary, make a difference not by facilitating the production of new interpretations but by seeking to advance an understanding of how interpretation occurs or how the institutions of literature and literary study function in a particular society? There is a good deal to be said for a resistance to theory that makes its promoters identify as explicitly as possible what sort of consequences a particular theoretical discourse might have so that its success in achieving these ends can be in some measure assessed. Otherwise, it becomes too easy for those interested in theory to assume that the importation into literary studies of some interesting theoretical discourse is itself necessarily an advance. Once we think of resistance to theory in this way, there is indeed a respectable or valuable side to resisting theory. It is the skeptical impulse itself, a desire to have something more fully worked out and, at its best, an alertness to what in texts resists a theoretical scheme.

But this broad conception of theory is not what de Man means by the term—though he begins "The Resistance to Theory" with the observations that part of the resistance to theory comes from the fact that it cannot be defined or delimited. Still, for him theory is not eclectically interdisciplinary. He writes,

Literary theory can be said to come into being when the approach to literary texts is no longer based on non-linguistic, that is to say historical and aesthetic, considerations or, to put it somewhat less crudely, when the object of discussion is no longer the meaning or the value but the modalities of production and of reception of meaning and of value prior to their establishment—the implication being that this establishment is problematic enough to require an autonomous discipline of critical investigation to consider its possibility and its status. (*RT*, 7)

De Man here takes theory not as systematic and speculative discourse applied outside the realm in which it originates but as reflection on the problems of the production of meaning in literary and other discourses—

in short, structuralism and its legacy, which we have called, in optimistic American fashion, "poststructuralism." Even the New Criticism, which certainly might be said to be interested in the production of meaning prior to its establishment, is seen by de Man as ultimately a form of resistance to theory, because of the social and ethical and aesthetic principles that it values above the text's resistance to its supposed meaning.[10] Barbara Johnson, looking at the terms in which Walter Jackson Bate and others set up an opposition between deconstructive reading and humanistic reading, remarks that it looks as though, whereas deconstruction is said to "go too far," humanism is, by contrast, supposed to stop reading when the text stops saying what it is supposed to say.[11] Historical and aesthetic assumptions about what works of a particular period or value may say and what would be inappropriate or anachronistic would be examples of a resistance to theory as a resistance to reading. Theory is contrasted with approaches that take meaning not as a problem but as something given, to be classified or evaluated, by placing works in historical schemes or discussing the ethical or political value of a work's meaning, for example.

Theory is identified with a focus on the problem of language and thus with reading attentive to the linguistic and rhetorical structures of a text. Even within approaches based on language, such as the structuralist attempt to work toward a "grammar" of narrative, or in reader-response theories, which link meaning to the process of reading, de Man finds that, however admirable these approaches may be, they are ultimately engaged in a resistance to reading that is a resistance to theory. Structuralist and semiological attempts to work out a grammar of narrative or generally to extend grammatical models beyond the sentence implicitly presume that the

10. See de Man, *The Resistance to Theory*, 6–7. New Criticism's rejection of paraphrase, as in "the heresy of paraphrase," would seem to mark an interest in the production of meaning prior to its establishment, and in "The Return to Philology" de Man praises the radical character of New Critical reading, as practiced in Reuben Brower's course at Harvard, in which de Man taught (*RT*, 23–24). But the New Criticism's aesthetic principle of the poem as organic whole and its commitment to the ethical value of the literary encounter prevent it from instantiating reading not based on nonlinguistic considerations. See also *RT*, 17.

11. Barbara Johnson, "Teaching Deconstructively," in *Writing and Reading Differently*, ed. G. Douglas Atkins and Michael Johnson (Lawrence: University Press of Kansas, 1985), 140.

meaning of texts is predictable or explicable in terms of linguistic structures or literary and linguistic conventions and thus elide the necessity of
reading, which is above all a coming to terms with rhetorical structures
where meaning cannot be determined by systematic considerations (deciding, for instance, whether something in a text is ironic or not is a problem of reading that cannot be resolved by grammatical models). "The resistance to theory is a resistance to the rhetorical or tropological dimension
of language," which comes into play even in structuralist and semiological
approaches that explicitly embrace rhetoric (*RT*, 17). And reader-oriented
approaches de Man sees as a strenuous avoidance of reading, whether by
postulating interpretive communities or historical circumstances of reception to explain or predict interpretive conclusions: "The resistance to theory, which as we saw, is a resistance to reading, appears in its most rigorous
and theoretically elaborated form among the theoreticians of reading who
dominate the contemporary theoretical scene" (*RT*, 17–18).

In this logic of small differences, where the resistance to theory seems
to become most prominent and most interesting in those discourses that
are reputed most theoretical, de Man takes a surprising step: instead of iso-
lating as true theory and true reading a deconstructive theory and practice of rhetorical reading—attentive to the obstacles to meaning, to the
unmasterable play of the referential functioning of language in texts—he
notes that these practices, too, ultimately involve an avoidance of reading.
Though they identify structures and functions that do not lead to a knowledge of an entity, are "consistently defective models of language's impossibility to be a model language" that would function without indeterminacy
or self-undermining, and "are theory and non-theory at the same time, the
universal theory of the impossibility of theory," still as theory, as teachable
and subject to systematization, "rhetorical readings, like the other kinds,
still avoid and resist the reading they advocate. Nothing can overcome the
resistance to theory since theory is itself this resistance" (*RT*, 19). A certain
resistance to reading and to theory is not just a lapse or a failure of theory
but is inherent in the theoretical enterprise, even as he has narrowly defined it.

How are we to understand this? In what sense can theory itself be a
resistance to theory? A brief detour through Freud might help. Laplanche
and Pontalis's *Dictionary of Psychoanalysis* reports that in psychoanalysis

"the name 'resistance' is given to everything in the words and actions of the analysand that obstructs his gaining access to his unconscious."[12] In *The Interpretation of Dreams*, the work that sets forth what Freud always regarded as his greatest discovery—about the meaning of dreams and the functioning of the dreamwork—the opening example is Freud's analysis of one of his own dreams, which has come to be known as the Dream of Irma's Injection. In describing how he analyzes the dream by looking for what he associates with its various elements when running over the day's residues and seeing how these apparently nonsensical elements actually do fit together and make sense, Freud reaches the conclusion that the dream was the expression of a wish, in this case the wish not to be held responsible for the failure of his patient Irma to get better, the wish for the fault to lie elsewhere.[13]

Lacan, in reanalyzing the dream and Freud's account of it, notes that this wish that Freud uncovers is scarcely an unconscious one: Freud tells us that he had spent the evening before the dream writing out an account of Irma's case in an attempt at self-justification. What Freud's interpretation of his own dream is resisting are aspects of the dreamwork that exceed and disrupt the narcissistic economy of the ego. Freud gives a semantic rather than syntactic interpretation of the dream; Lacan focuses on transferential relationships and on the most enigmatic moment of the dream, the chemical formula for trimethylamine, which Freud says appeared before him in bold type and which Lacan interprets as telling us that the essence of the dream is a formal structure. Insofar as Lacan focuses on the linguistic elements of the dream—in particular its inclusion of a chemical formula—his approach to the dream is no longer based on "non-linguistic considerations," to quote de Man. Freud's dream tells us about the nature of the unconscious, which, in a famous formulation of Lacan's, is structured like a language.[14]

12. Jean Laplanche and J.-B. Pontalis, *The Language of Psycho-Analysis*, trans. D. Nicholson-Smith (New York: Norton, 1973), 394.

13. Sigmund Freud, *The Interpretation of Dreams* (1900), in *The Standard Edition of the Complete Psychological Works of Sigmund Freud*, trans. James Strachey (London: Hogarth Press, 1953), 4:106–21.

14. Jacques Lacan, *The Ego in Freud's Theory and in the Technique of Psychoanalysis* (1954–55; repr., New York: Norton, 1988), 158–59.

The theory of dreams developed in this chapter of *The Interpretation of Dreams* (that the dream is the expression of a wish), and thus Freud's attempt to describe the workings of the unconscious, can be read as a case of resistance to the workings of the unconscious that theory seeks to describe, in fact as a characteristic defense of the ego that brings everything back to the desire of the subject, repressing the impersonal structures and processes in which it is caught up. The theory of the unconscious is resistance to the truth of the unconscious that it unwittingly exposes.

The example may help us understand how it could be that theory itself is a resistance to theory (thought of still as reflection on meaning as a problem rather than a given). The very attempt at understanding is a resistance to that which may not give rise to understanding—although these moments or elements can only be identified by the kind of attention we are calling theory—attention to meaning as a problem. In the case of literature, theory adequate to its linguistic object involves rhetorical reading—reading attentive to the functioning of tropes and figures and to the ways in which interpretation entails the imposition of meaning—but operations of theorization inexorably become a resistance to reading in this sense, transforming textual difficulties into examples of certain kinds of meaning, for instance.

One might, then, consider some of de Man's own work in the light of this problem or, rather, ask whether what is especially valuable or productive in his work for the future of literary criticism and theory may not be linked to this problem of resisting theory. We think of de Man as a literary theorist and so would be tempted to assume that his contribution must be a body of theory, but it may be that we should look, rather, to aspects of his resistance to theory (though for that, *theory* will still be the telling word).

One might identify five areas in which de Man made important contributions: the theorization of allegory, the revaluation of romanticism, his account of the relation between blindness and insight, his exploration of the relation between constative and performative dimensions of language, and his critique of the aesthetic ideology.[15]

15. There are excellent articles discussing various aspects of de Man's work in Lindsay Waters, ed., *Reading de Man Reading* (Minneapolis: University of Minnesota Press, 1989); and Tom Cohen, Barbara Cohen, J. Hillis Miller, and Andrzej Warminski, eds., *Material Events: Paul de Man and the Afterlife of Theory* (Minneapolis: University of Minnesota Press, 2001).

First, there is de Man's revaluation of allegory, which criticism, in the wake of Coleridge and Goethe, had treated as an undesirable and unsuccessful type of figuration, a product of the operations of fancy rather than imagination. An assumed superiority of the symbol underlay literary taste, critical analysis, and conceptions of literary history. Looking at the supposed shift from allegorical to symbolical imagery in late eighteenth-century poetry in *The Rhetoric of Temporality*, de Man challenges the view that romantic literature produces through the symbol a reconciliation of man and nature—an ethical and aesthetic theoretical conception—and instead identifies the allegorical structures at work in its most intense and lucid passages. Allegorizing tendencies "appear at the most original and profound moments . . . , when an authentic voice becomes audible," in works of European literature between 1760 and 1800. "The prevalence of allegory," he writes,

always corresponds to the unveiling of an authentically temporal destiny. This unveiling takes place in a subject that has sought refuge against the impact of time in a natural world to which, in truth, it bears no resemblance. . . .

Whereas symbol postulates the possibility of an identity or identification, allegory designates primarily a distance in relation to its own origin, and, renouncing the nostalgia and the desire to coincide, it establishes its language in the void of this temporal difference.[16]

This account of the relation between symbol and allegory, and its revaluation of allegory, has been central to recent work on romantic and postromantic literature in America, but the implications of de Man's reflection on allegory are not exhausted here. We can now see, as Minae Mizumura writes, that "[t]he tension between symbol and allegory is then already another name for the tension between a temptation of assuming the readability of a text, that is, of reconciling sign and meaning, and a renunciation of this temptation."[17] The exploration of allegory is a resistance to the theory (of literature) instantiated in the symbol, but to create a theory of allegory is to resist the irreconciliation of sign and meaning revealed by close reading.

But the further question that now may pose itself for us more pressingly is the relation between allegory, as a certain resistance to symbol-

16. Paul de Man, *Blindness and Insight*, 2nd ed. (Minneapolis: University of Minnesota Press, 1983), 206–7.

17. Minae Mizumura, "Renunciation," *Yale French Studies* 69 (1985): 91.

ic recuperation, and history. In the conclusion of the "Promises" chapter of *Allegories of Reading*, while arguing that the "redoubtable efficacy" of Rousseau's *Social Contract* is due to the rhetorical model of which it is a version, de Man writes, "textual allegories on this level of rhetorical complexity generate history," as if the historical effect or productivity of a text were an allegorical power, a power of allegory.[18] The relationship seems more intimate yet difficult to grasp in the last essays, where allegory seems an incomplete narrative of a nonfigurative occurrence that de Man associates with the "materiality of actual history" or "historical modes of language-power."[19] Here theory seems to focus above all on that which resists theory.

One of de Man's major achievements has certainly been the revaluation of romanticism, the demonstration through studies of Rousseau, Hölderlin, Wordsworth, Shelley, Keats, and Baudelaire that romanticism includes the boldest, most self-conscious writing of the Western tradition. The early romantics, Rousseau, Wordsworth, and Hölderlin, are "the first modern writers to have put into question, in the language of poetry, the ontological priority of the sensory object," for which later romantic and postromantic literature and critical discussions of it would remain nostalgic.[20] It is now apparent that other things are at stake in de Man's focus on romanticism, that the focus on it is crucial to an understanding of our recent past and our cultural situation. For instance, there is the problem of what Philippe Lacoue-Labarthe in *La fiction du politique* calls the "national aestheticism" that issues from a reading of romanticism but to which the work of a writer such as Hölderlin provides a divergence of crucial, critical force.[21]

18. Paul de Man, *Allegories of Reading: Figural Language in Rousseau, Nietzsche, Rilke, and Proust* (New Haven, CT: Yale University Press, 1979), 277.

19. Kevin Newmark's brilliant, difficult essay, "Paul de Man's History," in Waters, *Reading de Man Reading*, helps trace the elaboration of these terms. See also Jacques Derrida, "Typewriter Ribbon," and Andrzej Warminski, "'As the Poets Do It': On the Material Sublime," both in *Material Events: Paul de Man and the Afterlife of Theory*, ed. Tom Cohen, Barbara Cohen, J. Hillis Miller, and Andrzej Warminski (Minneapolis: University of Minnesota Press, 2001).

20. Paul de Man, *The Rhetoric of Romanticism* (New York: Columbia University Press, 1984), 16.

21. Philippe Lacoue-Labarthe, *La fiction du politique* (Paris: Christian Bourgois, 1987), 83, 147.

A critique of the reception of romanticism has been an activity of "deconstruction in America." An aestheticizing and monumentalizing interpretation of romanticism, institutionalized in the teaching of Wordsworth in American universities, has been challenged and in some measure dismantled by the deconstructive readings produced by de Man and his students.[22]

De Man insists that the question of romanticism is not just one of characterizing a period or a style. Discussion of romanticism is particularly difficult, he suggests, because it requires a coming to terms with a past from which we are not yet separated, a past whose poets' most intense questioning involves precisely this interpretive relation to their past experience—that is, the very structure on which our relation depends.[23] Descriptions of romanticism always miss the mark, for reasons that are structural rather than due to failures of intelligence. A further complication is introduced by the fact that the genetic categories on which literary history depends—the models of birth, development, death—are most decisively promoted but also exposed by the romantic works that they would be used to discuss: "one may well wonder what kind of historiography could do justice to the phenomenon of Romanticism, since Romanticism (itself a period concept) would then be the movement that challenges the genetic principle which necessarily underlies all historical narrative"—a certain resistance to theory.[24] As a result, he writes, "the interpretation of romanticism remains for us the most difficult and at the same time the most necessary of tasks," involving this double movement, of identifying what resists prior theorization and risking the resistance to reading that goes with the theoretical description of this structure.[25]

Another version of this structure of theory as resistance to theory is de Man's account of the relationship between blindness and insight. In the

22. The key role of this critique in de Man's own changes—the turn toward a linguistic terminology above all—emerges clearly in the dual version of his "Time and History in Wordsworth," published for the first time by Cynthia Chase and Andrzej Warminski in *Diacritics* 17, no. 4 (1987): 4–17.

23. De Man, *The Rhetoric of Romanticism*, 49–50. See Cynthia Chase, "Translating Romanticism: Literary Theory as the Criticism of Aesthetics in the Work of Paul de Man," *Textual Practice*, 4, no. 3 (winter 1990): 349–75.

24. De Man, *Allegories of Reading*, 82.

25. De Man, *The Rhetoric of Romanticism*, 50.

book of this title he argues that critics "owe their best insights to assumptions these insights disprove," a fact that "shows blindness to be a necessary correlative of the rhetorical nature of literary language."[26] A famous passage describes the way the New Critics' concentration on language (rather than authors, for example) was made possible by their conception of the work as organic form but led to insights into the role of irony that undermine the conception of literary works as harmonious, organic wholes. For them, as for other critics, an

insight could only be gained because the critics were in the grip of this peculiar blindness: their language could grope toward a certain degree of insight only because their method remained oblivious to the perception of this insight. The insight exists only for a reader in the privileged position of being able to observe the blindness as a phenomenon in its own right—the question of his own blindness being one which he is by definition incompetent to ask—and so being able to distinguish between statement and meaning. He has to undo the explicit results of a vision that is able to move toward the light only because, being already blind, it does not have to fear the power of this light. But the vision is unable to report correctly what it has perceived in the course of its journey. To write critically about critics thus becomes a way to reflect on the paradoxical effectiveness of a blinded vision that has to be rectified by means of insights that it unwittingly provides.[27]

This relation is structural, not psychological, for de Man. The blindness is not a product of the distinctive individual histories of critics.[28] And although "blindness" seems to belong to a phenomenological vocabulary of consciousness, de Man construes it as an impersonal mechanism of read-

26. De Man, *Blindness and Insight*, 141.

27. Ibid., 106.

28. De Man's is a theory about the dependency of truth on error, not simply about the pervasiveness of error. Thus, this is not de Man's attempt, as some have claimed, to make his own youthful blindness—his participation in a collaborationist newspaper in Belgium after the German invasion, until he quit in 1942—into an ineluctable necessity—at least not unless one can show some brilliant insight of his wartime journalism that was made possible by this blindness. For discussion see Werner Hamacher, Neil Hertz, and Thomas Keenan, eds., *Responses: On Paul de Man's Wartime Journalism* (Lincoln: University of Nebraska Press, 1989). For the articles themselves see Paul de Man, *Wartime Journalism, 1939–43*, ed. Werner Hamacher, Neil Hertz, and Thomas Keenan (Lincoln: University of Nebraska Press, 1988).

ing, a structure of the relation to texts. He speaks of what others would call the unconscious in terms of mechanisms of language: what happens independently of any intent or volition of subjects. He would interpret psychological accounts as defensive ways of creating intelligibility, of countering the threat of the random and of mechanical unintelligibility. An important question here is the possible impact of this way of thinking on a poststructuralist psychoanalytic criticism that explores how texts are structured by psychic conflicts or operations they theorize. At a time when psychoanalytic readings may become the refuge of a certain humanism, as in American ego psychology, which sees us as most human in our "unconscious selves," insistence on impersonal mechanisms may prove salutary.

This leads to a further, particularly important, topic, what one might call de Man's development of a materialist theory of language, or his investigation of what he calls, in "Shelley Disfigured," "the madness of words" ("No degree of knowledge can ever stop this madness, for it is the madness of words").[29] One might say that what de Man first described as the division at the heart of Being, and then as the complex relation between blindness and insight that prevents self-possession or self-presence, is, in *Allegories of Reading* and his subsequent writing, analyzed as a linguistic predicament, the figural structure of language that insures a division variously described as a gap between sign and meaning, between meaning and intent, between the performative and constative or "cognitive" functions of language, and between rhetoric as persuasion and rhetoric as trope.[30]

Although literary theory has to a considerable extent assimilated the demonstration that reading should focus on the discrepancies between the performative and constative dimensions of texts, between their explicit statement and the implications of their modes of utterance, criticism has not yet successfully explicated and worked with the more difficult and unsettling aspects of de Man's writing on language and occurrence. In emphasizing certain nonsemantic aspects of language, from the indeterminate significative status of the letter, as in Saussure's work on anagrams, to the referential moment of deixis, as in Hegel's reflections on "this piece of paper" in the preface to the *Phenomenology of Mind*, de Man stresses that

29. De Man, *The Rhetoric of Romanticism*, 122.

30. To observe this shift occurring, see de Man, "Time and History in Wordsworth."

language is not coextensive with meaning, and rhetorical reading becomes in part an exposure of the ideological imposition of meaning as a defense we build against language—specifically against the inhuman, mechanical aspects of language, the structures or grammatical possibilities that are independent of any intent or desire we might have yet are neither natural nor, in fact, phenomenal. How this resistance occurs in poetics or various forms of structural analysis is one of the distinctive and difficult segments of de Man's writing.

There are, in de Man's accounts, two levels of imposition. First there is the positing by language, which does not reflect but constitutes, which simply occurs. De Man speaks of "the absolute randomness of language, prior to any figuration or meaning."[31] This does not mean, as some commentators affect to believe, that somehow agents are not responsible for their words or actions; on the contrary, the possibility of their being responsible depends on the randomness of language itself, the blind occurrence of its positing. De Man writes, "The positing power of language is both entirely arbitrary, in having a strength that cannot be reduced to necessity, and entirely inexorable in that there is no alternative to it."[32] Then there is the conferring of sense or meaning on this positing, through figuration—as in allegorical narratives of law and desire, lurid figures of castrating and beheading, and less lurid figures as well. Positing does not belong to any sequence or have any status; these are imposed retrospectively. De Man asks, "How can a positional act, which relates to nothing that comes before or after, become inscribed in a sequential narrative? . . . It can only be because we impose, in our turn, on the senseless power of positional language the authority of sense and of meaning" (*RR*, 117). We transform language into historical and aesthetic objects, or embed discursive occurrences in narratives that provide continuities, in a process of troping that de Man calls "the endless prosopopoeia by which the dead are made to have a face and a voice which tells the allegory of their demise and allows us to apostrophize them in our turn" (*RR*, 122). "We can therefore not ask why it is that we, as subjects, choose to impose meaning, since we are ourselves defined by this very question" (*RR*, 118).

31. De Man, *Allegories of Reading*, 299.
32. De Man, *Rhetoric of Romanticism*, 116; hereafter abbreviated *RR* and cited parenthetically in the text.

For de Man the divergence between grammar and meaning becomes explicit when the linguistic structures are stated in political terms. De Man writes of "an unavoidable estrangement between political rights and laws on the one hand, and political action and history on the other. The grounds for this alienation are best understood in terms of the rhetorical structure that separates the one domain from the other."[33] That rhetorical structure is the discrepancy between language conceived as grammar and language as reference or intentional action, and the ineluctability and indeterminacy of this structural relationship is what de Man calls "text." "The structure of the entity with which we are concerned," writes de Man in his exposition of *The Social Contract*, "(be it as property, as national State, or as any other political institution) is most clearly revealed when it is considered as the general form that subsumes all these particular versions, namely as legal text" (*AR*, 267). (I return to this problem of the text in Chapter 4.) The problematical relationship between the generality of law, system, grammar, and its particularity of application, event, or reference is the textual structure Rousseau expounds in the relationship between the general will and the particular individual, or between the state as system and the sovereign as active principle. The tension between grammar and reference

is duplicated in the differentiation between the state as a defined entity (*État*) and the state as principle of action (*Souverain*) or, in linguistic terms, between the constative and the performative function of language. A text is defined by the necessity of considering a statement, at the same time, as performative and constative, and the logical tension between figure and grammar is repeated in the impossibility of distinguishing between two linguistic functions which are necessarily compatible. (*AR*, 274–75)

What is the significance of that aporia between performative and constative? It emerges clearly in Rousseau's question of whether "the body political possesses an organ with which it can state [*énoncer*] the will of the people." The constative function of stating a preexisting will and the performative positing or shaping of a will are at odds, and while the system requires that the organ only announce what the general will determines, the action of the state or "lawgiver" will in particular instances declare or posit a general will. This is especially so in the founding of the state, for though,

33. De Man, *Allegories of Reading*, 266; hereafter abbreviated *AR* and cited parenthetically in the text.

as Rousseau writes, "the people subject to the Law must be the authors of the Law," in fact, he asks, "how could a blind mob, which often does not know what it wants [promulgate] a system of Law?" The structural tension between performative and constative here in what de Man calls the text is determinative of history, with the violence of its positings, its tropological substitutions, and their "eventual denunciation, in the future undoing of any State or any political institution" (*AR*, 274–75).

Finally, de Man's late essays, collected in *Aesthetic Ideology*, undertake a critique of an aesthetic ideology that imposes, even violently, continuity between perception and cognition, form and idea, and which reading, pursued to its limits (as it occurs in texts), is always undoing. Retrospectively, we can now see this project in earlier writings as well, in de Man's discussions of Heidegger and in his critique of the "salvational poetics" which sees poetic imagination as a way of overcoming contradictions, and of the "naïve poetics," which "rests on the belief that poetry is capable of effecting reconciliation because it provides an immediate contact with substance through its own sensible form."[34] Much of de Man's writing is staked on the premise that rhetorical reading, attentive to the working of poetic language, will expose the totalizations undertaken in the name of meaning and unity.

The late essays in *Aesthetic Ideology* find in Kant's work on "the aesthetic" a critique of the ideology of the aesthetic developed, for instance, by Schiller and applied, or misapplied, both in humanistic conceptions of aesthetic education and in fascist conceptions of politics as an aesthetic project (Walter Benjamin called fascism the importation of aesthetics into politics). Traditionally, the aesthetic is the name of the attempt to find a bridge between the phenomenal and the intelligible, the sensuous and the conceptual. Aesthetic objects, with their union of sensuous form and spiritual content, serve as guarantors of the general possibility of articulating the material and the spiritual, a world of forces and magnitudes with a world of value. Literature, conceived here not as literary works but as the rhetorical character of language revealed by analytical reading, involves, de Man writes in *The Resistance to Theory*, "the voiding, rather than the affir-

34. De Man, *Blindness and Insight*, 244. See also Christopher Norris, *Paul de Man and the Critique of Aesthetic Ideology* (New York: Routledge, 1988).

mation of aesthetic categories." So, for example, the convergence of sound and meaning in literature is an effect that language can achieve "but which bears no substantial relationship, by analogy or by ontologically grounded imitation, to anything beyond that particular effect. It is a rhetorical rather than an aesthetic function of language, an identifiable trope (paronomasis) that operates on the level of the signifier and contains no responsible pronouncement on the nature of the world—despite its powerful potential to create the opposite illusion" (*RT*, 10). Literary theory, in its attention to the functioning of language, thus "raises the unavoidable question whether aesthetic values can be compatible with the linguistic structures that make up the entities from which these values are derived" (*RT*, 25). Literature itself raises this question in various ways, offering evidence of the autonomous potential of language, of the uncontrollable figural basis of forms, which cannot therefore serve as the basis of reliable cognition, or in some texts, allegorically exposing the violence that lies hidden behind the aesthetic and makes aesthetic education possible.

De Man's essay "Kant and Schiller" concludes with a quotation from a novel by Joseph Goebbels, which casts the leader as an artist working creatively on his material:

The statesman is an artist too. The people are for him what stone is for the sculptor. Leader and masses (*Fuhrer* and *Masse*) are as little of a problem to each other as color is to a painter. Politics are the plastic arts of the state as painting is the plastic art of color. Therefore politics without the people or against the people are nonsense. To transform a mass into a people and a people into a state—that has always been the deepest sense of a genuine political task.[35]

De Man's argument is that this aestheticization of politics, which seeks the fusion of form and idea, is "a grievous misreading of Schiller's aesthetic state" but that Schiller's conception is itself a similar misreading, which must be undone by an analysis that takes us back to Kant. Kant had "disarticulated the project of the aesthetic which he had undertaken and which he found, by the rigor of his own discourse to break down under the power of his own critical epistemological discourse."[36] To expose this disarticula-

---

35. Joseph Goebbels, *Michael: Ein deutsches Schicksal in Tagesbuchblättern*, quoted by de Man in "Kant and Schiller," in Paul de Man, *Aesthetic Ideology*, ed. Andrzej Warminski (Minneapolis: University of Minnesota Press, 1996), 154–55.

36. De Man, *Aesthetic Ideology*, 134.

tion is to expose the illicit imposition of unity through the aesthetic. De Man seeks to demonstrate how the most insightful literary and philosophical texts of the tradition expose the unwarranted violence required to fuse form and idea, cognition and performance.

"The critique of the aesthetic ends up, in Kant," de Man writes, "in a formal materialism that runs counter to all values and characteristics associated with aesthetic experience, including the aesthetic categories of the beautiful and the sublime."[37] That formal materialism of the letter, which he also calls the prosaic materiality of inscription, is the letter considered nonteleologically—that is, not as sign but as blank or mark of whose significance one cannot be assured. This "indeterminately significative mark"[38] or prosaic materiality of the letter is a puzzling concept, what de Man calls on the one hand "all we get" yet on the other hand impossible to experience as such, except as what is transformed when we confer sense and meaning—through the violent positings of the aesthetic and of understanding, for instance.[39] Though recent essays on de Man have helped to explicate his critique of aesthetic ideology, the nature of this materialist theory of language, with its emphasis on what resists meaning and theory, while proving endlessly seductive to theory, remains difficult to grasp.[40]

De Man's writing grants great authority to texts—a power of illumination that is a power of disruption—but little authority to meaning. This highly original combination of respect for texts and suspicion of meaning will give his writing a continuing power, though its effects are not easily calculable. His essays commit themselves to major literary and philosophical works for their relentless undoing of the meanings that usually pass for their value. His analyses, with their deployment of a set of key terms that

37. De Man, "Phenomenality and Materiality in Kant," in *Aesthetic Ideology*, 83.

38. Cynthia Chase, "Primary Narcissism and the Giving of Figure: Kristeva with Hertz and de Man," in *Abjection, Melancholia, and Love: The Work of Julia Kristeva*, ed. John Fletcher and Andrew Benjamin (London: Routledge, 1990), 128.

39. Cynthia Chase, "Giving a Face to a Name: De Man's Figures," in *Decomposing Figures: Rhetorical Readings in the Romantic Tradition* (Baltimore: Johns Hopkins University Press, 1986), 95–105.

40. See, however, Marc Redfield, "Humanizing de Man," *Diacritics* 19 (summer 1989): 35; Warminski, "'As the Poets Do It'"; and Derrida, "Typewriter Ribbon," both in Cohen et al., *Material Events*.

take on special resonance, effectively teach suspicion of meaning and "the danger of unwarranted hopeful solutions," while demanding, as the price of possible insight, a commitment to the authority of the text.

Especially important is de Man's insistence that we not give in to the desire for meaning, that reading follow the suspensions of meaning, the resistances to meaning, and his encouragement of a questioning of any stopping place, any moment that might convince us that we have attained a demystified knowledge. This frequently puts us in an uncomfortable "precarious" situation, as he would put it, precisely at what might seem a programmatic moment. "More than any other mode of inquiry, including economics," de Man writes, in *The Resistance to Theory*, "the linguistics of literariness is a powerful and indispensable tool in the unmasking of ideological aberrations, as well as a determining factor in accounting for their occurrence" (11). That formulation—"determining factor"—seems to me to carry a warning: to suggest that we should remain alert to the possibility that the tools for unmasking may also be determining factors, factors that determine and thus help account for ideological aberrations. As so often with de Man, one cannot be sure whether this formulation is a subtle warning or a grammatical ambiguity. The linguistics of literariness is an important factor in accounting for ideological aberrations, but to call it a determining factor—may this not suggest that it determines them and accounts for them because it produces them, as well as helping to analyze and explain them? As so often, when confronted with indeterminately significative dimensions of language on which we cannot but confer sense and meaning, we are left with that more-than-grammatical problem. Nothing can overcome the resistance to theory, for it is itself that resistance. But, as de Man goes on to say, in a sentence less frequently quoted, "Literary theory is in no danger of going under; it cannot help but flourish, and the more it is resisted the more it flourishes, since the language it speaks is the language of self-resistance" (*RT*, 19–20). This is not a matter for celebration—promise of a rosy future for literary theory—but a recognition that we are inexorably in theory, whether we champion or deplore it.

CONCEPTS

4

Text: Its Vicissitudes

The concept of text, which has been central to literary studies, has undergone many mutations as it has traveled from the work of classical philologists, for whom it was and is the object of a powerful disciplinary formation, to postmodern theorists of the text, for whom the concept might be summed up by the title of a fine book by John Mowatt: *Text: The Genealogy of an Antidisciplinary Object.* Of course, the interesting thing about a traveling concept is not that it travels—travelers' tales can be quite boring and unprofitable—but what it reveals through its travels. One very striking point in the itinerary of *text*, though—unparalleled, to my knowledge in the travels of other concepts—is that in Oswald Ducrot's and Tzvetan Todorov's *Dictionnaire encyclopédique des sciences du langage* of 1972, *texte* has two contradictory entries. In the main body of the dictionary it is defined as an organization of the utterance beyond the sentence, which "may coincide with a sentence, as well as with an entire book; it is defined by its autonomy and its closure (even if, in another sense, certain texts are not 'closed')."[1] But then the appendix, which seeks to take account of recent developments that had challenged the idea of a *science* of language, also contains an entry for *texte*, under the heading "le texte comme productivité." Citing the recent work of Jacques Derrida and others, but especially Julia Kristeva, this entry tells us that "in opposition to any com-

1. Oswald Ducrot and Tzvetan Todorov, *Encyclopedic Dictionary of the Sciences of Language*, trans. Catherine Porter (Baltimore: Johns Hopkins University Press, 1979), 294.

municational and representational use of language, the text is defined here essentially as *productivity*":

Defining the text as productivity amounts to saying . . . that the text has always functioned as *transgressive* with regard to the system according to which our perception, our grammar, our metaphysics, and even our scientific knowledge are organized, a system according to which a subject, situated in the center of a world that provides it with a horizon, learns to decipher the *supposedly prior meaning* of this world, a meaning that is indeed understood as originary with regard to the subject's experience.[2]

Field of a "dynamic infinity," text "differentiates itself from the common sentence and 'doubles' it with an operation that is other to such an extent that it will have to be called translinguistic."[3]

The double inscription of *text*, as a key concept in the reorganization of the human sciences around the linguistic model and in the almost immediate and gleeful critique of the possibility of a scientific model, is a measure of the importance, of the pivotal nature, of this concept. Today one no longer sees as many books as one formerly did with *text* or *textual* in their title, and "textualism," as it is sometimes called, is often considered a sin or at least an insult. But declining to speak of text and textuality will not solve any of the problems of literary and cultural study. If we fail to confront the problems clustered around the notions of text, we are going to be programmed by our own unexamined assumptions, for the problem of the text is always with us.

Let me briefly sketch what I take to be the principal vicissitudes of *text* as a way of taking up major issues we approach through it. In philology the notion of the text—as in the idea of "the establishment of the text"—is already dual. Textual critics or textual editors contrasted the object before them, a text, with the text that they seek to establish (often by comparing versions) and thus with the text in the putatively perfect state in which it left the author's hands and to which the editor aspires to restore it. The text is thus both the pure origin, the manifestation of the final intention of the author, and an object marked by a history of material practices of transmission, which bring corruption. Textual scholarship was and indeed still is a process of reconstruction, based on methods that are much open to debate,

2. Ibid., 357.
3. Ibid., 358.

but it is only recently that the idea of the text as the corrupted material form in which the original intentions must be divined has been challenged. Modern textual scholars such as Jerome McGann have sought to reconceive the text as social act and to focus on the social practices and materials of transmission and publication, from inks and papers to book prices and editorial practices, and study these things as socially significant.[4] McGann thus tries to move away from the idea that the material practices involving texts are above all so many possible forms of corruption that may befall the final authorial intention, of which the text ought to be the manifestation.

Through these recent developments the idea of text in textual scholarship may come to intersect with other modern ideas of text, but we have yet to see how far this may go or how much of a rapprochement there will turn out to be. What I would stress here is that the idea of text in traditional textual scholarship presents a duality that will reappear in different forms. The notion of text is that of a material object but also of the very form of the work, in its original, ideal state. Thus the term *text* gestures toward matter, manifestation; indeed, this is the colloquial notion of "text": the text is the writing that you see before you, "the text of this law," for instance. But texts are of interest above all because of that which is or ought to be carried by or manifested in the material text and are thus seldom identified unreservedly with what appears on paper.

In Anglo-American New Criticism the notion of "the text itself" comes into its own in its most useful form—in an opposition: the text itself, the aesthetic object of literary study, as opposed to what it is said to mean or reflect or manifest; as opposed to history or biography. Students are enjoined to pay attention to the text itself, to cite evidence from the text itself, to set aside what is said about it or about the author. They are urged to focus on what the text says or, better, does, as opposed to what it is supposed to say. "The text itself"—the emphatic pronoun so often accompanies it—is a complicated positivity. The text itself is words on the page, but despite the banning of the intentional fallacy (confusing what something means with what someone is supposed to have meant by it), and despite the rule that arguments about meaning are not settled by con-

4. See Jerome McGann, *The Textual Condition* (Princeton, NJ: Princeton University Press, 1991), 12.

sulting the oracle (that is, asking the author, directly or indirectly),[5] the New Critical notion of the text is not wholly divorced from authorial intention, which takes the form of a powerful posited teleology. The text is the words on the page, yes, but these words are presumed to be organized as a complex whole—otherwise we would not speak of the text but just of writing.

Michael Riffaterre, best known for his theorization of intertextuality nonetheless inherits and articulates this concept of the text: "By textuality I mean the complex of formal and semantic features that characterize a self-sufficient, coherent, unified text, and legitimize its forms, however aberrant they may be, by removing any hint of the gratuitous."[6] The textuality of a text (its essence as text) is the complex internal organization that sets it off from any context. If aesthetic objects are, in Kant's phrase, purposive wholes without purpose, it is the artistic intention embodied in the text that warrants our expecting that the parts will be related to each other, that obscurities will have their reasons, and that everything will contribute to the effect of the whole. Having said this, we have to stress that the work itself reveals that artistic intention in ways that no information about the writer and his or her plans or intentions can, so that the text itself, though subtended by an artistic purpose, is separate from any other kinds of information, which can all be regarded as ancillary and set aside through various oppositions (intrinsic/extrinsic, and so forth).

It was in the inherited context of this idea of the text—an autotelic whole governed by a powerful aesthetic teleology—that Derrida's lapidary formula, "il n'y a pas de hors texte" [there is no outside-the-text] was interpreted to mean something like "everything outside the actual text or texts we are considering is irrelevant and doesn't really exist," whereas in Derrida's argument it means something like the opposite, that there is only text, since you cannot get outside of text.[7] But I am getting ahead of my text.

The structuralist moment is the turning point in the interdisciplinary fortunes of the text, and the most important, both for interdisciplinar-

5. W. K. Wimsatt and Monroe Beardsley, "The Intentional Fallacy," in *The Verbal Icon* (Lexington: University Press of Kentucky, 1954), 18.

6. Michael Riffaterre, "Textuality: W. H. Auden's 'Musée des beaux arts,'" in *Textual Analysis*, ed. Mary Ann Caws (New York: MLA, 1986), 1.

7. Jacques Derrida, *Of Grammatology*, trans. Gayatri Spivak (Baltimore: Johns Hopkins University Press, 1976), 158.

ity and for the general projects of the humanities and social sciences. The crucial first step was considering human activities as so many languages—sign systems whose functioning needs to be explained: how is it that their products have the meanings they do? Just as the task of the linguist is to describe the system of rules, conventions, and practices that enable human beings to produce and understand sentences, so it is the task of the structuralist or semiotician to reconstruct the other sign systems through which culture takes place.[8] A wide range of activities and their productions are considered in similar ways, as products of systems of signification and thus as texts. The first consequence, then, is the equivalence, through the notion of sign systems and of text, of different cultural products, whether literary works, fashion captions, advertisements, films, or religious rituals: all can be considered as texts. In the structuralist-semiotic perspective anything can be a text.

The second result is that *text* can even come to be a neutral term: to refer to "Hugo's text" is in many cases noncommittal, in that it does not specify a genre (such as play, poem, novel) nor does it decide between the literary and nonliterary or between the purely verbal, the behavioral, and the visual. *Text* is both a technical term that carries a lot of theoretical weight and an apparently neutral term to designate a cultural production. Of course, this usage does have implications: it carries a certain insistence that we are dealing with something exact; when it is used for a nonverbal entity it has a programmatic edge (don't think of this just as a painting!); and above all, it implies a framework in which the idea of text is basic. But *text* is here opposed to some sort of generic specification or reference to a particular medium.[9]

It is also opposed to the idea of objects that do not require interpretation or do not depend on conceptual frameworks or sign systems. In "The Ideology of the Text" Fredric Jameson writes, "Textuality may be rapidly described as a methodological hypothesis whereby the objects of study of

8. For discussion see Jonathan Culler, *Structuralist Poetics: Structuralism, Linguistics, and the Study of Literature* (London: Routledge, 1976), esp. 27–31.

9. In a book that calls for a return to traditional criticism, Roger Shattuck offers "Nineteen Theses on Literature," of which number 8 reads: "Let us eschew the freestanding word *text.* Its indiscriminate use today provides evidence of deadening stylistic conformity. Rather, let us take advantage of the full range of terms like *book, work, poem, play, novel, essay*" (Roger Shattuck, *Candor and Perversion* [New York: Norton, 2000], 5).

the human sciences are considered to constitute so many texts that we *decipher* and *interpret*, as distinguished from older views of these objects as realities or existents or substances that we in one way or another attempt to *know*."[10] The advantages of this concept are, of course, greatest in non-literary disciplines, where we could say that the concept of text does three things:

1. it suggests that the items under consideration should not be taken as given and that one should consider how they come to be produced, isolated, presented to attention;

2. it marks the meaning of these objects as a problem that needs to be explored; and

3. it posits that the analyst's methods need to be considered, not just prior to the inquiry to decide what steps will be carried out, but in the process of treating the objects of study themselves.

Jameson writes, for instance, "the notion of textuality, whatever fundamental objections may be made to it, has at least the advantage as a strategy of cutting across both epistemology and the subject/object antithesis in such a way as to neutralize both, and of focusing the attention of the analyst on her own position as *reader* and on her own mental operations as *interpretation*."[11] Above all, in the social sciences the notion of text challenges the idea that data are separate from theory and interpretation. Clifford Geertz, who did much to establish the idea of text in anthropology, explains that "the text analogy . . . the broadest of the recent reconfigurations of social theory," involving "a thoroughgoing conceptual wrench," trains attention "on how the inscription of social action is brought about, what its vehicles are and how they work, and on what the fixation of meaning from the flow of events—history from what happened, thought from thinking, culture from behavior—implies for sociological interpretation."[12] To treat a Balinese cockfight as a text (rather than as a rite or a pastime) is to focus on how deep social meanings are inscribed in a practice of watching a chicken

10. Fredric Jameson, "The Ideology of the Text," in *The Ideologies of Theory* (Minneapolis: University of Minnesota Press, 1987), 18. This important essay was first published in 1975 but was greatly expanded for the 1987 publication.

11. Ibid.

12. Clifford Geertz, *Local Knowledge: Further Essays in Interpretive Anthropology* (New York: Basic Books, 1983), 30–31.

hack another to bits. "What it says is not merely that risk is exciting, loss depressing, or triumph gratifying, banal tautologies of affect, but that it is of these emotions, thus exampled, that society is built and individuals put together."[13]

Roland Barthes links the rise of the concept of text to interdisciplinary encounters: people from different fields could have productive exchanges when they treated their objects of study as texts. He insists that we are not dealing with a radical mutation but with "an epistemological shift [glissement épistémologique] more than a real break."[14] The concept of the text as the product of a sign system that must be interrogated has been extremely productive, first for the sort of interdisciplinary cultural study inaugurated by structuralism and carried on (once we are said to have entered a poststructuralist age) by a cultural studies that strangely inclines to conceal such theoretical antecedents.[15]

The best-known essay about the concept of the text from this period is no doubt Roland Barthes' "De l'œuvre au texte" [From Work to Text] of 1971. Although the ideas it draws on were certainly in the air—none of the characterizations of the text are at all surprising—Barthes' distinctive articulation of them is highly idiosyncratic and not conducive, as Barthes himself might be the first to admit, to the advancement of methodological clarity or of an analytical program in literary and cultural studies. Barthes describes the notion of the text through an opposition between text and work on a number of different parameters. The persistence of this opposition gives his essay its clarity and force: the text is always being opposed to the work. But what Barthes seems to wish to resist above all is the idea that the concept of text can replace the concept of work; for him it isn't a matter of changing our view of objects previously treated as works and con-

13. Clifford Geertz, *The Interpretation of Cultures* (New York: Basic Books, 1973), 449.

14. Roland Barthes, "From Work to Text," in *The Rustle of Language*, trans. Richard Howard (Berkeley: University of California Press, 1989), 56.

15. One field this concept of text entered and where it has enjoyed picaresque adventures is film studies. I lack the expertise to describe the vicissitudes of the idea of the filmic text or textual analysis in the work of Christian Metz, Raymond Bellour, Maire-Claire Ropars, and others. John Mowatt provides an overview in the chapter "The Textual Analysis of Film," in *Text: The Genealogy of an Antidisciplinary Object* (Durham, NC: Duke University Press, 1992), 141–76.

ceiving them instead in a new way, tempting though this idea might be. It is as though the text is a new thing, previously unglimpsed. What constitutes the text, for instance, is "its force of subversion with regard to the old classifications." Text is "what is situated at the limit of the rules of the speech-act [des règles de l'énonciation], (rationality, readability, etc.)."[16] It is irreducibly plural, a practice or play of the signifier generating the infinite deferral of the signified; it is not consumed by the reader but solicits collaboration on the part of the reader and functions not as an object of consumption yielding *plaisir* but as a practice of disruptive and self-disruptive *jouissance*.

Text, then, introduces a new concept of the literary object, but the status of the opposition between *œuvre* [work] and *texte* is not entirely clear. Barthes' claim is not that literary studies used to operate with one notion of its object, that of the work, which now it has reason to contest, so that it now thinks of the objects of its study as texts, with myriad consequences. On the contrary, he wants to insist that there are indeed *œuvres*—writings that we continue rightly to describe and analyze as such, which are locatable, describable—and then there is *texte*. Although he speaks here and there in the essay of *texts* in the plural, he insists that texts are not countable, computable, locatable, and he generally speaks of *le Texte*, singular, with a capital *T* and treats it as a mass noun rather than a count noun, maintaining that there is "du Texte" [Text] to be located here and there in *œuvres*. The "texte en soi," pure text, is not something that can be found or analyzed, so that we cannot say that writings on one list are oeuvres and these others are texts. And he insists from the outset, knowing that this is how we are inclined to interpret his essay, "We must not permit ourselves to say: the work is classical, the text is avant-garde." We mustn't because there can be "Text in a very old work, and many products of contemporary literature are not texts at all."[17] But of course this argument reinforces the idea that the oeuvre is something like "normal literature" and that text is something avant-garde, just so radical that it cannot be pinned down.

In an essay of 1972 entitled "Research: The Young" [Jeunes chercheurs], Barthes writes, "[L]et us make no mistake about either this singular or this capital letter; when we say *the Text*, it is not in order to divinize

16. Barthes, "From Work to Text," 58.
17. Ibid., 57.

it, to make it the deity of a new mystique, but to denote a mass, a field, requiring a partitive and not a numerative expression: all that can be said of a work is that there is Text in it."[18] But this usage certainly does make *Text* an honorific concept, if not quite a God. And indeed, an objection to Barthes' formulations in "De l'œuvre au texte" is that while remaining within a logic of opposition, they work precisely to generate a mystique of the text: it is something so radical, disruptive, indeterminate, that it is not even an object but a practice or process, at best identifiable in certain moments. If you can show that there is "du Texte" in works of the past, you have shown that they are radical, exciting, worthy of attention.

Barthes describes accurately, I think, what was actually happening in the field of criticism: *jeunes chercheurs*, as he notes, saw it as their task to "explore what Text there can be [repérer ce qu'il y peut avoir de Texte] in Diderot, in Chateaubriand." It is a matter of finding "what, in previous work, is Literature and what is Text."[19] Barthes is always up front and undefensive, to the point of undermining his own concepts and projects and those of his students. His description does indeed evoke a lot of work done in this domain-that of finding what one might call disruptive, indeterminate, or perhaps "postmodern" moments or elements in works of the past. My objection is not at all to this sort of critical writing itself, of which I have done my share, and which may, like any other sort of critical writing, be surprising or predictable, dubious or convincing. My doubts bear, rather, on the theoretical framework: is this a good way to theorize this domain?

There seem two eminently defensible possibilities here. The first would distinguish between two different ideas of literary and cultural objects, that of the work and that of the text, two different ways of conceiving them. People used to treat *Madame Bovary* as an oeuvre, product of an authorial intention, with a meaning that had to be sought, an aesthetic unity to be valued, and so forth. But we now see that such things can and perhaps should be treated as texts, which means: as products of sign systems and intertextuality, instances of the indeterminate functioning of language, products of historical processes of production and reception. Thus *work* and *text* would be two different concepts of the object of study. It is

18. Barthes, "Research: The Young," in *The Rustle of Language*, by Roland Barthes, trans. Richard Howard (Berkeley: University of California Press, 1989), 73.
19. Ibid.

not that some writings would be one and some the other, though obviously *jeunes chercheurs* would find it more interesting to argue that writings celebrated as oeuvres should really be treated as texts rather than to continue to treat them as oeuvres. And note that within this perspective the idea of text could be charged with all the radical potential that Barthes wants to give it. The claim would be that we should stop reading books in relation to the idea of *l'œuvre* and conceive of them according to this impossible model of *le texte*.

Alternatively, *œuvre* and *texte* could be two different classes of objects (roughly the traditional and the avant-garde). Barthes rejects this conception more vigorously than the first sort, perhaps because this is what it is easiest to understand him to be saying: avant-garde products are radical, disruptive, indeterminate, good, and thus merit the appellation *texte*, whereas traditional ones do not, though some of them have some textual good in them. When Barthes insists that lots of contemporary writing is in fact nothing but *œuvres*, not *texte*, it certainly strengthens the idea that this is above all an honorific distinction.

The problem here is one that runs through Barthes' book *S/Z*, with its analogous distinction between *le lisible*, "the readerly," and *le scriptible*, "the writerly," which Barthes will not let us take either as two types of writing or as two ways of thinking of writing. But in *S/Z* this constitutes an interesting paradox in the methodological framework of his engagement with Balzac's novella: one that enriches the book and illuminates some of the paradoxes of critical procedures generally, as when the supposed refusal of interpretation becomes an interpretation. But in "From Work to Text," a brief expository essay that does nothing other than propose to illuminate a methodological framework, the indeterminate character of this opposition becomes an unavoidable problem, not to say methodological incoherence. While opposing work and text, Barthes refuses to let text and work be concepts that operate at the same level or in the same way.

One consequence of this is that while Barthes' account of the distinctions helps students find *du Texte* in older works, it does not help much for dealing with avant-garde works, which always fall short of the radical ideal and which are not much illuminated by accounts showing them to fall short. His insistence that the move to *text* is not just a methodological shift but that there are indeed works (which sometimes contain *du texte*) makes the idea of the text seem something of a fetish, an ideal object so radical and disruptive that no actual discourse is adequate to the idea (while of course *works* really do exist). The asymmetry helps animate the classic texts, in which one finds *du moderne*, but does not provide a good framework for dealing with the texts on which Barthes' scheme claims to set highest value. The best rationale for Barthes' asymmetrical opposition, in fact, is that by valorizing *text* it functions above all to enable critics to approach classic oeuvres in a new way, which rescues them from monumentalization, releases various sorts of intertextual and semiotic energies, and generally revitalizes the study of what Barthes later admitted was his first love, French literature of the nineteenth century.[20] And in this context the fact that *text* is valued so highly that actual avant-garde works fail to accede to the condition of *text* prevents this opposition from working to value contemporary, experimental works over the great writings of the past.

Is short, the practical results of Barthes' asymmetrical opposition may be quite admirable, but as a theoretical, methodological claim it creates difficulties. The concept of text that he develops might function well in a univocal model, where we now read works as texts, but he insists on maintaining the binary model where there are still *works*. Barthes' essay thus seems to undermine the idea of text that it claims to advance and that it presents so vividly.

One way to take Barthes' essay is to try to reduce the asymmetry of the concepts of work and text and to note that each is a model, a conception of how things might in principle function. It is important to remember that the idea of the work as the realization of an authorial intention and as an organic whole is also something of an impossible ideal, and thus a goal of analysis, so that it may function symmetrically to that Barthesean ideal of the text that is systematically set against it.[21]

Barthes' essay is, perhaps unfortunately, the most celebrated piece on

20. See Jonathan Culler, *Roland Barthes: A Very Short Introduction* (Oxford: Oxford University Press, 2002), 106–7.

21. Interestingly, Jacques Derrida develops the idea of *oeuvre* in two essays, "Typewriter Ribbon" and "The University Without Condition," in *Without Alibi*, ed. and trans. Peggy Kamuf (Stanford, CA: Stanford University Press, 2002), 133, 217. *Oeuvres* are signed, are products of an author, and are cut off from context in Kantian fashion, but the *oeuvre* also cuts. See Peggy Kamuf, "Introduction: Event of Resistance," in *Without Alibi*, 17–22.

the concept of the text and in some respects has had the effect of bringing the idea of the text into disrepute, as something extremely recondite,
ideologically charged, and so on. Others had tried to define the idea more
perspicuously. Julia Kristeva, for instance, in a number of places put the
methodological concept of text in opposition to notions of representation
and communication: they belong to different methodological networks.[22]
But she avoids any idea that modern writings are texts while old-fashioned
writings are not (she writes about medieval narrative, for instance). Kristeva sought to treat language in general through the concept of text, which
stresses that discourse is not simply expression by a subject but produces
the subject and that it is fundamentally intertextual, related to other discourses. She writes, for instance, "If one grants that *every* signifying practice is a field of transpositions of various signifying systems (an intertextuality), one then understands that its 'place' of enunciation and its denoted
'object' are never single, complete, and identical to themselves, but always
plural, shattered."[23] The text discloses the mechanisms through which language produces its effects and dislodges speakers from strictly representational relations to language, thus threatening the identities of speakers by
treating them as constructed, not given.

Jacques Derrida, in remarks such as the famous "il n'y a pas de hors-
texte," articulates a conception that might be used to rescue the notion of
text from the characterizations Barthes had given it, to make it more cen-
trally normative of language in general. In the afterword to *Limited Inc*,
entitled "Towards an Ethic of Discussion," Derrida writes:

[T]he concept of text I propose is limited neither to the graphic, nor to the book,
nor even to discourse, and even less to the semantic, representational, symbolic, ideal, or ideological sphere. What I call "text" implies all the structures called
"real," "economic," "historical," socio-institutional, in short: all possible referents.
Another way of recalling, once again, that "there is nothing outside the text" [qu'il
n'y a pas de hors-texte]. That does not mean that all referents are suspended, denied, or enclosed in a book, as people have claimed, or have been naïve enough to
believe or to have accused me of believing. But it does mean that every referent,

22. See, e.g., Julia Kristeva, "La productivité dite texte," in *Semeiotike: Re-
cherches pour une sémanalyse* (Paris: Seuil, 1969), 208–45.
23. Julia Kristeva, *The Revolution in Poetic Language*, trans. Margaret Waller
(New York: Columbia University Press, 1984), 59–60.

all reality, has the structure of a differential trace, and that one cannot refer to [se rapporter à] this real except in an interpretive experience. The latter neither yields meaning nor assumes it except in a movement of differential referring. [Celle-ci ne donne ou ne prend sens que dans ce mouvement de renvoi différantiel (*sic*).] That's all.[24]

The argument that the referent has the structure of a differential trace, that it is textualized and not something of a different nature, has been conducted in many places. One of the more striking comes in Derrida's discussion of Rousseau's *Confessions*, where Rousseau characterizes writing and signs in general as "suppléments" to the thing itself but in fact shows that his experience is, in Derrida's words, "an endless linked series, ineluctably multiplying the supplementary mediations that produce the sense of the very thing that they defer: the impression of the thing itself, of immediate presence, or originary perception. Immediacy is derived. Everything begins with the intermediary" [Tout commence par l'intermédiaire].[25]

The more these texts want to tell us of the importance of the presence of the thing itself, the more they show the necessity of intermediaries. These signs or supplements are in fact responsible for the sense that there is something to grasp. What we learn from these texts is that the copies create the idea of the original and that the original is always deferred—never to be grasped. Experience is always mediated by signs, and the "original" is produced as an effect of signs, of supplements.

For Derrida, Rousseau's texts, like many others, propose that instead of thinking of life as something to which signs and thus texts are added to represent it, we should conceive of life itself as suffused with signs, made what it is by processes of signification. Writings may claim that reality is prior to signification, but in fact they show that "il n'y a pas de hors-texte": when you think you are getting outside signs and text, to "reality itself," what you find is more text, more signs, chains of supplements.

It is this interweaving of signs and supplements, of language with what we call real life, that provides the most elementary rationale for the notion of text: if language or logos were a separate stratum that were found-

24. Jacques Derrida, "Towards an Ethic of Discussion," in *Limited Inc* (Evanston, IL: Northwestern University Press, 1988), 148. See also the French version: "Vers une éthique de la discussion," in *Limited Inc* (Paris: Galilée, 1990), 273.

25. Derrida, *Of Grammatology*, 157.

ed on something else, then it might indeed be conceivable, as traditional accounts seem to do, to set aside signs or discourse so as to accede directly to that other thing, whether it be thought, action, or reality itself. But this is what is not possible. One level or stratum interacts with the other and cannot be separated except provisionally or artificially. This is why the notion of the text as woven of different strands is superior to the geological metaphor of strata or levels: the text is not a series of layers but the interweaving of language with other threads of experience. In one of Derrida's early texts on Husserl, "Form and Meaning [le vouloir-dire]: A Note on the Phenomenology of Language," where he notes Husserl's own distrust of the metaphor of layers or strata, with which Husserl is nevertheless inextricably implicated, Derrida writes:

The *interweaving* (*Verwebung*) of language, of what is purely linguistic in language, with the other threads of experience, constitutes one fabric [un tissu]. . . . If the stratum of the logos were simply *founded*, one could set it aside so as to let the underlying substratum of non-expressive acts and contents appear beneath it. But since this superstructure reacts in an essential and decisive way upon the *Unterschicht* (substratum), one is obliged, from the start of the description, to associate the geological metaphor with a properly *textual* metaphor, for *fabric* or *textile* means *text*. *Verweben* here means *texere*. The discursive refers to the non-discursive, the linguistic "stratum" is intermixed with the pre-linguistic "stratum" according to the controlled system of a sort of *text*.[26]

The phenomenologist's attempt to unravel the confusion and to found speech on a ground of perception or intuition and thus "in the primordial given presence of the thing itself" leads not to the isolation of levels but to the recognition of interweaving, *Verwebung*, and thus to the conclusion that "the texture of the text is irreducible."[27]

Here, or in the concept of "the general text," a textuality that underlies and makes possible particular texts, the focus is not interdisciplinary inquiry; nevertheless, the idea of a general textuality certainly encourages thinking of all cultural objects as texts and hence a measure of interdisciplinarity. Sometimes the claim is made that this idea of text is an instance of literary studies seeking to extend its empire by seeing everything as a

26. Jacques Derrida, "Form and Meaning: A Note on the Phenomenology of Language," in *Speech and Phenomena and Other Essays on Husserl's Theory of Signs* (Evanston, IL: Northwestern University Press, 1973), III–12.

27. Ibid., 113.

text and that therefore what we have is not so much interdisciplinarity as the imperialism of literary studies. But the extension of the idea of text has transformed literary studies as much as, if not more than, any of the other disciplines, so it is not the case, for instance, that other disciplines have been assimilated to or had imposed on them a traditional idea of the literary. (That would, in any event, involve the idea of *l'œuvre* rather than *texte*.) And could one not maintain that insofar as the idea of the text has challenged positivistic models in anthropology and sociology or straightforward representational models in history or art history, this is a major intellectual advance in those disciplines rather than the imperialism of the literary?

I want to conclude by pursuing the interdisciplinary potential of the idea of the text in Paul de Man's *Allegories of Reading*. The second half of de Man's book is devoted to Rousseau, and as we near the end, he undertakes a complex reading of *The Social Contract*. Rousseau describes what he calls the "double relation" in which an individual is engaged: "Each individual . . . is committed in a double relationship, namely as member of the sovereign authority with regard to individuals and as a member of the state with regard to the sovereign authority"—on the one hand, helping to constitute the general will and thus part of the sovereign authority of the state and on the other hand a member of the community *subject to* the sovereign authority of the state.[28] "Indeed," writes Rousseau, "each individual can, as a man, have a private will contrary to or differing from the general will he has as a citizen."[29] As part of the general will, the citizen is alienated from the particular desires and interests that animate him or her as an individual, and this double relationship extends throughout political life: a piece of land, for instance, may be considered part of the state or private property. The same estrangement that separates the citizen as contributor to the sovereign authority of the state from the citizen as individual separates political rights and laws, on the one hand, from political action and history, on the other.

Working through Rousseau's account of these relations, de Man

28. Jean-Jacques Rousseau, *Du contrat social, ou Essai sur la forme de la république* [1760], in *Œuvres complètes*, ed. Bernard Gagnebin and Marcel Raymond, Bibliothèque de la Pléiade (Paris: Gallimard, 1964), 3:290.

29. Ibid., 291.

writes, "[T]he structure of the entity with which we are concerned (be it as property, as national State, or any other political institution) is most clearly revealed when it is considered as the general form that subsumes all these particular versions, namely as legal text"; and after discussion of the problematical relation of the generality of law and its particular applications (a point Rousseau stresses), he writes,

[W]e have moved closer and closer to the "definition" of *text*, the entity we are trying to circumscribe. . . . The system of relationships that generates the text and that functions independently of its referential meaning is its grammar. To the extent that a text is grammatical, it is a logical code or machine. . . . But just as no text is conceivable without grammar, no grammar is conceivable without the suspension of referential meaning. . . . [G]rammatical logic can function only if its referential consequences are disregarded.[30]

A law must be general, without reference to particular individuals— only to the empty *chacun* [each]. But, de Man continues, "no law is a law unless it also applies to particular individuals." And Rousseau writes that the general will functions only because "there is no one who does not secretly appropriate the term *each* and think of himself when he votes for all [il n'y a personne qui ne s'approprie en secret ce mot *chacun* et qui ne songe qu'à lui-même en votant pour tous]. Which proves that the equality of right and the notion of justice that follows from it derive from the preference that each man gives to himself and therefore from the nature of man."[31] Rousseau stresses that "the general will, to be truly such, should be general in its object as well as in its essence, . . . and that it loses its natural rectitude when it is directed toward any individual, determinate object," yet it is this mechanism of secretly referring *chacun* to oneself that allows the general will to function. "There can be no text without grammar," writes de Man; "the logic of grammar generates texts only in the absence of referential meaning, but every text generates a referent that subverts the grammatical principle to which it owed its constitution."[32]

It is this contradictory or duplicitous structure that relates text and

30. Paul de Man, *Allegories of Reading: Figural Language in Rousseau, Nietzsche, Rilke, and Proust* (New Haven, CT: Yale University Press, 1979), 267, 268–69.

31. In the second version of *Du contrat social* Rousseau suppressed the "en secret" in this passage. Otherwise, all the passages quoted are identical in the first and second versions. Rousseau, *Du contrat social*, 306. Quoted in de Man, *Allegories of Reading*, 269.

32. De Man, *Allegories of Reading*, 269.

law: in the passage from *The Social Contract* it is the duplicitous production of a referent ("en secret") that bridges the gap between the elaboration
of the law and its application. De Man then links the general model of figurative language, where there is a gap between grammatical and referential
meaning, to Rousseau's account of the state:

> In the description of the structure of political society, the "definition" of a text as
> the contradictory interference of the grammatical with the figural field emerges in
> its most systematic form. . . . We call *text* any entity that can be considered from
> such a double perspective: as a generative, open-ended non-referential system and
> as a figural system closed off by a transcendental signification that subverts the
> grammatical code to which the text owes its existence.[33]

An impossible object, joining perspectives whose compatibility is by no
means assured. De Man continues: "[T]he tension between figural and
grammatical language is duplicated in the differentiation between the State
as a defined entity (*état*) and the State as a principle of action (*souverain*),
or, in linguistic terms, between the constative and performative function
of language. A text is defined by the necessity of considering a statement,
at the same time, as performative and constative."[34]

In de Man we thus find that the text has become the name for and
the model of a pervasive structural relationship to which we have in recent
memory given many names, both in thinking about language (performa-
tive/constative, langue/parole) and in thinking about the most basic matters of action, identity, and institutions (the relationship between structure
and event, for example). The concept of text thus offers the possibility of
functioning as the basis for wide-ranging interdisciplinary study. But it is
striking that de Man's conception of *text* is based not on aesthetic or literary structures but on a legal structure requiring judgment and exercising power through its referentiality. There is no organic and aesthetic totalization, as with the New Critical conception of the text. As in de Man's
account of the *double rapport* of the individual to the state, the concept
of text captures a ubiquitous and paradoxical structural relationship between the generality of law, grammar, system, and the particularity of act
or event.[35]

33. Ibid., 270.

34. Ibid.

35. For a powerful reading of de Man's reading of Rousseau that takes up
this and other questions see Derrida, "Typewriter Ribbon," in *Without Alibi*, especially 150–54.

As the varied examples I have adduced suggest, the notion of text seems to serve, above all, to foreground the complexity of the semiotic productions that we undertake to study. Preserved in these vicissitudes is stress on the etymological connotations of wovenness—multiple strands that can be pursued and whose relation needs to be considered—whether these strands are considered to be things like the codes that Barthes describes or the inextricability of language from the reality that it performatively helps to structure. Whether there are incompatibilities between the complex concepts of text in Derrida and de Man is not clear; for both, text is a structural relationship between ineluctable but incompatible perspectives. What Derrida and de Man do certainly share, though, in contrast to Barthes, is a preference for monadic rather than dualistic models: the text as impossible object in its integration of incompatible modes of functioning—an impossibility we generally succeed in ignoring.

Both the New Critical notion of text as an organic totality and Barthes' conception of text as a highly charged impossible ideal have been eclipsed, I believe, and rightly so, by Derrida and de Man's aporetic structure, but *text* can still function as in the early days of the structuralist enterprise, as a relatively neutral way of naming objects of inquiry whose meaning cannot be taken for granted and where, as Geertz puts it, one needs to focus on the fixation of meaning from the flow of events. *Text*, then, is both one of the most complex theoretical constructions in theory and an incomparable interdisciplinary operator, offering analytic possibilities for a wide range of fields.

5

The Sign: Saussure and Derrida
on Arbitrariness

The arbitrary nature of the sign lies at the root of modern theory: Saussure's *Cours de linguistique générale* makes this the first principle of part 1 of the *Course*, "Principes généraux." "This principle dominates the whole of the linguistics of *la langue*; its consequences are innumerable."[1] One of these consequences is broached in the chapter on the immutability and mutability of the sign: "the arbitrariness of its signs theoretically entails the freedom of establishing just any relationship [n'importe quel rapport] between phonic substance and ideas. The result is that each of the two elements united in the sign maintains its own life to a degree unknown elsewhere, and that language changes, or rather evolves, under the influence of all the forces which can affect either sounds or meanings" (F 110; E 76). The essential nature of the history of languages depends on the arbitrariness of the sign.

But of course the most important consequence comes in the chap-

1. Ferdinand de Saussure, *Cours de linguistique générale*, ed. Tullio de Mauro (Paris: Payot, 1973), 100 (my translation). Henceforth I will cite page references to this French edition, as well as to Wade Baskin's English translation, *Course in General Linguistics* (London: Peter Owen, 1974), in the form (F 12; E 13), though I sometimes silently modify the English translation. Roy Harris's more recent translation, *Course in General Linguistics* (London: Duckworth, 1983), is astute but tendentious and idiosyncratic. Since his translation gives the page numbers of the French edition, my references can lead to the correct page in his volume.

ter on linguistic value, one of the most difficult of the *Course*. If the sign were not arbitrary, one could not say that "dans la langue il n'y a que des différences" [in the linguistic system there are only differences], but "arbitrary and differential are correlated qualities" (F 166, 163; E 120, 118). In the linguistic system, instead of ideas given in advance, we have "values emanating from the system." These values are entirely relative (a consequence of the arbitrariness of the sign), and it is therefore the articulation by language of the plane of ideas and of sound that instantiates the arbitrariness of the sign in its most "radical" form.[2] It is not just the relationship between the signifier *love* and the signified "love" that is arbitrary but also the distinction between the signified "to love" and the signified "to like," both of which are rendered in French by *aimer*. Language is not a nomenclature, and the articulations of each plane are themselves arbitrary and conventional.

Thus for Saussure the arbitrary nature of the sign determines what is most distinctive about language both synchronically and diachronically. Moreover, the *Course* seems determined to insist on the *essential* character of this arbitrariness. At the beginning of part 1, an objection to the principle of arbitrariness is raised and swiftly rejected:

On pourrait s'appuyer sur les onomatopées pour dire que le choix du signifiant n'est pas toujours arbitraire. Mais elles ne sont jamais des éléments organiques d'un système linguistique. Leur nombre est d'ailleurs bien moins grand qu'on ne le croit. Des mots comme *fouet* ou *glas* peuvent frapper certaines oreilles par une sonorité suggestive; mais pour voir qu'elles n'ont pas ce caractère dès l'origine, il suffit de remonter à leur formes latines (*fouet* dérive de *fagus*, "hêtre," *glas* de *classicum*); la qualité de leur sons actuels, ou plutôt celle qu'on leur attribue, est un résultat fortuit de l'évolution phonétique.

Quant aux onomatopées authentiques (celles du type *glou-glou, tic-tac*), non seulement elles sont peu nombreuses, mais leur choix est déjà en quelque mesure arbitraire, puisqu'elles ne sont que l'imitation approximative et à demi conventionnelle de certaines bruits. (F 101–2)

Onomatopoeias might be used to prove that the choice of the signifier is not always arbitrary. But they are never organic elements of a linguistic system. Besides, their number is much smaller than is generally supposed. Words like French *fouet*

2. The *Cours* speaks of "le plan indéfini des idées" and "celui non moins indéterminé des sons" [the undefined plane of ideas and that no less determined of sounds] that must be articulated by differences (F 156; E 112).

"whip" or *glas* "knell" may strike certain ears with a suggestive sonority, but to see that they have not always had this character, we need only go back to their Latin forms (*fouet* is derived from *fagus*, "beech tree," *glas* = *classicum*). The quality of their present sounds, or rather the quality that is attributed to them, is a fortuitous result of phonetic evolution.

As for authentic onomatopoeias (e.g. *glou-glou*, *tic-tac*, etc.), not only are they limited in number but also they are already chosen somewhat arbitrarily, for they are only approximate and already more or less conventional imitations of certain noises. (E 69)

Moreover, since these onomatopoeias become caught up in the phonological and morphological evolution that other words undergo, "elles ont perdu quelque chose de leur caractère premier pour revêtir celui du signe linguistique en général, qui est immotivé" [they lose something of their original character in order to assume that of the linguistic sign in general, which is unmotivated] (F 102; E 69).

Derrida cites this passage in *Glas* and offers a compelling analysis of it, to which I will return later. For the moment what interests me is the way in which the *Course* rejects fortuitous motivation in order to preserve the essential arbitrariness of the sign and deems apparently motivated signs not to be organic elements of the system, so that they might even be ignored by linguistics. To think language is to think the arbitrary nature of the sign.

The idea that the essential quality of the sign is its arbitrariness may not have been crucial to the development of linguistics, but it would no exaggeration to say that in semiology and literary and cultural studies, the arbitrary nature of the sign presided over the reception of Saussure and structuralism generally. The *Course's* famous remarks on semiology directly follow this discussion of the arbitrary nature of the sign. The possibility of natural signs, as in pantomime, is granted, but if semiology admits them, the *Course* declares, "its principal object will nonetheless be the set of systems founded on the arbitrary nature of the sign" (F 100; E 68). One might imagine, then, that motivated signs could be assigned to a different discipline, but the *Course* goes on to treat arbitrary signs as the general norm, arguing that in society any means of expression depends on a collective habit or convention. Signs of politeness, for instance, often endowed with a certain natural expressivity, are nonetheless established by a rule, and it is the rule that obliges us to use them, not their intrinsic value. "One can therefore say that entirely arbitrary signs realize better than others the se-miological ideal" (F 100–101; E 68). And this is why linguistics can become "le patron général de toute sémiologie," both the model or template and the boss of semiology.

There is a delicate operation underway here, as in the case of ono-matopoeias: do not deny the possibility of motivated signs but make arbi-trary signs the norm, so that the goal of linguistic and semiological analysis becomes to demonstrate the arbitrary and conventional nature of suppos-edly motivated signs. It is as if Saussure had realized that the passion that might best drive semiology and its heir, cultural studies, would be the de-sire to expose the arbitrary and conventional nature of whatever is present-ed as natural or motivated. The drive to demystify the natural or the mo-tivated, to uncover the true conventionality of the allegedly natural, has been essential to the fortunes of literary and cultural studies in the past few decades.

Saussure himself recognized that the arbitrariness of the sign distin-guishes language from other sign systems: "Even the fashion that deter-mines our dress is not entirely arbitrary—one cannot depart too far from the conditions dictated by the human body. Language, on the contrary, is limited in no way" (F 110; E 75–76). But the idea of the arbitrary sign as semiological norm triumphed over this other line of reflection. In Barthes' *Mythologies*, for example, the presence of motivation is recognized: "pas de mythe sans forme motivée" [no myth without motivated forms].[3] But this motivation, this allegedly natural relation between form and meaning, is treated as an "alibi" that permits us to get away with denying the contin-gency and historical character of our practices—claiming that I choose my clothes for fit and comfort, not for the meanings they bear.

The famous photo on the cover of *Paris-Match* of a black soldier in French uniform saluting the flag signifies, on the semiological plane Barthes calls "mythique," that France is a great empire and that all its sons, without distinction of color, serve faithfully under its flag. The re-semblance between this salute, this uniform, and those of white soldiers is a motivation that makes the image seem to give rise "naturally" to the concept and allows historical contingency to mask itself as Nature. "Nous sommes ici au principe même du mythe" [We are here at the very prin-ciple of myth].[4]

3. Roland Barthes, *Mythologies* (Paris, Seuil, 1957), 212.
4. Ibid., 215.

This naturalizing tendency of semiological systems is what semiologists and practitioners of cultural studies fight against: to unmask the cultural operations and reveal the arbitrary and conventional nature of the sign. "From an ethical point of view," Barthes writes, "what is disturbing in myth is its motivation. If there is a health of language, it is based on the arbitrary nature of the sign."[5] So we can devote ourselves to diagnosing all the ways the languages of our cultures, present and past, fail to be healthy. Thus, for instance, Judith Butler's vital work in gender studies has been based on a distrust of any signifying distinction presented as natural and the desire to reveal the conventional forms of the signifying operations by which we are daily obliged to enact "man" or "woman."[6]

The position briefly expounded in the *Course* has been a crucial presupposition of a range of projects in literary and cultural studies, driven by the suspicion of motivated signs and the presumption that if one finds in texts distinctions or categories presented as natural, they have not been analyzed with sufficiently sophisticated methods or else that the author is in the thrall of a dubious ideology.

Insofar as this distrust of motivation derives from Saussure, it is worth returning to the *Course*—and to the curious reflection on motivation I cited earlier. Derrida comments on this passage in the section of *Glas* beginning, "Le glas acharne une lecture grammatologique de Saussure." *Glas* provokes, gives a taste for, a grammatological reading of Saussure:

Le *glas* acharne une lecture grammatologique de Saussure, toujours de cette page du *Cours*, précisément, qui établit la linguistique dans son patronage ("On peut donc dire que les signes entièrement arbitraires réalisent mieux que les autres l'idéal du procédé sémiologique; c'est pourquoi la langue, le plus complexe et le plus répandu des systèmes d'expression, est aussi le plus caractéristique de tous; en ce sens la linguistique peut devenir le patron général de toute sémiologie, *bien que* la langue ne soit qu'un système particulier"). J'ai souligné *bien que*: l'institution violent du patronat.

The *glas* fleshes a grammatological reading of Saussure, always, precisely of that page of the *Course* that establishes linguistics in its patronage ("So signs, it can be said, that are wholly arbitrary realize better than the others the ideal of the semiological process; that is why language, the most complex and universal of all sys-

5. Ibid., 212.

6. Judith Butler, *Gender Trouble: Feminism and the Subversion of Identity* (London: Routledge, 1990); and Judith Butler, *Bodies That Matter: On the Discursive Limits of "Sex"* (London: Routledge, 1993). See chapter 6 below.

tems of expression, is also the most characteristic; in this sense linguistics can become the general patron[7] for all branches of semiology, *although* language is only one particular semiological system"). I have underlined *although*: the violent institution of the patronate.[8]

Derrida notes Saussure's dubious claim to know what are "authentic" onomatopoeia, which would require, in violation of the principle of the priority of synchronic analysis, identifying an origin that would determine the essence of a sign. Moreover, the claim that onomatopoeias are not "organic elements of a linguistic system" uses, in quasi-tautological fashion, the definition of the linguistic sign as arbitrary to distinguish elements that truly belong to the system from those that do not. But since we see, on the one hand, that so-called ordinary words can become onomatopoeic and, on the other hand, that onomatopoeias can become ordinary words, the distinction between what belongs to the system and what does not breaks down. And, Derrida continues, since what Saussure calls these signs being caught up in the system, "'l'entraînement' a toujours déjà commencé, qu'il n'est ni un accident ni un dehors du système, les juges, les soi-disant détenteurs des critères systématiques, ne savent plus ce qui appartient à quoi et à qui" [since the process of being "drawn" has always already begun, which is neither an accident nor something outside the system, the judges, the self-proclaimed keepers of systematic criteria, no longer know what belongs to what and to whom].[9]

But Saussure appears to claim to know, and instead of taking an interest in what *Glas* calls "the *contaminated* effects of onomatopoeia or of arbitrariness," he seems determined to preserve at all costs the thesis of the essentially arbitrary nature of the sign, a pure and essential arbitrariness whose fortuitous contamination is set aside as insignificant, though in fact, as Derrida argues, the possibility of contamination shows that the arbitrary was not pure to begin with. But could the elimination of contamination ever succeed? "Que restera-t-il du système interne de la langue, des 'éléments organiques d'un système linguistique', quand on l'aura purifié, dépouillé de toutes ses qualités, de ces attributions, de cette évolution?"

7. *Le patron* means both boss and model.

8. Jacques Derrida, *Glas* (Paris: Galilée, 1974), 105; Jacques Derrida, *Glas*, trans. John Leavey and Richard Rand (Lincoln: University of Nebraska Press, 1986), 90.

9. Ibid., 107; English 93.

[What will remain of the internal system of the language, of the "organic elements of a linguistics system," when it will have been purified, stripped of all those qualities, of those attributions, of that evolution?].[10]

The examples offered by Saussure only reinforce doubts about the possibility of distinguishing the system from fortuitous effects. "The examples are chosen too poorly or too well." There is no empirical rigor to these particular examples: on the one hand, no one calls *fouet* or *glas* authentic onomatopoeias—the claim is only that they "may be suggestive to certain ears"—and on the other hand, the mimetic effect seems generated above all by and in the figurative discourse of exemplification: the words *fouet* and *glas* "can strike" the ear, as whips and bells strike, and it is in this—that the words can be said to act as the objects act—more than in any similarity between the sound of a bell and the sound of the word *glas*, that there is resemblance. "One wonders why Saussure chose these 'words' as examples of presumed onomatopoeias."[11] Derrida suspected something was wrong here, though he stresses that he is reading the influential published text of the *Course*, not exploring Saussure's thought.

In fact, when you look at the students' notes from which the *Course* was constructed, you discover that these examples were invented by the editors, who, I imagine, were pleased at their own resourcefulness: whips and bells, so much more striking than Saussure's feeble example, Latin *pluit*, "it rains."

The fullest notes for the discussion of onomatopoeia are Emile Constantin's. His notes for what became the whole paragraph in the *Cours* read as follows:

In connection with this there is the question of onomatopoeias (words of which the sound has something that evokes the actual concept they are called on to represent). Here the choice, it is said, would not be arbitrary. Here there would indeed be an internal connection. In general people greatly exaggerate the number of onomatopoeias. It is sometimes said for example that *pluit* represents the sound of the rain, but if you go a little way further back, it becomes clear that this is not the case (earlier *plovit*, etc.).[12]

10. Ibid., 108; English 94.

11. Ibid., 107; English 93.

12. Ferdinand de Saussure, *Troisième cours de linguistique générale (1910–1911), d'après les cahiers d'Emile Constantin*, ed. and trans. Eisuke Komatsu and Roy Harris (Oxford, UK: Pergamon, 1993), 77. The standard source of the stu-

The other student notes that report on this subject have the same example. None mention *fouet* or *glas*, none talk about *fortuitous* results of phonetic evolution, and none speak of "authentic onomatopoeias." Saussure's point is that he does not deny the existence of onomatopoeias: "But it is evident," say the notes, "that there are some of these: *tick-tock*, *glub-glub*, but so subsumed in the mass that they pass into the regime of ordinary words."[13] The editors, trying to render emphatic what they take to be Saussure's point—that the motivations of onomatopoeias do not alter the fundamental nature of the sign—created a text that tries too hard to protect the essential arbitrariness of the sign, in effect dismissing onomatopoeia from the linguistic system. In so doing the editors introduced examples and formulations that trip over themselves and, as Derrida shows, undermine the points they seem to have been designed to make.

Derrida asks whether, on the contrary, the examples of motivation and demotivation provided by the making and unmaking of onomatopoeias should not lead one to think differently about the linguistic system and the frame it seems to impose, where some things are said to be inside and others outside. Don't effects of motivation and naturalization operate in ways that disrupt the distinction between what is internal to the linguistic system and what is external to it? What if the play of remotivation and resemblance

faisait que le système interne de la langue n'existe pas ou que l'on ne s'en serve jamais ou que du moins l'on ne s'en serve qu'en le contaminant et que cette contamination soit inévitable, donc régulière et "normale," fasse partie du système et de son fonctionnement, en fasse partie, c'est-à-dire aussi bien fasse de lui, qui est le tout, une partie d'un tout plus grand que lui.

---

dents' notes from which the editors constructed the text of the *Course* is Engler's critical edition: Saussure, *Cours de linguistique générale*, ed. Rudolf Engler (Wiesbaden: Harrassowitz, 1967). I will provide references to this edition in the form "Engler x.y.z," where x = page number, y = column, and z = segment number. Constantin's notes are generally in column 5. The passage quoted here is Engler 156.5.1147–50. Translations of Engler are my own.

It is easier, however, to follow Constantin's notes in Saussure, *Troisième cours*, ed. Eisuke Komatsu, which prints them in order and also contains an English translation. For Constantin's notes, thus, I use this edition, cited as *Troisième cours*.

13. Engler, *Cours*, 156.2.1152–56.

And what if *mimesis* so arranged it that language's internal system did not exist, or that it is never used, or at least that it is used only by contaminating it, and that this contamination is inevitable, hence regular and "normal," makes up a part of it, that is, also, makes of it, which is the whole, a part of a whole that is greater than it.[14]

This deconstruction of the act of positing a system based on the exclusion of motivation from the mechanisms of language inaugurates the kind of pursuit of signs that Derrida conducts in *Glas*, where every kind of "mimesis without imitation"—association, agglutination, graft, "contiguïté gluante," and above all the transformation of word into proper name or into signature—is adduced and explored as a textual mechanism. In this way *Glas* points toward a linguistics that is not a linguistics of the sign: "Les glas, tels que nous les aurons entendus, sonnent la fin de la signification, du sens et du signifiant" [The *glas*'s, such as we shall have heard them, toll the end of signification, of sense and of the signifier].[15] This is a linguistics of motivation that cannot be pinned down in signs.

But surprisingly, if we go back to the notes from which the *Course in General Linguistics* was composed, aided by Derrida's critique of the position developed in the published text of the *Course*, we find a line of argument that is not at all foreign to Derrida's explorations. In his third course of lectures, according to the students' notes, Saussure moved expeditiously from his account of the arbitrariness of the sign (in "Nature of the Linguistic Sign") to another chapter entitled "Absolute and Relative Arbitrariness in the Linguistic System."[16] This is a chapter that has been neglected by readers of Saussure because in the published *Course* it is moved out of Part 1, General Principles, and relegated to the end of Part 2, Synchronic Linguistics, after the chapters on linguistic units, linguistic identity, syntagmatic and paradigmatic relations, and the crucial chapter on linguistic value. In the published *Course* the discussion of absolute and relative arbitrariness thus appears as an afterthought, not even a separate chapter but the last section in a chapter entitled "The Mechanism of a Language," where it is explicitly designated as "another angle": "le mécanisme de la langue peut être présenté sous un autre angle." "The fundamental principle of the arbitrariness of the sign *does not prevent* our distinguishing

14. Derrida, *Glas*, 109; English 93.
15. Ibid., 39; English 31.
16. Saussure, *Troisième cours*, 85.

[*n'empêche pas de distinguer*] what in each language is radically arbitrary, that is to say unmotivated, from what is only relatively arbitrary" (F 180; E 131, my italics). This distinction is one that the fundamental nature of the sign *does not prevent one* from making but that, implicitly, is not germane to the basic nature of the system. In the course notes, however, it is presented as fundamental in the logical development of the argument that leads us from the principle that the relation between signifier and signified is "radicalement arbitraire"—that is to say, arbitrary in its root—to the notion of value (based on difference) and to the description of the linguistic system, which, surprisingly, is based on motivation. "Everything that makes a language a system or an organism needs to be approached from this point of view, which is not done in general: as *a limitation of arbitrariness* [comme une *limitation de l'arbitraire*] in relation to the idea."[17] Far from being an option that one is merely not prevented from pursuing, this line of thought is presented in the notes as required by the nature of the linguistic system, despite the fact that it has been generally neglected. (It continues to be so neglected.)

A version of this key sentence appears in the published *Course*, but since it does not come until after the discussions of syntagmatic and associative relations and linguistic value, it has seemed ancillary, especially since the editors immediately offer a gloss: "But the mind contrives to introduce a principle of order and regularity into certain parts of the mass of signs, and this is the role of relative motivation" (F 182; E 133). The editors thus make it very plausible to treat motivation as a minor principle at work in certain portions of the system—perhaps portions of the lexicon (*dix* "ten" is arbitrary; *dix-neuf* "nineteen" is motivated)—rather than what Saussure declares it to be: the perspective from which everything that makes a language a system must be approached. And commentators have followed the editors' lead in downgrading this perspective. Roy Harris, more outspoken than most, maintains that the distinction between absolute and relative arbitrariness "is a fudge, which serves the primary purpose of maintaining the 'first principle' [of the arbitrariness of the sign] at all costs."[18] I confess that I, too, in my own book on Saussure, take the dis-

17. Ibid., 87, Constantin's italics; Engler, *Cours*, 301.5.2108.
18. Roy Harris, *Reading Saussure: A Critical Commentary on the "Cours de linguistique générale"* (London: Duckworth, 1987), 133.

cussion of absolute and relative arbitrariness as a concession to the obvious fact that some lexical items are motivated with respect to others but not as a point having much bearing on the nature of the linguistic system itself, since these other signs to which the relatively motivated ones are related are themselves arbitrary signs.[19]

The crucial point can be stated simply: for Saussure the sign is in its foundations arbitrary but the linguistic system is a system of motivation, and the two principles are interdependent. It is because the relation between signifier and signified is unmotivated that *la langue* becomes a system of motivation.

In the notes Saussure makes it clear that he does not subscribe to the principle, suggested by the comments on onomatopoeia analyzed by Derrida, that the origin of a sign determines its nature: in the development of French out of Latin, the Latin *inimicus* is motivated (*in* + *amicus*) but the French *ennemi*, which evolved from it, "does not refer to other signs [ne fait appel à rien]. It has gone back to the absolute arbitrariness that is in any case the elementary condition of linguistic signs."[20] Derrida would say, rightly, that arbitrariness cannot be called absolute if it emerges out of motivation and is always open to remotivation, but Saussure's "absolu" is to be interpreted differentially as contrasting with "relatif": arbitrariness is the fundamental condition of signs, and in the synchronic state of a language, some will be completely (absolutely) arbitrary (unmotivated), whereas some will be relatively motivated, though cases of motivation will change with the evolution of the language. "The whole process of evolution of a language can be represented as a fluctuation [va-et-vient] between

19. Jonathan Culler, *Ferdinand de Saussure*, rev. ed. (Ithaca, NY: Cornell University Press, 1986), 30. Françoise Gadet is the exception among commentators. She introduces the concept of relative arbitrariness in her initial discussion of the arbitrary nature of the sign as a sense of arbitrariness that "suggests the preconditions for the establishment of a distinctly linguistic terrain; the whole Saussurian enterprise is geared to constructing this terrain through the definition of the relations between signs" (Françoise Gadet, *Saussure and Contemporary Culture*, trans. Gregory Elliott [London: Hutchinson, 1989], 37). See also Akatane Suenga, "Des deux arbitraires, absolu et relatif, à un arbitraire 'primaire'—le fait linguistique et le devenir du signe chez Saussure," *Cahiers Ferdinand de Saussure* 52 (1999): 189–200.

20. Saussure, *Troisième cours*, 88.

the respective proportions of the entirely unmotivated and the relatively motivated."[21] What is entirely unmotivated at one point can become relatively motivated at another.

Saussure broaches the topic of absolute and relative arbitrariness not just with examples of lexical motivation but with diverse grammatical and morphological examples, from verb tenses to plurals: "The English plural *ships* suggests through its formation the whole series *flags, birds, books,* etc., while *men* and *sheep* suggest nothing" (F 191; E 132). Constantin's notes conclude that in treating the linguistic system as "*une limitation de l'arbitraire* par rapport à l'idée" [a limitation of arbitrariness in relation to the idea], "[i]mplicitly you will thus proceed on the best possible basis, since the fundamental given of the linguistic sign is arbitrariness. Thus we are not choosing the first ground available, but taking as ground the fundamental principle, just as the language has necessarily taken it as the ground on which everything is to be built up."[22] Far from excluding motivation from *la langue*, Saussure makes it the very principle of the linguistic system, "la meilleure base possible" for conceptualizing the systematicity of language. The fundamental nature of the linguistic sign is its arbitrariness, but the linguistic system provides motivation that makes it possible, for instance, to infer the meaning of words, phrases, and sentences from the arbitrary meanings of their parts. It is not, Saussure adds, that *grammar* and *motivation* are synonymous but "they share something of the same principle." *Grammar*, which means "system," is the motivation of signs that are at root arbitrary and thus available for motivation. The system of motivation is what makes it possible to understand utterances: a form one has never heard before can be related to other forms and a meaning inferred only because the language is a system of motivation.

Saussure's discussion of motivation adduces many lexical pairs, where one is unmotivated and the other motivated. "*Ormeau* 'elm,' unmotivated; *poirier* 'pear tree,' relatively motivated, refers to a coexisting term, *poire* 'pear,' and also the ending *ier*. It attempts to motivate itself."[23] This last phrase, "Il essaie de se motiver," is a striking formulation. We are inclined to think of it as a personification, purely figurative, as if only people, not

21. Ibid., 87.
22. Ibid.
23. Engler, *Cours*, 299.2.2995.

words, could try to do something; but Saussure repeatedly avers that language escapes conscious control, does things on its own, and Derrida is interested in how the functioning of texts makes irrelevant or problematic the distinction between what might be deliberately chosen and what might not. "Language motivating itself" might well be an apposite description of the play of language.

The published *Course* pursues this problem of *poire/poirier*, noting that sometimes, as here, the formative elements are clear, whereas "others are vague or meaningless. For instance, does the suffix *-ot* really correspond to a meaningful element in French *cachot* 'dungeon'?" (F 181–82; E 132). Does "dungeon" equal *cache* (hide) plus *ot*? The *Course* then continues with an example not attested in the notes: "On comparing words like *coutelas* 'cutlass,' *fatras* 'pile,' *platras* 'rubbish,' *canevas* 'canvas,' etc., one has the vague feeling that *-as* is a formative element characteristic of substantives, without being able to define it more precisely." The editors, who previously invented the example of *glas*, here produce a whole series in *as*. In raising the question of the identity of this possible formative element, *-as*, the *Course* pursues the problem raised by *Glas* itself à propos of *glas*'s other formative element, *gl-* (*glose, glaieul, glaive, glaviaux, glaireux, glouton, glu, glace*, not to mention *aigle* and *sanglot*):

GL

je ne dis pas le signifiant GL, ni le phonème GL, ni le graphème GL. La marque ce serait mieux si l'on entendait bien ce mot ou si on lui ouvrait les oreilles; ni même la marque donc.

Il est aussi imprudent d'avancer ou de mettre en branle *le* ou *la* GL, de l'écrire ou de l'articuler en majuscules. Cela n'a pas d'identité, de sexe, de genre, ne fait pas de sens, ce n'est ni un tout défini, ni la partie détachée d'un tout

gl reste gl

GL

I do not say either the signifier GL or the phoneme GL, or the grapheme GL. Mark would be better, if the word were well understood, or if one's ears were open to it; not even the mark then.

It is also imprudent to advance or to set GL swinging in the masculine or feminine, to write or to articulate it in capital letters. That has no identity, sex, gender, makes no sense, is neither a definite whole nor a part detached from a whole.

gl remain(s) gl[24]

Gl, like *-as*, is an inscribed object of uncertain status, where the question of whether it is an element of the language at all remains open. Derrida leaves it open, focusing instead on its iterability and implying, I take it, that such entities, which might conceivably be called *marks* if that term were understood as originary rather than derived, are the "primordial" linguistic soup—prior to any definition of signifiers, phonemes, or graphemes—out of which linguistic and discursive entities are formed. Words where *gl* plays illustrate the workings of what Derrida calls the originary trace, a structure of *différance* that is the condition of possibility of signs.

But *Glas*, unlike Saussure's *Cours*, is interested above all in textual effects. Derrida writes, "L'association est une sorte de contiguïté gluante, jamais un raisonnement ou un appel symbolique; la glu de l'aléa fait sens, et le progrès se rythme par *petites secousses*, agippement et succions, placage—en tout les sens—et pénétration glissante. Dans l'embouchure ou le long de la colonne" [Association is a sort of gluing contiguity, never a process of reasoning or symbolic appeal; the glue of chance makes sense, and progress is rhythmed by *little jerks*, gripping and suctions, patchwork taking—in every sense and every direction—and gliding penetration. In the embouchure or along the column].[25] If the goal is to show how metonymic association, "la glu de l'aléa," makes sense—to show this by miming it in the graftings of critical description—then the implication is that it is through the work of the various texts, citing and cited, in their grippings and suctions, that elements are articulated. Saussure takes a different approach, concerned less with the effects of association within and between texts than with the question of how to decide when something becomes a linguistic element, given what appear to be repetitions. Though not theorizing iterability or *différance*, in attempting to work out the conditions of possibility of linguistic units he is grappling with the effects that make such thinking necessary.

A long sequence from the notes of another student, Riedlinger, takes up, by reflecting on the problem of the prefix, the question of how far one

24. Derrida, *Glas*, 137; English 119.
25. Ibid., 161; English 142.

can posit linguistic elements when one senses, discerns, or imagines repetition (a problem particularly germane to *Glas*). "How far is there a prefix recognized by the linguistic system [*connu à la langue*] in *séparer, séduire, sélection*?"[26] The situation is far from clear. Is *sé* like *re*? And what about *gl*, which seems to escape the category of prefix? "It is possible, as far as such a prefix is concerned, that there is no definite meaning and that analysis of this is reduced to a purely morphological distinction, to the *vague* consciousness that there is here an element that one cannot confuse with other categories of elements. This prefix can be recognized more or less clearly by the language without possessing definite meaning."[27]

For Saussure, finally, the test of whether elements are recognized by the language is the extent to which one can employ them in a new formation: "What is the absolute, peremptory proof that these prefixes are living elements of the language? It can only be analogical creation. It is because I can form *redémissionnner* [resign again], *recontempler* [recontemplate], without ever having heard them (cf. all the *re*'s people place before words that according to the dictionary do not take it!)."[28] Though the appeal here is to the performative possibilities inscribed in the structure of the system, and especially to "creative analogy," the logic gestures also toward what texts are able to do—what they are able to bring off. Whereas linguists have conceived of creative analogy as "false analogy," which introduces new forms on the analogy with others when there are historically attested forms that should have sufficed, Saussure argues that, on the contrary, so-called false analogy, with its productivity, is a true manifestation of the structure of the language. "Tout est grammatical dans l'analogie" [Analogy is grammatical throughout] (F 226; E 165). Analogical creation reveals the language's sense of its operative constituents, its structure.

"La création analogique," which Saussure calls an "immense phenomenon," is itself only a special case of the general operation of interpretation, whereby "the linguistic system represents its units to itself [se représente les unités] and organizes them for itself in this or that fashion, and then it can use them for creation by analogy."[29] "La langue ne se trompe pas" [A language never errs] (F 251; E 183).

26. Engler, *Cours*, 299.2.2100.
27. Ibid.
28. Ibid., 390.2.2590.
29. Ibid., 379.2.2527.

"La langue ne se trompe pas," and linguists need to try to find out what distinctions it makes, with what units it operates. "The language spends its time interpreting and decomposing what in it is the contribution of preceding generations—that's its career! [c'est là sa carrière!]—so as to then with the sub-units it has obtained combine them in new constructions. Thus *somnoler* [doze] could only be formed by decomposing the verbs in *-er* and *somnolent* in a particular way."[30] The adjective *somnolent* [sleepy] comes from Latin *somnolentus*, "smelling of sleep," composed of *somn* + *olentus* "sleep" + "smelling," but in modern French *somnolent* is analyzed *somnol* + *ent*, as if it were an adjective deriving from a present participle; and therefore the verb of which it *would* be the participle, *somnoler*, has been created. This is an example of how language—the linguistic system—leads a life of its own, representing itself to itself.

All of these issues—the status of prefixes, analogy versus false analogy, and the system's decomposition or self-analysis—lead us back to the same point, which is Saussure's view of the linguistic system, a view that is, finally, startling in its simplicity. He speaks of "the fundamentally identical character of all synchronic facts" (F 187; E 136) and maintains that "units and grammatical facts are only different names for designating diverse aspects of the same general fact: the functioning [jeu] of linguistic oppositions" (F 168; E 122). Riedlinger's notes for the second course sum it up nicely:

What does everything that exists in a state of the language consist in? [En quoi consiste tout ce qui se trouve dans un état de langue?] I said that it was the play of differences (comes from the fact that the word is arbitrarily chosen!). There is a perpetual opposition of values by means of phonic differences, but these are always differences which are manifested in a relative unit; within a vaster unit that brings them together we have sub-units which are opposed to each other. Everything comes down to differences, to groupings. Now here we must posit a fundamental distinction—which I have said nothing about up to now—if we wish to make any progress: . . . There are two ways for a word to be near, coordinated with, related to, in contact with another; we can call this the two spaces of existence of words, or the two spheres of relations among words.[31]

30. Ibid., 386.2.2573.

31. Ferdinand de Saussure, *Deuxième cours de linguistique générale d'après les cahiers d'Albert Riedlinger et Charles Patois*, ed. and trans. Eisuke Komatsu and George Wolf (Oxford, UK: Pergamon, 1997), 51–52.

These two spheres of relations are the associative (or paradigmatic) and the syntagmatic. The notes call the former "le trésor intérieur qui équivaut au casier de la mémoire" [the inner wealth or treasury that is equivalent to the pigeonholes of memory] and the latter the speech chain or discourse. Traditional distinctions between morphology, syntax, and lexicology are illusory; all these matters involve the same phenomena. "There are groupings of syntagmatic differences and groupings of associative, mental differences. In the linguistic system there are only differences and no positive quantity. But these differences can operate on these two axes: the line of speech and that of internal, mental comparisons, of form with form."[32]

The linguistic system is the play of two sorts of differences, made possible by associations in discourse and in the stock of forms, and this play is to be conceived of as a process of motivation, which makes it possible to produce and understand sequences. And, as the preceding discussions make clear, Saussure does not assign any limits to these processes of association. "Each element makes us think of the other: everything which is similar and dissimilar in some way appears in the vicinity of each word, otherwise the mechanism of the language would be impossible."[33] Or again, "Un mot quelconque évoque inévitablement par association tout ce qui peut lui ressembler" [Any word inevitably evokes by association everything that can resemble it].[34] We are certainly closer to the world of *Glas* than we might have expected.

Commenting on the remarks about *glas* in the *Course in General Linguistics*, Derrida asks, in a passage I quoted earlier, "What will remain of the internal system of the language, of the 'organic elements of a linguistics system,' when it will have been purified, stripped of all those qualities, of those attributions, of that evolution?"[35] The answer, we can now see, is not just that in denying the motivation of signs, one would eliminate a significant aspect of language but rather that one would deny the nature of the fundamental mechanisms of the linguistic system, since the system can be conceived as a mechanism of motivation. Saussure's conception of the mechanisms of the linguistic system—the play of differences, the opera-

32. Engler, *Cours*, 304.2.2132.
33. Saussure, *Deuxième cours*, 53.
34. Engler, *Cours*, 312.2.2181.
35. Derrida, *Glas*, 108; English 94.

tion of analogy, the series that generate units of indeterminate status and, above all, grammar as a process of motivation—precludes a theory based on signs purified of motivation or a theory that does not permit a structural "openness" of this "système interne de la langue."

Derrida had also asked,

> Et si le système interne de la langue n'existe pas ou que l'on ne s'en serve jamais ou que du moins l'on ne s'en serve qu'en le contaminant et que cette contamination soit inévitable, donc régulière et "normale," fasse partie du système et de son fonctionnement, en fasse partie, c'est-à-dire aussi bien fasse de lui, qui est le tout, une partie d'un tout plus grand que lui.

> And what if the internal system of a language did not exist, or that it is never used, or at least that it is used only by contaminating it, and that this contamination is inevitable, hence regular and "normal," makes up a part of it, that is, also, makes of it, which is the whole, a part of a whole that is greater than it.[36]

We might now hazard an answer to this question, whose logic of diminishing hyperbole (from the denial of existence of the system, to the denial that one uses it, to the suggestion that one uses it only in contaminating it) has a quite different status in our day, when the idea of a linguistic system is well entrenched, than it could have had for a Saussure struggling to establish the idea of language as a synchronic system rather than a history. Saussure's discussions of multiple languages, which occupied a much greater place in his lectures than they do in the published *Course*, cite plenty of evidence of the indeterminacy of a language—its boundaries, the shading of dialects into one another and of dialect into language—and of the difficulty of determining what might count as the features and the structure of a language at any point in its history. Still, he asserts the need to take a language or linguistic system—*la langue*—as the principal object of investigation, even if strictly speaking it does not exist. For Saussure, "le système interne de la langue," however undeterminable, is still a reality for speakers, an inexorable, unavoidable feature of their lives and their world. It is what they encounter, and they use it, as it uses them. Moreover, creative, innovative possibilities, such as those of analogy, especially so-called false analogy, depend on a linguistic system—a point Saussure particularly stresses. The contamination of the linguistic system is indeed a feature of

36. Ibid., 109; English 94.

its use—normal and regular, part of the system—and it makes the system an instance of motivation, of which there are other instances, such as those put forward by Saussure's work on anagrams. Linguistic motivation, a part of the system, might thus indeed be said to exceed the linguistic system, as Derrida posits.

If this is so, then we need to think differently about language and not conceive of motivation as an irrelevant accident that fortuitously befalls a system of arbitrary signs. Saussure would encourage us to think of the functioning of this system, which is larger than what is encompassed by the idea of "normal" language, not in terms of transgression and contamination but in terms of different kinds of differences and of motivation, suggesting that we should attempt to theorize the different kinds of motivation that mobilize, that can mobilize, differences.

Saussure is attempting to theorize this object whose nature is always to remain paradoxically ungraspable, undelimitable. The well-known principle that in the linguistic system there are only differences without positive terms is one such theoretical formulation, of a condition that by definition makes a language undelimitable, because differences are uncircumscribable. But the separating of *langue* from *parole* and of synchronic from diachronic—the asserting of the priority of synchronic description wholly necessary in Saussure's day as counterweight to the predominance of a historical philology that neglected to inquire about the nature of the linguistic system itself—has led to the idea that Saussure dogmatically posits an idealized, self-contained linguistic system and imperiously sets aside everything, from linguistic performance to motivation to historical evolution, that is not part of this system. But the processes of motivation that he identifies as the grammar of the language (which governs combinations) are the same as those at work in historical evolution driven by analogy, in which elements are decomposed and recomposed. Saussure highlights the difficulty of separating *langue* from *parole*, synchronic from diachronic, precisely at the point of linguistic creativity governed by the processes of analogizing. It is not just that it is difficult for the analyst to delimit this object, the language. Saussure declares that this structural indeterminacy is a property of the system itself: "The hesitations, the almosts, the half-analyses, the indecisions are a constant feature of the results which the linguistic system reaches by its activity" [Les hésitations, les à-peu-près, les demi-analyses, les flottements sont un caractère constant des résultats auxquels arrive la langue par son activité].[37] The linguistic system is not a self-contained entity but a process that by its fundamental mechanisms is engaged in the "flottement" of which *Glas* gives us a taste.

Simon Bouquet notes that Saussure broke off his work on the anagrams that he believed were concealed in Latin verse in order to prepare the introduction to his second Course, where his philosophy of language takes off, and that "it is not forbidden to hypothesize, against the usual story, that this search for anagrams leads to the theory of value."[38] This is an idea that would demand a good deal of work and remains to be explored, but what one can say is that since the theory of value displaces meaning in its insistence that signifieds depend on the infinite network of signs, it brings us back to the Saussurean formulation quoted earlier: "Un mot quelconque évoque inévitablement par association tout ce qui peut lui ressembler." If this is so, then the task for a theory of language is to explore what weight to give to *peut* here. What can *can* mean? Resemblance is uncircumscribable but still to be explored, and to see what resemblance can mean and what can be possible as an effect of resemblance requires the sort of radical writing and reading undertaken in *Glas*.

37. Engler, *Cours*, 392.2.2602.
38. Simon Bouquet, *Introduction à la lecture de Saussure* (Paris: Payot, 1997), 371.

6

The Performative

I propose to consider the vicissitudes of a concept that has flourished in literary and cultural theory in the United States in recent years. The concept of the performative has developed in unexpected ways since it was first introduced by the philosopher J. L. Austin in 1955 to describe a special kind of speech act: an utterance that accomplishes the action to which it appears to refer. At roughly the same time the notion of performance was emerging, quite independently, as central in an innovative strand of work in the social sciences. Gregory Bateson's seminal "A Theory of Play and Fantasy" (1955) established an approach to behavior as variously framed performance, pursued in his collection *Steps Toward an Ecology of Mind*; and Irving Goffman's pioneering *The Presentation of Self in Everyday Life* (1956) adopted a framework of theatricalized action. Goffman writes in his introduction, "The perspective employed in this report is that of the theatrical performance; the principles derived are dramaturgical ones."[1] And later in the same work we read, "A status, a position, a social place is not a material thing, to be possessed and then displayed; it is a pattern of appropriate conduct, coherent, embellished, well-articulated. Performed with ease or clumsiness, awareness or not, guile or good faith, it is nonetheless something that must be enacted and portrayed, something that must be realized" (75). Goffman cites Sartre's famous example of the waiter who is playing the waiter, performing the role. Social structure is to

1. Irving Goffman, *The Presentation of Self in Everyday Life* (1956; repr., New York: Doubleday, 1959), xi.

be analyzed through the patterns of behavior made evident in the performance of roles.

What the social scientists Goffman, Bateson, Victor Turner, and others share is a focus on the construction of meaning as a social process, in which analysis needs to identify the frames, scripts, and boundaries that make possible the play of meaning. The ascription of normativity to social roles and scriptings goes along with an interest in processes of reframing, the generation of meaning by the violation of scriptings. Theater provides sociologists and anthropologists with models for thinking about how social structures are embodied and negotiated in the actual behavior of individuals; social relations emerge above all in the enactments of roles.

If we take the root notion of performance to be theatrical or musical, then we have as our point of departure a concept that combines creativity and constraint: we have access to a work through its performances (as is more obviously the case with a musical composition); we can compare performances of the same work. Each performance involves both a script and interpretation. The concept of performance in the theater focuses attention on production rather than text—on event, for which there is also an audience to be considered: there is no performance without an audience, at least potential, and thus social circumstances.

Since the pioneering work of Goffman, Austin, and others, the sense of the importance of a performative dimension of language, behavior, and identity itself has only grown, though the relations among various thinkers' notions of the performative and performance are scarcely clear. One way to view the situation would be from the vantage point of theater studies, as the coming into its own of a root notion of performance that has long served as a general figure for life itself: "All the world's a stage / And all the men and women merely players."[2] Marvin Carlson, in his authoritative survey, *Performance: A Critical Introduction*, writes, "With performance as a kind of critical wedge, the metaphor of theatricality has moved out of the arts into almost every aspect of modern attempts to understand our condition and activities, into almost every branch of the human sciences—sociology, anthropology, ethnography, psychology, linguistics."[3] Writing about

2. William Shakespeare, *As You Like It*, act 2, scene 7.
3. Marvin Carlson, *Performance: A Critical Introduction*, 2nd ed. (New York: Routledge, 2004), 6.

the new field of performance studies, which is centered on the theater but expands beyond it in various directions, Carlson observes that while performance enters social science disciplines as a metaphor of theatricality and then is developed into a critical concept, the results of work in social science fields on performance and performativity have provided stimulus and inspiration to practitioners of performance studies in the humanities. There is an orderly loop of enrichment. But from Carlson's perspective the development of the concept of the performative is a side issue,[4] which certainly is not the case in literary and cultural studies.

But there is a third sense of performance, not explicitly connected to the theatrical or the social-scientific usage but lurking in the background, and who can say what surreptitious, unconscious influence it exercises? This is the idea of performance associated with modern capitalism. Performance is what counts; pay should follow performance. Executives have to perform, where performance is related to the bottom line (frequently tied to eliminating other people's jobs). Capitalist performance is occasionally linked to a certain theatricality—of the superstar CEO who makes a splash on the public stage—but this sense is not foregrounded, and the sexual innuendo is doubtless stronger than the theatrical: you want your executives to perform as you want a male lover to perform.

In a related sense Jean-François Lyotard, in *The Postmodern Condition*, takes performativity to be what has replaced grand narratives: we have lost our faith in narratives of progress, of the unity of knowledge, or of emancipation, and believe instead in "performativity"; efficiency replaces narrative projections as the determining value. Lyotard says that Austin's sense of the performative and "the new current sense of efficiency measured according to an input/output ratio . . . are not far apart."[5] Lyotard's analysis is not usually cited in discussions of performance and performativity, but one might wonder whether it does not lurk somewhere in the background of our contemporary interest in performance and performativity: we want the objects of our attention to perform, to deserve to be

4. The index does not contain a listing for *performative* but indicates that 9 pages of this 275-page book are devoted to performativity. Carlson discusses Austin's concept of the performative and others' reinterpretation of it in a section of a chapter entitled "The Performance of Language: Linguistic Approaches," in part 1, devoted to "Performance and the Social Sciences."

5. Jean-François Lyotard, *The Postmodern Condition* (Minneapolis: University of Minnesota Press, 1984), 88n30.

kept on and not terminated. Behind the formulations in the English translation of Lyotard lies French usage: while *le performatif* as substantive is a
neologism, it is perfectly colloquial to desire your concepts or machines to
be *performants*—to do their work well.[6]

If we focus not on the figure of performance in general but on the
concept of the performative, then we no longer have the orderly feedback
loop of mutual enrichment that Carlson happily describes. Eve Sedgwick
and Andrew Parker, in their introduction to a collection entitled *Performativity and Performance*, speak instead of "a carnivalesque echolalia of what
might be described as extraordinarily productive cross-purposes. One of
the most fecund, as well as the most underarticulated, of such crossings has
been the oblique connection between performativity and the loose cluster
of theatrical practices, relations, and traditions known as performance."[7]

This chapter seeks to provide some articulation, looking at what happens when the notion of the performative is extracted from Austin's theory
of speech acts and adopted by literary theorists and critics to describe first
literary discourse and later a wide range of discursive productions, including identity itself. It is striking, for instance, how the theatrical reference
has been repeatedly attenuated so that one ends up with a performativity
that is very different from one modeled on theatrical performance. The
performative becomes part of a basic aporetic structure of texts of all sorts
and a condition of invention or inauguration, and then, in the debates of
feminist theory, gay and lesbian studies, and queer theory, it becomes a fo-
cal point for questions about agency and identity. But recent developments
in the thinking of performativity may be leading us back toward concepts
of performance, in which a certain sense of theatricality is revived. At any
rate, this point of arrival, with talk of a performative concept of gender, is
very different from the point of departure, Austin's conception of performative utterances, but the performative, like the picaresque hero, travels
far to make its fortune.

6. Jacques Derrida links the *performante* to the efficiency of a machine, but
"performativity will never be reduced to technical performance" (see Jacques Derrida, "Typewriter Ribbon," in *Without Alibi*, trans. Peggy Kamuf [Stanford, CA:
Stanford University Press, 2002], 74).

7. Eve Sedgwick and Andrew Parker, eds., *Performativity and Performance*
(New York: Routledge, 1995), 1.

The notion of the performative is proposed by J. L. Austin, in a book published posthumously, *How to Do Things with Words*. "It was for too long the assumption of philosophers," he writes, "that the business of a 'statement' can only be to 'describe some state of affairs,' or to state some fact, which it must do either truly or falsely."[8] The normal utterance was conceived as a true or false representation of a state of affairs, and utterances that failed to fit this model were treated either as unimportant exceptions or as deviant "pseudo-statements." "Yet," Austin continues, "we, that is, even philosophers, set some limits to the amount of nonsense we are prepared to admit that we talk, so that it was natural to go on to ask, as a second stage, whether many apparently pseudo-statements really set out to be 'statements' at all" (2).

Austin thus proposes to attend to cases treated as marginal and to take them as an independent type. He proposes a distinction between *constative* utterances, which make a statement, describe a state of affairs, and are true or false, and another class of utterances, which are not true or false and which actually perform the action to which they refer: *performatives*. To say "I promise to pay you" is not to describe a state of affairs but to perform the act of promising; the utterance is itself the act.

The example Austin uses to illustrate the performative (and this will be significant for some later theorists) is the utterance "I do," by which bride and groom in the Anglo-American wedding ceremony undertake to wed one another. When the priest or civil official asks, "Do you take this woman to be your lawful wedded wife," and I respond "I do," I do not describe anything, says Austin; I do it. "I am not reporting on a marriage: I am indulging in it" (*How*, 6). When I say "I promise to pay you tomorrow" or "I order you to stop," these performative utterances are neither true nor false; they will be, depending on the circumstances, appropriate or inappropriate, "felicitous" or "infelicitous" in Austin's terminology. If I say "I order you" but have no right to do so, or if you are not doing the thing I order you to stop doing, my utterance will be inappropriate, infelicitous, a failure. If I say "I do," I may not succeed in marrying—if, for example, I am married already or if the person performing the ceremony is not authorized to perform weddings in this community. The utterance will

8. J. L. Austin, *How to Do Things with Words* (Cambridge, MA: Harvard University Press, 1975), 1; hereafter abbreviated *How* and cited parenthetically in the text.

"misfire," says Austin. The utterance will be unhappy—and so, no doubt, will the bride or groom, or perhaps both. The essential thing about performative utterances is that they do not describe but perform—successfully or unsuccessfully—the action they designate. It is in pronouncing these words that I promise, order, or marry. A simple test for the performative is the possibility of adding "hereby" in English before the verb: "I hereby promise"; "We hereby declare our independence"; "I hereby order you"; but not "I hereby walk to town." I cannot perform the act of walking by pronouncing certain words.

The distinction between performative and constative captures an important difference between types of utterances ("The distinction will have been a great event of the century," writes Derrida).[9] It has the great virtue of alerting us to the extent to which language performs actions rather than merely reporting them. But in *How to Do Things with Words*, as Austin pushes further in his account of the performative, he encounters difficulties. It seemed initially that to identify performatives, one might draw up a list of the "performative verbs": verbs that in the first person of the present indicative (I promise, I order, I declare) perform the action they designate but in other persons and tenses behave differently and describe actions rather than perform them, as in: "I promis*ed* to come"; "*You* order*ed* him to stop"; "*He will* declare war if they continue." But Austin notes that you cannot define the performative by listing the verbs that behave in this way because, for instance, the utterance "Stop it at once!" can constitute the act of ordering you to stop just as much as can "I order you to stop." And the apparently constative statement, "I will pay you tomorrow," which certainly looks as though it will become either true or false, depending on what happens tomorrow, can, under the right conditions, be a promise to pay you rather than a description or prediction like "he will pay you tomorrow." But once you allow for the existence of such "implicit performatives," where there is no explicitly performative verb, you have to admit that *any* utterance can be an implicit performative. For example, in English the sentence "The cat is on the mat" is for some reason the stock example of a simple declarative sentence, your basic constative utterance. But "The cat is on the mat" could be seen, rather, as the elliptical version of "I hereby affirm that the cat is on the mat," a performative

9. Jacques Derrida, "The University Without Condition," in *Without Alibi*, trans. Peggy Kamuf (Stanford, CA: Stanford University Press, 2002), 209.

utterance that accomplishes the act of affirming to which it refers. Austin concludes, "What we need to do for the case of stating, and by the same token describing and reporting, is to take them a bit off their pedestal, to realize that they are speech acts no less than all those other speech acts that we have been mentioning and talking about as performative."[10] Constative utterances also perform actions—actions of stating, affirming, describing, and so on. They are a kind of performative. Moreover, for many constative statements—"The cat is on the mat," "Boston is populous," "It's a nice day today"—the interesting question may not be whether the utterance is true or false but why I might be saying it. What speech act am I performing by uttering these words? In brief, Austin starts from a situation where performatives are seen as a special case of the constative—pseudo-statements—and arrives at a perspective from which constatives are a particular type of performative.

Given the difficulty of finding solid criteria for maintaining the distinction between constatives and performatives, Austin changes tack, abandoning "the initial distinction between performatives and constatives and the program of finding a list of explicit performative words" and considering instead "the senses in which to say something is to do something" (*How*, 121). He distinguishes the locutionary act, which is the act of speaking a sentence, from the illocutionary act, which is the act we perform *by* speaking this sentence, and from the perlocutionary act, which is an act accomplished (effects secured) by performing the illocutionary act. Thus uttering the sentence "I promise" is a locutionary act. By performing the act of uttering this sentence under certain circumstances I will perform the illocutionary act of promising, and finally, by promising I may perform the perlocutionary act of reassuring you, for example. Or when I perform the illocutionary act of affirming that Montpellier is in France, I may accomplish the perlocutionary act of bringing you to know it. Thus, instead of two types of utterance, constative and performative, we end up with three dimensions or aspects of every speech act, of which the locutionary and illocutionary are particularly important to a theory of language.

The result of Austin's heuristic trajectory is radically to change the status of the constative statement: it began as the model for all language use; then it became one of two general uses of language, and finally, with

10. J. L. Austin, "Performative Utterances," in *Philosophical Papers* (London: Oxford University Press, 1970), 249–50.

the identification of aporias that prevent the firm separation of constative from performative, it subsists not as an independent class of utterance but as one aspect of language use.

For literary critics, though, it has not made much difference whether we think of performative language as a special type, as in Austin's original characterization, or whether we focus instead on the performative dimension of all speech acts. The essential thing is that, against the philosophical model for which the norm for language is to make statements about what is the case, Austin has provided an account of the active, productive functioning of language.

Critics have found the idea of performative language valuable for characterizing literary discourse.[11] Since literary criticism involves attending to what literary language does as much as to what it says, the concept of the performative seems to provide a linguistic and philosophical justification for this idea: there are utterances that above all do something. Moreover, like the performative, the literary utterance does not refer to a prior state of affairs and is not true or false. Instead of starting with the question of truth or falsity, and having to defend a literary utterance as true in some higher sense despite its apparent falsity, one could ask whether it was successful or unsuccessful, felicitous or infelicitous. An act of appointing—"I appoint you three as a committee to consider this problem"— brings into being the entity, the committee, to which it refers, so a literary work performatively brings into being what it purports to describe. The literary utterance, too, brings into being the fictional characters and states of affairs to which it refers. The beginning of Joyce's *Ulysses*, "Stately plump Buck Mulligan came from the stairhead bearing a bowl of lather on which a mirror and a razor lay crossed," does not refer to some prior state of affairs but creates this character and this situation. And literary works bring into being ideas, concepts, which they deploy. La Rochefoucauld claims that no one would ever have thought of being in love if they had not read about it in books, and the notion of romantic love (and of its centrality to the lives of individuals) is arguably a massive literary creation.

11. The bibliography here is vast, but highlights of the past twenty-five years might be Mary Louise Pratt, *Toward a Speech Act Theory of Literary Discourse* (Bloomington: Indiana University Press, 1977); Sandy Petrey, *Speech Acts and Literary Theory* (New York: Routledge, 1990); and J. Hillis Miller, *Speech Acts in Literature* (Stanford, CA: Stanford University Press, 2002).

Certainly novels themselves, from *Don Quixote* to *Madame Bovary* and beyond, blame romantic ideas, in all their cultural power, on literature. Such fictions, which also go by the name of ideology and include such basic fictions as the "hour" that so regulates our lives, cannot be separated from the performativity of literary fiction.[12]

In short, the first result of the performative is to bring to center stage a use of language previously considered marginal—an active, world-making use of language, which resembles literary language—and to help us to conceive of literature as act. The notion of literature as performative contributes to a defense of literature: no longer made up of frivolous pseudo-statements, it takes its place among the acts of language that bring into being what they name.

Second, for Austin, in principle at least, the performative breaks the link between meaning and the intention of the speaker, for what act I perform with my words is not determined by my intention but by social and linguistic conventions.[13] The utterance, Austin insists, should not be considered as the outward sign of some inward act that it represents truly or falsely. If I say "I promise" under appropriate conditions, I have promised, have performed the act of promising, whatever intention I may have had in my head at the time. Since literary utterances are also events where the intention of the author is not thought to be what determines the meaning, here is another way in which the model of the performative seems highly pertinent.

The concept of the performative thus seems to provide a model of language that suits the analysis of literature better than competing models. This result is ironic, though, for two reasons. First, Austin's account of performatives, far from having literature in view, explicitly *excludes* literature. His analysis, he explains, applies only to words spoken seriously. "I

12. For a powerful reflection on the "as if" of fiction and its relation to the event see Derrida, "The University Without Condition," 205–37; for "the hour" see 228.

13. Derrida and others have argued that in fact Austin reintroduces the controlling role of intention through the insistence that the utterance be "serious," but his denial that the speech act be construed as the outward representation of an inner act is helpful for critical theory. See Derrida, *Limited Inc* (Evanston, IL: Northwestern University Press, 1988), 19; Jonathan Culler, *On Deconstruction: Theory and Criticism After Structuralism* (Ithaca, NY: Cornell University Press, 1982), 110–34.

must not be joking, for example, or writing a poem" (*How*, 9).[14] He continues with a formulation that treats dramatic performance not as a model for performatives but as a special type of miscarriage that should lead to its exclusion from consideration:

> A performative utterance will, for example, be in a peculiar way hollow or void if said by an actor on the stage, or introduced in a poem, or spoken in a soliloquy. This applies in a similar manner to any and every utterance—a sea change in special circumstances. Language in such circumstances is in special ways—intelligibly—used not seriously, but in ways parasitic upon its normal use—ways which fall under the doctrine of the etiolations of language. All this we are excluding at present from consideration. Our performative utterances, felicitous or not, are to be understood as issued in ordinary circumstances. (*How*, 22)[15]

For Austin literature had to be excluded in order to get at the fundamental nature of the performative; for literary theorists literature is a primary example of the performative functioning of language. This is no

14. Shoshana Felman asks whether Austin might not be joking here: "Coming from a jester like Austin, might not that sentence be taken as a denegation—as a joke?" (Shoshana Felman, *The Scandal of the Speaking Body: Don Juan with Austin, or Seduction in Two Languages* [Stanford, CA: Stanford University Press, 2003], 95). This book is a reprint, with a title more faithful to the French original of 1980 and with an introduction by Stanley Cavell and an afterword by Judith Butler, of Felman's *The Literary Speech Act: Seduction in Two Languages* (Ithaca, NY: Cornell University Press, 1983). No doubt modeled on Barbara Johnson's brilliant defense of Lacan of 1977, which seeks to show that Lacan already says everything that Derrida says in his critique of him (see "The Frame of Reference," in Johnson's *The Critical Difference* [Baltimore: Johns Hopkins University Press, 1980]), Felman's discussion is a fascinating attempt to attribute to Austin everything she has learned from Derrida. She argues that critics who reproach Austin for excluding jokes exclude his joking, but what is at issue is not Austin's undoubted playfulness but the particular economy of his project, which can admit infelicities and exploit them so profitably only by excluding the fictional and the nonserious. For discussion see Culler, *On Deconstruction*, 110–34; see also J. Hillis Miller, "J. L. Austin," in *Speech Acts in Literature*, esp. 28–40, for excellent treatment of this issue, though without reference to Felman.

15. Since *etiolation* means a making pale, sickly, by exclusion of sunlight, it activates the negative connotations of "parasitic": literature as sickly parasite on healthy normal linguistic activity. Literary critics have understandably not been happy with this view of language, though they have been happy to adopt the performative.

small mutation. In his essay "Performative Utterances" Austin again invokes the stage, the joke, and the poem but offers an example that repays serious attention:

We could be issuing any of these utterances, as we can issue an utterance of any kind whatsoever, in the course, for example, of acting a play or making a joke or writing a poem—in which case of course it would not be seriously meant and we shall not be able to say that we seriously performed the act concerned. If the poet says "Go and catch a falling star" or whatever it may be, he doesn't seriously issue an order.[16]

In fact, the example ultimately undermines the point he is trying to make. In Donne's "Song," if the order to go and catch a falling star is not serious, it is because it is presented as an impossibility. It is only the first of a series of tasks that one could not reasonably be ordered to do because they cannot be accomplished. One could argue, though, that it needs to be taken seriously in order to be appreciated as an impossibility. These tasks, the poem ultimately reveals, are as impossible as finding a woman who is both beautiful and faithful:

Goe and catche a falling starre,
   Get with child a mandrake root,
Tell me, where all past yeares are,
   Or who cleft the Divils foot.
Teach me to heare Mermaides singing
Or to keep off envies stinging,
     And finde,
     What winde,
Serves t'advance an honest minde.[17]

The next stanza urges the addressee to depart on this impossible quest: "Ride ten thousand days and nights" until your hair turns white, and when you return to recount the wonders you have seen, you will "sweare / No where / Lives a woman true, and faire." Barbara Johnson writes, "The very nonseriousness of the order is in fact what constitutes its fundamental seriousness; if finding a faithful woman is like catching a falling star, this is

16. Austin, *Philosophical Papers*, 241.
17. John Donne, "Song," in *The Complete Poetry of John Donne*, ed. J. Shawcross (New York: Anchor, 1967), 90.

apparently very serious indeed."[18] If, at one level, the explicitly impossible "Goe and catche a falling starre" is not a serious command, this is not because it occurs in a poem. Poems *are* full of serious commands, from the "Stay, traveler," of the epitaph, to addresses to the beloved. They are full also of performatives seriously accomplished: Virgil's "Arma virumque cano" [Arms and the man I sing] is a perfect performative, to which a "hereby" could be added: it accomplishes the act to which it refers. One might suspect that, ultimately, what Austin objects to is not the use of the performative verb in a literary context but the status of the subject: the actor onstage or the author in a poem speaks through a persona. But, as Johnson writes, once we consider "the conventionality of all performative utterances (on which Austin often insists), can it really be said that the chairman who opens a discussion or a priest who baptizes a baby or the judge who pronounces a verdict are persons rather than personae . . .? The performative utterance automatically fictionalizes its utterer when it makes him the mouthpiece for a conventionalized authority."[19] The suspicion that people are all too often performing a role when they issue performatives and that the fictionality of literary performatives might be a model for "serious" performatives could be what makes Austin determined to set aside the nonserious and the fictional—as if he could preserve the serious performative from the charge of theatricality by deeming theatrical and literary performatives quite a different matter. It is not, I would stress, that there is no difference between the command of a general on the battlefield and a command in a poem, but both, doing things with words, have a performative power, and both involve the problems of iterability and citationality.

The second irony of the literary fortunes of the performative is that for Austin the notion of the performative situates language in concrete social contexts and functions, such as getting married, christening a boat, calling a meeting to order, thanking, apologizing, promising, warning. To talk about performative utterances is, for him, to adopt a perspective opposing that of theorists who try to analyze language without concern for its contexts of use. His program would go along with the Wittgensteinian

18. Barbara Johnson, "Poetry and Performative Language: Mallarmé and Austin," in Johnson, *The Critical Difference*, 59.

19. Ibid., 60.

slogan, don't ask for the meaning; look at the use. But for literary theorists the notion of the performative stresses above all the self-reflexive character of language, the fact that the utterance itself is the reality or the event to which the utterance refers—when I say "I promise," the promise I refer to is the promise I perform in saying those words. The performative—a socially embedded act? or a self-reflexive act? The same concept thus sustains two rather different notions of the basic nature of language.

The idea of the performative nature of literature directs our attention to two problems or issues. The first is this: if, as performative, an utterance is not true or false but felicitous or infelicitous, what does it mean for a literary utterance to be felicitous or infelicitous? This turns out to be a complicated matter. On the one hand, one could ask whether *felicity* isn't just another name for what generally concerns critics. When confronted, say, with the opening of Shakespeare's sonnet "My mistress' eyes are nothing like the sun," we ask not whether this utterance is true or false but what it does, how it fits in with the rest of the poem, and whether it works happily with the other lines. That might be one conception of felicity. But the model of the performative also directs our attention to the conventions that enable an utterance to be a promise or a poem—the conventions of the sonnet, say. The felicitousness of a literary utterance might thus involve its relation to the conventions of a genre. Does it comply and thus succeed in being a sonnet rather than a misfire? But more than that, one might imagine, a literary composition is felicitous only when it fully accedes to the condition of literature by being published, read, and accepted as a literary work, just as a bet becomes a bet only when it is accepted. Mary Louise Pratt's *Toward a Speech Act Theory of Literary Discourse* leads us in this direction. In sum, the notion of literature as performative enjoins us to reflect on the complex problem of what it is for a literary sequence to succeed.

Second, and more difficult, there is the question of what is the act that a literary performative accomplishes, for part of the value of literature lies in its freedom, in the fact that it "makes nothing happen," as W. H. Auden puts it.[20] I will return to this question.

20. W. H. Auden, "In Memory of W. B. Yeats," in *Selected Poems* (New York: Random House, 1979), 82. The poem continues:

The next key moment in the fortunes of the performative comes in the work of Jacques Derrida and Paul de Man. Austin's analysis is taken up by Derrida, particularly in "Signature Event Context" of 1971.[21] This text is not primarily devoted to Austin; written for a philosophical colloquium on communication, it turns at the end to Austin to show how a very promising approach to language, which resists the notion of language as fundamentally a series of true or false representations, encounters difficulties from not taking account of the extent to which language is necessarily a set of iterable marks. Derrida praises Austin's project of exploring the force of language through an analysis that does not focus on truth or falsity of representation or make meaning dependent on intention, but he shows that Austin, concentrating on seriously intended first-person present-tense utterances of the general form "I hereby do X . . . " and excluding what he regarded as falling outside of "normal circumstances," including the nonserious, failed to recognize the citational, ritualistic character of speech acts in general. Austin sets aside as anomalous, nonserious, or exceptional particular instances of what Derrida calls a general iterability that should be considered a law of language—general and fundamental because for some-

---

it survives

In the valley of its saying . . .

. . .

it survives

A way of happening, a mouth.

Auden later changed "saying" to "making."

21. Delivered to a philosophy conference in Montreal, Derrida's lecture appeared in *Marges de la philosophie* (Paris: Minuit, 1972) and was published in English in *Glyph* 1 (1977), together with a vigorous reply by the speech-act theorist John Searle. Derrida responded at length in "Limited Inc, a, b, c . . . ," *Glyph* 2 (1977). These two texts of Derrida's, together with "Afterword: Toward an Ethics of Discussion," a substantial piece that ten years later reflects on issues raised in this exchange, are published as Jacques Derrida, *Limited Inc* (Evanston, IL: Northwestern University Press, 1988). Gordon Bearn's "Derrida Dry: Iterating Iterability Analytically," *Diacritics* 25, no. 3 (fall 1995): 3–25, is a brilliant translation of Derrida's argument in "Signature Event Context" into the vocabulary of analytical philosophy. For discussion of the notorious exchange between Derrida and Searle see Culler, *On Deconstruction*, 110–28; Stanley Fish, "How to Do Things with Austin and Searle," in *Is There a Text in This Class?* (Cambridge, MA: Harvard University Press, 1980), 197–245; and Miller, *Speech Acts in Literature*, 69–111.

thing to be a sign it must be able to be cited and repeated in all sorts of circumstances, including "nonserious" ones.

"Could a performative utterance succeed," Derrida writes, "if its formulation did not repeat a 'codified' or iterable form, in other words if the formula that I utter to open a meeting, christen a boat, or undertake marriage were not identifiable as conforming to an iterable model, if it were not thus identifiable as a kind of citation?"[22] The possibility of serious performatives depends upon performance of a script. Despite Austin's radical challenge to traditional philosophy of language and pursuit of the idea of linguistic force, he backed away by excluding the citationality that Derrida sees as the most general condition of possibility for performative utterances. Though recognizing that performatives can always misfire or fail, Austin failed to follow this perpetual possibility of misfire to the general iterability of all signs that it implies. Derrida argues that, rather than opposing serious to nonserious or citational utterances, as Austin does, one should work to identify different sorts of iteration or citation within the framework of a general iterability. One would end up with "different types of marks or chains of iterable marks and not an opposition between citational utterances on the one hand and singular and original utterance events on the other."[23] Austin, in bringing in "the serious" to buttress his attempt not to make meaning dependent on intention, and focusing on deliberate self-conscious acts of the "I hereby . . . " sort, fails to grasp the extent to which such actions are a special case of a more general performativity of language.

In the Derridean revision and, for example, in Paul de Man's use of the distinction between the performative and constative functioning of language, the performative is linked to the power of language to posit, to name. By using a noun, we posit the existence of a referent. Naming is one of Austin's performative speech acts, but his example is "I hereby name this ship the Mr. Stalin," where the question focuses on whether I am the properly authorized person and whether this is in fact the right name, both conditions of felicity of this official act (*How*, 23). He does not seem interested in the way in which, by reiterated naming, we articulate the world, even though we are not officially authorized to do so. The Académie française develops French terms for technical inventions, such as the "toile

22. Jacques Derrida, "Signature Event Context," *Limited Inc*, 18.
23. Ibid.

d'araignée mondiale" for the World Wide Web, or "un courriel" for an e-mail, but "unauthorized" French speakers persist in speaking of sending each other "un mail," and they invariably prevail.

Derrida's broadly based account accomplishes something scarcely evident in Austin's more narrowly drawn specification of the performative: to link the concept of performative language to the creative power of language and to the problem of origination in general. Austin's title is *How to Do Things with Words*, but his account can imply that we are doing things with words primarily when we gather ourselves hereby to perform a public, authorized act, according to socially stipulated rules, whereas language acts in singular yet iterable ways all the time.

The performative thus relates to the general problem of acts that originate or inaugurate, acts that create something new, in the political as well as literary sphere. In literature, Derrida writes,

this experience of writing is "subject" to an imperative: to give space for singular events, to invent something new in the form of acts of writing which no longer consist in a theoretical knowledge, in new constative statements, to give oneself to a poetico-literary performativity at least analogous to that of promises, orders, or acts of constitution or legislation which do not only change language or which, in changing language, change more than language.[24]

Not only is the performativity of literature analogous to that of constitutions and other acts of inauguration; literature, he observes, is "a system of performative possibilities that accompanied the modern form of democracy. Political constitutions have a discursive regime identical to that of the constitution of literary structures."[25]

One way to explicate this claim is to say that the act of constitution, like that of literature, depends on a complex and paradoxical combination of the performative and constative, where in order to succeed, the act must convince by referring to states of affairs but where success consists of bringing into being the condition to which it refers. Literary works claim to tell us about the world, but if they succeed, they do so by bringing into being the characters and events they relate. Something similar is at work in inau-

24. Jacques Derrida, "This Strange Institution Called Literature," interview by Derek Attridge, in Derrida, *Acts of Literature*, ed. Derek Attridge (New York: Routledge, 1992), 55.
25. Ibid.

gural acts in the political sphere. Derrida asks, of the Declaration of Independence of the United States, made in the name of the "good People" of the colonies, whether

> the good people have already freed themselves in fact and are only stating the fact of this emancipation in [*par*] the Declaration? Or is it rather that they free themselves at the instant of and by [*par*] the signature of this Declaration? . . . This obscurity, this undecidability between, let's say, a performative structure and a constative structure, is *required* in order to produce the sought-after effect. It is essential to the very positing or position of a right as such.[26]

In fact, this "good people," in whose name the declaration is issued, "does *not* exist *before* this declaration, not *as such*. If it gives birth to itself, as free and independent subject, as possible signer, this can hold only in the act of the signature. The signature invents the signer."[27] The people become a people only through the declaration their representatives sign on their behalf, yet the declaration depends on its being made in the name of a people that does not exist as such until their autonomy is declared. Moreover, in the Declaration of Independence the key sentence reads, "We, therefore, the Representatives of the united States of America, in General Congress Assembled, . . . do, in the Name, and by the Authority of the good People of these Colonies, solemnly publish and declare, That these United Colonies are, and of Right ought to be Free and Independent States." Is independence stated or produced by this utterance? The declaration that these states *are* independent looks constative but is a performative that is supposed to create the new reality to which it refers, but to support this claim, the assertion is made (fundamentally constative, as a claim about a state of affairs) that they *ought* to be independent.[28] A similar structure underlies the famous "We hold these truths to be self-evident," where the truth of self-evidence is buttressed by a performative holding or deeming that nevertheless puts in question their alleged self-evidence. It is

26. Jacques Derrida, "Declarations of Independence," *New Political Science* 15 (summer 1986): 9.

27. Ibid., 10.

28. Derrida's analysis seems to me to reverse or at least to blur this point. He writes of this sentence, "the 'and' articulates and conjoins here the two discursive modalities: the to be and the ought to be, the constation [constat] and the prescription, the fact and the right" (ibid., 11). But it is the assertion of what ought to be that is constative and the declaration that it is the case that is performative.

this impossible combination of performative and constative that particularly interests Derrida as he explores the possibility of acts of inauguration or invention. Unlike Austin, who took the impossibility of distinguishing rigorously between performative and constative as grounds for a retreat, Derrida insists that inaugural events require both—that the contradictory combination, "a performative structure and a constative structure, is *required* in order to produce the sought-after effect."

The tension between the performative and constative dimensions of literary and philosophical utterance is what emerges, in all its philosophical and political ramifications, in the analyses of Paul de Man. De Man, one might say, starts from the difficulty Austin encounters of separating performative and constative but takes this difficulty to be a crucial feature of the functioning of language that cannot be remedied by approaching the matter differently, as Austin tried to do. If every utterance is both performative and constative, including at least an implicit assertion of a state of affairs and a linguistic act, the relation between what an utterance says and what it does is not necessarily harmonious or cooperative. On the contrary. For de Man the moments that show us language at its most characteristic are utterances that exhibit a paradoxical or self-undermining relationship between performative and constative, between what they do and what they state.

Recall the Frost poem discussed in Chapter 1:

The Secret Sits

We dance round in a ring and suppose,
But the Secret sits in the middle and knows.[29]

This poem depends on the opposition between supposing and knowing. To explore what attitude the poem takes to this opposition, what values it attaches to its opposing terms, we can ask whether the poem itself is in the mode of supposing or of knowing. Does the poem suppose, like "we" who dance round, or does it know, like the secret? As a product of the human imagination, the poem might seem an example of supposing, a case of dancing around, but its gnomic, proverbial character and its confident

29. Robert Frost, *The Complete Poems* (New York: Holt, Rinehart, 1958), 495.

assertion of the fact that the secret "knows" make it seem very knowing indeed. So we can't be sure. But what does the poem show us about knowing? The secret, which is something that one knows or does not know—thus, an object of knowing—here becomes by metonymy the subject of knowing, *what knows* rather than what is or is not known. By capitalizing and personifying the entity, the Secret, the poem performs a rhetorical operation that promotes the object of knowledge to the position of subject; it presents knowing as something produced by a rhetorical supposition or personification. The knowing secret is produced by an act of supposing. The poem thus foregrounds the dependency of its constative assertion, that the secret knows, on a performative supposing that creates the subject supposed to know—a remarkable involution for an apparently simple couplet, but such are the intricacies of the struggle between performative and constative.

In de Man's essays, whether on Nietzsche, Rousseau, or Proust, the constative is the inescapable claim of language to transparency, to represent things as they are, to name things that are already there (sometimes he substitutes *cognitive* for *constative* to emphasize the epistemological stakes: "The interest of Rousseau's text is that it functions performatively as well as cognitively").[30] The performative for de Man consists of the rhetorical operations, the acts of language, that undermine this claim by imposing linguistic categories, organizing the world rather than simply representing what is. In Nietzsche, he writes, "[t]he critique of metaphysics is structured as an aporia between performative and constative language."[31] The "aporia," the "impasse" of an undecidable oscillation, as when the chicken depends on the egg but the egg depends on the chicken, here entails that the only way to claim that language functions performatively to shape the world is through a constative, such as "Language shapes the world"; but on the other hand, there is no way to claim the constative transparency of language except by a speech act. The propositions that perform the illocutionary act of stating necessarily claim to do nothing but merely display things as they are; yet if you want to show the contrary—that claims to represent things as they are in fact impose their categories on the world—you have no way to do this except through claims about what is or is not the case. So

30. Paul de Man, *Allegories of Reading: Figural Language in Rousseau, Nietzsche, Rilke, and Proust* (New Haven, CT: Yale University Press, 1979), 282.

31. Ibid., 131. See also my discussion of de Man in Chapter 3 above.

when Nietzsche claims that truth is but a moving army of metaphors and metonymies whose metaphoricity has been forgotten, he can only do this in statements that seem to claim to be true. More generally, the claim that declarations are acts of language that suppose and impose the categories rather than refer to what exists independently of language cannot avoid recourse to a language of declaration. "The deconstruction," writes de Man, "states the fallacy of reference in a necessarily referential mode."[32] The argument that the language of philosophical constatation is in fact performative takes the form of constative statements. For de Man, then, there is no question of *celebrating* performativity in general or the performativity of literature in particular. All one can say is that literature is perhaps more likely than philosophy to be alert to the undecidable relation between performative and constative that both subtends and undermines philosophical statement.

For de Man the structural tension between performative and constative is also adduced, as I explained in Chapters 3 and 4, to describe and account for the problematic relationship between the generality of law, system, grammar, and its particularity of application, event, or reference. Citing "an unavoidable estrangement between political rights and laws on the one hand, and political action and history on the other," de Man writes that "the grounds for this alienation are best understood in terms of the rhetorical structure that separates the one domain from the other."[33] The rhetorical structure to which de Man refers is the discrepancy between language conceived as grammar and language as reference or intentional action, which is best elucidated as the structural tension between performative and constative. As we saw, the ineluctability and indeterminacy of this structural relationship is what de Man calls "text," what he sees as determinative of history, with the violence of its positings. Although he does not stress, as Derrida is led to, the possibilities of inauguration and invention, he too links the possibility of the event to the positings of the performative, but he stresses the unintelligibility of the aporetic structure more than the potentially affirmative character of imposition.

In the next moment of the history of the performative there is a singular turn in its fortunes, with the emergence in feminist theory and in

32. De Man, *Allegories of Reading*, 205.
33. Ibid., 266.

gay and lesbian studies of a "performative theory of gender and sexuality" in immensely influential books of the philosopher Judith Butler: *Gender Trouble: Feminism and the Subversion of Identity* and *Bodies That Matter: On the Discursive Limits of "Sex."*

Concerned with how best to "trouble the gender categories that support gender hierarchy and compulsory heterosexuality," *Gender Trouble* takes issue with the notion that a feminist politics requires a notion of feminine identity, of essential features that women share as women and that give them common interests and goals.[34] For Butler, on the contrary, the fundamental categories of identity are cultural and social productions, more likely to be the *result* of political cooperation than its condition of possibility—more performative effect than constative truth. *Gender Trouble* does not deny that there are biological differences between the sexes (though it argues that *accounts* of biological difference are cultural projections of sexual and gender differences and is critical of the cultural production of sex as prediscursive); but one can take gender to be the cultural interpretation of biological difference. Butler proposes that we consider gender as performative in the sense that it is not what one is but what one does. A man is not what one is but something one does, a condition one enacts. Identity is an effect.[35] Gender is created by one's acts, in the way that a promise is created by the act of promising. You become a man or a woman by repeated acts, which, like Austin's performatives, depend on social conventions, habitual ways of doing something in a culture. Just as there are regular, socially established ways of promising, making a bet, giving orders, and getting married, so there are socially established ways of being a man or being a woman.

In *Gender Trouble* the idea that gender is performative seems to be linked to a notion of theatrical performance: "gender is a kind of persistent impersonation that passes as the real."[36] You become a man or woman by playing a role. This gave rise to the idea that Butler was treating gender as something one could choose freely and led to charges that she was slighting the real weight of gender identities. The performative account of gender was seen as wrongly linking gender to a freely chosen performance.

34. Judith Butler, *Gender Trouble: Feminism and the Subversion of Identity* (New York: Routledge, 1990), x–xi.

35. Ibid., 147.

36. Ibid., x.

Bodies That Matter seeks to refute this charge and rejects the notion

that gender is a choice, or that gender is a role, or that gender is a construction that one puts on, as one puts on clothes in the morning, that there is a "one" who is prior to this gender, a one who goes into the wardrobe of gender and decides with deliberation which gender it will be today. This is a voluntaristic account of gender which presumes a subject, intact, prior to its gendering. The sense of gender performativity that I meant to convey is something quite different.[37]

Butler makes two claims here. First, that there is not a subject, already constituted, prior to gender, who chooses. When one is constituted as a subject, one is already constituted as a boy or girl. As soon as a child is spoken to or about, for example, he or she receives a gender. "Indeed, there is no 'one' who takes on a gender norm. On the contrary, this citation of a gender norm is necessary in order to qualify as a 'one,' to become viable as a 'one,' where subject-formation is dependent on the prior operation of legitimating gender norms."[38]

The second issue is choice. Butler writes,

Gender performativity is not a matter of choosing which gender one will be today. Performativity is a matter of reiterating or repeating the norms by which one is constituted: it is not a radical fabrication of a gendered self. It is a compulsory repetition of prior and subjectivating norms, ones which cannot be thrown off at will, but which work, animate, and constrain the gendered subject, and which are also the resources from which resistance, subversion, displacement are to be forged.[39]

Gender is an obligatory practice, an assignment, say, but—and this is important for Butler—"an assignment which is never quite carried out according to expectation, whose addressee never quite inhabits the ideal s/he is compelled to approximate" (*Bodies*, 231). In that gap lie possibilities for resistance and change.

Butler poses the question of the difference between the performing of gender norms and the performative use of language: "Are these two different senses of performativity or do they converge as modes of citation-

37. Judith Butler, "Critically Queer," *GLQ* 1, no. 1 (1993): 21. This paragraph is repeated, in somewhat altered form, in *Bodies That Matter: On the Discursive Limits of "Sex"* (New York: Routledge, 1993), x; subsequent references to *Bodies That Matter* will be abbreviated *Bodies* and cited parenthetically in the text.

38. Butler, "Critically Queer," 23.

39. Ibid., 22.

ality in which the compulsory character of certain social imperatives becomes subject to a more promising deregulation?" (*Bodies*, 233). Butler takes care not to answer this question directly, but it is the notion of the citation of norms, crucial to Derrida's account of the performative, that brings together the performative utterance and the gender performative. The utterance "It's a girl!" or "It's a boy!" by which a baby is, in English, welcomed into the world, is for Butler less a constative utterance (true or false, according to the situation) than the first in a long series of performatives that will create the subject whose arrival they announce. The naming of the girl, she writes, "initiates the process by which a certain 'girling' is compelled" (*Bodies*, 232).

By insisting on the importance of the repetition of obligatory norms in the production of performative effects, Butler takes up the model of authoritative speech: the utterances of judges, umpires, and others who declare what is what: "Performative acts are forms of authoritative speech: most performatives, for instance, are statements which, in the uttering, also perform a certain action and exercise binding power. Implicated in a network of authorization and punishment, performatives tend to include legal sentences, baptisms, inaugurations, declarations of ownership, statements that not only perform an action but confer a binding power on the action performed" (*Bodies*, 235). These are cases where one generally supposes that the utterance creates the situation it names because of the authority of the speaker—judge, umpire, or other authority. But Butler insists, rightly I think, that, on the contrary, it is *in* the repeated citation of norms, the application of rules, that the authority of a mode of speaking is generated. "There is no power construed as subject that acts, but only a reiterated acting that is power in its persistence and instability" (*Bodies*, 225).

Whereas Austin takes the existence of proper authority for granted as a condition of possibility of successful speech acts, he does not reflect on the role of speech acts or their citationality in supporting or creating such authority. Citation helps create authority. Similarly, and here Butler brings a new dimension to the analysis of performative utterance, the force of the insult "Queer!" comes not from the intention or authority of the speaker, who is most likely some fool quite unknown to the victim, but from the fact that the shout "Queer!" repeats shouted insults of the past, interpellations or acts of address that produce the homosexual object through reiterated shaming or abjection and whose citationality lends some authority to the wielder of insults. "'Queer!' derives its force precisely through the repeated invocation by which a social bond among homophobic communities is formed through time. The interpellation echoes past interpellations, and binds the speakers, as if they spoke in unison across time. In this sense it is always an imaginary chorus that taunts 'queer!'" (*Bodies*, 227). Not the repetition itself but the fact that it is recognized as conforming to a model, a norm, linked with a history of exclusion, is what gives the insult its performative force. Conventional insults such as "Fag!" or "Nigger!" accumulate, Butler writes, "the force of authority through the repetition or citation of a prior, authoritative set of practices," speaking as if with the voice of all the taunts of the past (*Bodies*, 227).[40]

Eve Sedgwick, in an article entitled "Queer Performativity," notes the centrality of the marriage performative in Austin and suggests that a productive shift might occur if one took as key examples not the explicit, public, or state-sanctioned production of heterosexual identity in the performatives of the marriage ceremony but rather the innumerable minor performative acts that shape subjects against their will, of which the model might be the familiar exclamation, "Shame on you!"[41] This utterance is an act by which the parent or teacher performatively confers shame, creating the situation to which the utterance refers, installing the child in an identity constituted in relation to the social norms that are supposedly being violated. Unlike Austin's first-person indicative performatives, which are deliberate acts of a speaker who promises, marries, orders, or judges, "Shame on you!" is a performative that conceals the actor or agent who confers shame on the child, and in this it is related to insults like "Queer!" It draws its force from the repeated echo of norms.

It is this historical dimension of performatives that implies the possibility of deflecting or redirecting the weight of the past, by attempting to capture and redeploy the terms that bear an oppressive signification, as in the adoption of "Queer" by homosexuals themselves, or in the theatrical citation of norms of femininity in drag performances. Butler insists that you do not become autonomous by choosing your name, for names always

40. For further discussion of the problem of hate speech as action see Butler's *Excitable Speech: A Politics of the Performative* (New York: Routledge, 1997).

41. Eve Sedgwick, "Queer Performativity," *GLQ* 1, no. 1 (1993): 4.

carry historical weight and are subject to the uses others will make of them in the future: you cannot control the terms that you choose to name yourselves. But the historical character of the performative process creates the possibility of a political struggle.

Now it is obvious that the distance between the beginning and the (provisional) end of this story so far—between Austin and Butler—is very great. It is not, I should emphasize, a difference between philosophy and literary studies, for Butler herself is a philosopher, even though her books do contain occasional readings of literary works, which may contribute to the breadth of her claims.[42] But her polysyllabic prose seems more philosophical, less literary than the extremely playful writing of Austin—who paradoxically sets aside the literary and the nonserious.

There is, first, a difference between what is at stake for Austin and for Butler. For Austin the concept of the performative, by helping us to think about an aspect of language neglected by prior philosophers, starts a process of rethinking what language is and how it should be studied; for Butler it is a model for thinking about crucial social processes where a number of matters are at stake: (1) the nature of identity and how it is produced, (2) the functioning of social norms, (3) the fundamental problem of what today we call "agency" in English: how far and under what conditions can I be a responsible subject who chooses my acts, and (4) the relationship between the individual and social change.

There is also a difference in the conception of the performative itself. One might ask what it would mean for Butler's performatives to be felicitous or infelicitous. Obviously, she does not take as the goal of her performatives a happy, successful performing of femininity, in acts that fulfill all the conditions of this social idea. If hers is a theory that locates success in the perturbation of gender norms, that seems a different conception of the performative. Indeed, here is where we can see a fundamental difference inaugurated by Derrida. Whereas Austin is interested in cases of misfire and failure as ways of identifying what are the rules or the socially accepted procedures for the performance of certain speech acts, he shows no ex-

42. See readings of Willa Cather and Nella Larsen in *Bodies That Matter* and also, especially, *Antigone's Claim: Kinship Between Life and Death* (New York: Columbia University Press, 2000), discussed briefly in Chapter 1 above.

plicit interest in how speech acts might actually do something by breaking or evading the rules.[43] For Derrida himself, though, particularly interested in how things often fail to go quite as expected or prescribed, the performativity of language is fundamental to the possibility of inauguration, change, which is precisely not rule-*governed*, though of course made possible by rules and procedures in place, which language cites as it attempts something new. This interest in the link between iterability and transformation is Butler's Derridean inheritance.[44]

In fact, Austin and Butler seem to have two different sorts of acts in view. Austin's examples appear to be singular acts, which can be accomplished once and for all, if I meet the conditions of felicity. If I am the umpire of a soccer match in progress, I can, by declaring that a kick was good, make it a goal. In the performative theory of gender, by contrast, no act in itself brings something about. I become a man only through massive, daily repetition of conventional procedures.

But the notion of the speech act itself raises questions about this distinction, between singular acts and iteration. As Derrida shows in his reading of Austin, the iterability that is the condition of possibility of performatives introduces a gap that puts in question a rigorous distinction between singular events and repetitions. But this apparent difference between two sorts of act brings us back to the problem of the nature of the literary event, accentuating a distinction that was concealed in the appropriation of the notion of performative for thinking about literature. On the one hand, the literary work seems to accomplish a singular, specific act. It creates that reality that is the work, and its sentences accomplish something in particular in that work. For each work, one can try to specify what it and its parts accomplish, just as one can try to spell out what is promised

43. Hillis Miller is certainly right to stress that Austin's own attempt to do something radically new in philosophy needs to be taken into account in drawing such a contrast (see Miller, *Speech Acts in Literature*), but it is nonetheless true that Austin never tries to theorize how something not allowed for by the rules might take place or how one does something one is not authorized to do (as in a declaration of independence).

44. It is important to recognize, though, that the performative cannot account for the event, which, if it is truly an event, erupts. "The event belongs to a perhaps that is in keeping not with the possible but with the impossible. And its force is therefore irreducible to the force or power of the performative" (Derrida, *Without Alibi*, 235).

in a particular act of promising. This, one might say, is the Austinian version of the literary event.

But on the other hand, thinking of Butler's model, we could say that a work succeeds, becomes an event, by a massive repetition that takes up norms and, possibly, changes things. If a novel happens, it does so because, in its singularity, it inspires a passion that gives life to these forms, in acts of reading and recollection, repeating its inflection of the conventions of the novel and, perhaps, effecting an alteration in the norms or the forms through which readers go on to confront the world. A poem may very well disappear without a trace, but it may also trace itself in memories and give rise to acts of repetition. Its performativity, then, is less a singular act accomplished once and for all than a repetition that gives life to forms that it repeats.

This double approach may help us to reflect on the nature of literature as event. Derrida notes that literature is

an institution that consists in transgressing and transforming, thus in producing its constitutional law; or, to put it better, in producing discursive forms, "works," and "events" in which the very possibility of a fundamental constitution is at least "fictionally" contested, threatened, deconstructed, presented in its very precariousness. Hence, while literature shares a certain power and a certain destiny with "jurisdiction," with the juridico-political production of institutional foundations, the constitutions of states, fundamental legislation, and even the theological-juridico performatives which occur at the beginning of law, at a certain point it can only exceed them, interrogate them, "fictionalize" them: with nothing, or almost nothing, in view, of course, and by producing events whose "reality" or duration is never assured, but which by that very fact are more thought-provoking, if that still means something.[45]

Butler's model helps us—although this is in no way her goal—to conceive of this unusual performativity that interrogates by repeating foundational acts—in a repetition that can have critical value, as it animates and alters forms that it repeats.

The fortunes of the performative are striking in the disparities among the various conceptions and assumptions. Austin's initial challenge to a philosophical assumption that language was above all a means of representation and that truth or falsity must thus be the primary categories of

45. Derrida, "This Strange Institution Called Literature," 73.

evaluation made possible a broadly based rethinking not just of how language works but of signifying action generally. Austin's setting aside of theater, poetry, and jokes provides an easy route for such rethinking, leading us to ask what is accomplished by this act of exclusion and whether the marginal is not central, so that the literary, the theatrical, the fictionalized performatives make themselves felt on the scene of the generalized performative. This legacy of reconfiguration, despite its divergences (Derrida and de Man, for instance, stress rather different aspects of the problem of the performative), enables us to address key problems in literary and cultural studies.

Let me, in conclusion, list some of these issues.

—First, how to think about the shaping role of language: do we try to limit it to certain specific acts, where we think we can say with confidence what it does, or do we try to gauge its broader effects, as it organizes our encounters with the world? Obviously, we ought to do both, while attempting to specify the level at which we are working.

—Second, how should we conceive of the relation, in the cultural realm, between social conventions—the constitutive conventions that make possible social life—and individual acts? It is tempting, but clearly too simple, to imagine that social conventions are like the scenery or background against which we decide how to act; the various accounts of the performative offer more complicated accounts of the entanglement of norm and action, whether presenting conventions as the condition of possibility of events, as in Austin, or, as in Butler, seeing action as an assignment of repetition, which may nevertheless occasionally deviate from the norms. Literature, which is supposed to "make it new" in a space of convention, provides yet another case. Grasping this relationship through appropriately complex models is surely crucial for any truly pertinent cultural studies, as well as for literary studies.

—Third, how should one conceive of the relation between what language does and what it says? This is the basic problem of the performative—the question, yet to be resolved, of whether there can be a harmonious fusion of doing and saying or whether there is an ineluctable tension here that governs and undermines all textual activity. Whereas once it was assumed that aesthetic achievement depended on harmonious fusion, the ineluctability of tension now seems better established.

—Finally, how, in this postmodern age, should we think of the event? It has become commonplace in the United States, for instance, in this age of mass media, to say that what happens on television "happens, period," is a real event. Whether the image corresponds to a reality or not, the media event is an event to be reckoned with. The problematic of the performative can help us to explore in a more sophisticated way the issues that are often crudely addressed in terms of the modern blurring of the boundaries between fact and fiction or the problem of pseudoevents, but Derrida's reminder that the true event is the unforeseen, that "the force of the event is always stronger than the force of a performative," can prevent a simple celebration of performativity as creativity. And the problem of the nature of the literary event, of literature as act, because of its obvious complexity, may help us to avoid the temptation to oversimplify the problem in other domains.

In sum, rather than try to restrict or simplify the performative's domain, by choosing one strand of reflection as the correct one, we ought to accentuate and pursue the differences between them—so as to increase our chances of grasping the different levels and modes in which events occur. This is a project requiring the cooperation—albeit the inevitably contentious cooperation—of philosophy and literary theory and the possibility of reconnecting with the domain of performance theory in theater studies and the social sciences, so that in the "carnivalesque echolalia of what might be described as extraordinarily productive cross-purposes," of which Parker and Sedgwick speak, we might indeed come both to enjoy the carnivalesque and to find these cross purposes productive.

7

Interpretation: Defending
"Overinterpretation"

Since 1975 I have from time to time argued that one of the major problems of literary studies is the assumption, all too infrequently challenged, that the goal of literary studies is the interpretation of literary works and that the test of any theoretical discourse is whether it makes possible new and convincing interpretations of individual works.[1] This presumption produces a rather odd situation: although we have vast numbers of interpretations of every major work and of very many minor ones, we lack adequate accounts of how literature itself works: what are the norms and conventions that enable literary works to have the meanings they do for members of a culture? As Northrop Frye pointed out long ago in *The Anatomy of Criticism*, we lack the understanding and agreement that would enable us to write the opening pages of a textbook about literature, explaining what the basic divisions, types, or categories of literature are. While we have histories of some genres, we lack convincing theories of the importance or roles of genres or of what genres there are or of the constitutive conventions of each. But instead of working on such problems, critics see their task as producing new interpretations of the works that interest them and, naturally, in the quest to avoid tedious, unsurprising interpretations, often produce interpretations that seem outlandish, excessive.

1. See Jonathan Culler, *Structuralist Poetics* (Ithaca, NY: Cornell University Press, 1975), viii, 114–30; and Jonathan Culler, "Beyond Interpretation," in *The Pursuit of Signs* (Ithaca, NY: Cornell University Press, 1981), 3–17.

I am scarcely a partisan of interpretation, then (although I have certainly done my share of it), but when I was invited to act as a respondent to Umberto Eco, who was to deliver three lectures on the topic "Interpretation and Overinterpretation," I somehow sensed what my role was supposed to be: to defend overinterpretation.[2] Since I had often heard Umberto Eco lecture, and well knew the wit and exuberant narrative skill he could bring to the mockery of whatever he chose to call "overinterpretation," I could see that defending overinterpretation might well prove uncomfortable, but in fact I found myself happy to accept my allotted role, to defend overinterpretation on principle.

Interpretation itself needs no defense; it is with us always, but like most intellectual activities, interpretation is interesting only when it is extreme. Moderate interpretation, which articulates a consensus, though it may have value in some circumstances, especially pedagogical ones, is of little interest. A good statement of this view comes from G. K. Chesterton, who observes, "Either criticism is no good at all (a very defensible position) or else criticism means saying about an author the very things that would have made him jump out of his boots."[3] The production of interpretations of literary works should not be thought of as the supreme goal, much less the only goal of literary studies, but if critics are going to spend their time working out and proposing interpretations, then they should apply as much interpretive pressure as they can, should carry their thinking as far as it can go. Many "extreme" interpretations, like many moderate interpretations, will no doubt have little impact, because they are judged unpersuasive or redundant or irrelevant or boring, but if they are extreme, they have a better chance, it seems to me, of bringing to light connections or implications not previously noticed or reflected on than if they strive to remain "sound" or moderate.

Let me add that, whatever Umberto Eco may say, what he in fact does in the three lectures of *Interpretation and Overinterpretation*, as well

2. The Tanner Lectures at Robinson College, Cambridge, published as Umberto Eco, *Interpretation and Overinterpretation*, with Richard Rorty, Jonathan Culler, and Christine Brooke-Rose, ed. Stefan Collini (Cambridge, UK: Cambridge University Press, 1992); hereafter abbreviated *IO* and cited parenthetically in the text.

3. G. K. Chesterton, *Appreciations and Criticisms of the Works of Charles Dickens*, vol. 15 of *Collected Works of G. K. Chesterton* (San Francisco: Ignatius Press, 1986), 272.

as what he has written in his novels and his works of semiotic theory, convinces me that deep down, in his hermetical soul, which draws him to those interpreters whom he calls the "followers of the veil," *Adepti del Velame* (those who believe in a hidden, hermetic meaning), he too believes that overinterpretation is more interesting and intellectually valuable than "sound," moderate interpretation. One who was not deeply attracted to overinterpretation could not create the characters and the interpretive obsessions that animate his novels. Eco spends no time in his three lectures telling us what a sound, proper, moderate interpretation of Dante would say but a good deal of time reviving, breathing life into, an outrageous nineteenth-century Rosicrucian interpretation of Dante—an interpretation that, as he says, had had no impact on literary criticism and had been completely ignored until Eco uncovered it and set his students to work on this interesting semiotic practice. "The bibliography of the Followers of the Veil is incredibly rich," he writes. "And it is incredible to what extent the mainstream of Dantesque criticism has ignored or disregarded it. Recently I encouraged selected young researchers to read—maybe for the first time—all those books" (*IO*, 52). If sound interpretation were the goal of literary studies and overinterpretation an abuse to be shunned or stigmatized, then why send one's students to read what is justly forgotten and ignored? Apparently Eco recognizes that these texts might in various ways be more interesting than conventional, sound Dante criticism.

But if we are to make any progress in thinking about interpretation and overinterpretation, we must consider the opposition itself, which is rather tendentious. The idea of "overinterpretation" not only begs the question of which is to be preferred, but it also, I believe, fails to capture the problems Eco himself wishes to address. One might imagine *overinterpretation* to be like *overeating*: there is proper eating or interpreting, but some people don't stop when they should. They go on eating or interpreting in excess, with bad results. Consider, though, the two principal cases Eco gives us in the lecture entitled "Overinterpreting Texts." The writing on Dante by Gabriele Rossetti (the father of the better-known Victorian poet Dante Gabriel Rossetti) did not produce a normal, proper interpretation and then go too far, interpret too much, or interpret excessively. On the contrary, it started from a premise radically different from normal, proper interpretation: that Dante was really a Freemason, Templar, and Rosicrucian, even though there is no evidence that Freemasonry existed in Dante's day. Rossetti sets out to interpret the *Divina Commedia* in terms of hidden references to Masonic-Rosicrucian motifs. According to Eco he "assumes that a Masonic-Rosicrucian symbol would be as follows: a rose with a cross inside of it, under which appears a pelican" (*IO*, 55). As I understand Eco's argument, what vitiates Rossetti's attempt to interpret Dante as a Freemason-Rosicrucian are two problems, the combination of which is lethal and ensured his neglect until Professor Eco revived him. First, Rossetti attempted to draw a Rosicrucian thematics from elements of a motif that in fact never appear together in Dante and some of which appear rarely anywhere in the poem (the pelican appears only once), so that his argument is not persuasive. "Rossetti, in his desperate and rather pathetic fowling, could find in the divine poem seven fowls and eleven birds and ascribe them all to the pelican family; but he would find them all far from the rose" (*IO*, 55). Second, Rossetti sought to explain the importance of these motifs (which he had failed to demonstrate) as the influence of a supposedly prior tradition, for which no independent evidence exists (*IO*, 54–60). The problem here is scarcely overinterpretation. If anything it is underinterpretation: a failure to interpret enough elements of the poem and a failure to look at actual prior texts to find in them concealed Rosicrucianism and determine possible relations of influence.

The second example Eco offers in his second lecture is a piece of belletristic interpretation of Wordsworth's "A slumber did my spirit seal" by Geoffrey Hartman, whom Eco calls "one of the leaders of the Yale deconstructionists" (*IO*, 61), but who is better seen as linked to deconstruction by metonymy—by his contiguity at Yale to people such as Paul de Man, Barbara Johnson, J. Hillis Miller, and Jacques Derrida, who were engaged in deconstructive reading. Hartman is in this example displaying what has been known as literary sensibility or sensitivity: hearing in a verse echoes of other words or images.

The poem runs as follows, with Eco's italics:

A slumber did my spirit seal,
I had no human *fears*
She seemed a thing that could not feel
The touch of earthly *years.*

No motion has she now, no force,

She neither *hears* nor sees,
Rolled round in earth's *diurnal course*
With rocks, and stones, and *trees.*

Hartman finds "Wordsworth's language penetrated by an inappropriate subliminal punning. So 'diurnal' divides into 'die' and 'urn,' and 'course' may recall the older pronunciation of 'corpse.'"[4] Certainly *diurnal*, as a Latinate word, does call attention to itself in the context of the simple diction of Wordsworth's poem, and who is to deny a thematically appropriate subliminal pun?

In the second stanza, Hartman writes, we find

the euphemistic displacement of the word "grave" by an image of gravitation ("Rolled round in earth's diurnal course"). And though there is no agreement on the tone of this stanza, it is clear that a subvocal word is uttered without being written out. It is a word that rhymes with "fears" and "years" and "hears," but which is closed off by the very last syllable of the poem, "trees." Read "tears" and the animating, cosmic metaphor comes alive, the poet's lament echos through nature, as in pastoral elegy. "Tears," however, must give way to what is written, to a dull yet definitive sound, the anagram "trees."[5]

Eco points out that *tears* is not an anagram of *trees*—it is one letter off—and that "gravitation" does not appear in the text. The argument about "gravitation" might be that now that Lucy is dead, without motion, the reader expects to hear that she is in her grave, whereas what we get instead is a strange, contradictory image (she has no motion but nevertheless is "rolled") that requires some sort of explanation. That she, like the rocks, stones, and trees, is held on the rolling earth by gravitation is perhaps as good an explanation as any (hence the displacement of "grave" by gravitation). It is these two claims of Hartman's that make Eco see this passage, which treats *tears* as potentially evoked by the rhyming series of *fears, hears, years,* as an example of overinterpretation.

Hartman's substitution of *tears* for *trees* might seem strained, especially since "rocks and stones and tears" would not make much sense, but he seems not to want to indulge in what would be regarded as overinterpretation, acknowledging that *tears* "must give way to what is written."

4. Geoffrey Hartman, *Easy Pieces* (New York: Columbia University Press, 1985), 149–50. Quoted in Eco, *Interpretation and Overinterpretation*, 61.

5. Hartman, *Easy Pieces*, 150.

His interpretive passage might rise to overinterpretation if he were to make stronger claims—arguing, for instance, that "trees" does not belong in the last line of the poem because trees do not roll as rocks and stones and tears do. Further, he might have argued, the more natural order of an earlier line ("She neither hears nor sees") would have been "She neither sees nor *hears*" (given the usual priority of sight), which would have demanded as the concluding rhyme word *tears*, instead of *trees*. Therefore he might have concluded, like a good "Follower of the Veil," the secret meaning of this little poem is really the repression of *tears*, for which *trees* has been substituted. That might have been overinterpretation, but it also might have been more interesting and illuminating of the poem (even if we were finally to reject it) than the more moderate interpretation Hartman produced, which seems an admirable traditional exercise of literary sensibility to identify suggestions lurking in and behind the language of the poem.[6]

Clearer instances of overinterpretation might be strained reflections on the significance of set or idiomatic phrases that have a regular social meaning.[7] If I greet an acquaintance by saying, as we pass on the sidewalk, "Hello, nice day, isn't it?" I don't expect him to walk on muttering something like, "I wonder what on earth he meant by that? Is he so committed to undecidability that he can't tell whether it is a nice day or not and has to seek confirmation from me? Then why didn't he wait for an answer, or does he think *I* can't tell what sort of day it is so that he has to tell me? Is he suggesting that *today*, when he passed me without stopping, is a nice day by contrast with yesterday, when we had a long conversation? etc." This is what Eco would call *paranoid interpretation* (*IO*, 48), and if our interest is in simply receiving messages that are sent, then paranoid interpretation

6. In his third lecture Eco writes that "if a normal English-speaking human being is seduced by the semantic relationship between words *in praesentia* and words *in absentia*, why should one not believe that Wordsworth was unconsciously seduced by these echo-effects?" (*IO*, 70). Does the question then become whether Geoffrey Hartman is "normal"?

7. Eco's example of this is an unusual interpretation of *believe me*: "the Followers of the Veil evoke someone who, upon being told, 'Sir, you are a thief, believe me!' replies with: 'What do you mean by "believe me"? Do you perhaps wish to insinuate that I am distrustful?'" (*IO*, 54). This seems not so much overinterpretation as deliberately missing the point, ignoring a serious accusation (thievery) by detecting a potential minor charge (you think I am distrustful?). But the general phenomenon is certainly pertinent to overinterpretation.

may be counterproductive, but with things the way they are, a little paranoia may be essential to the just appreciation of things. What here emerges in paranoid overinterpretation is at least an engaged reflection on the possible implications of speech acts and structures of social interaction.

If our interest is not so much in the receiving of intended messages but in understanding, say, the mechanisms of linguistic and social interaction, then it is eminently useful from time to time to stand back and ask why someone said some perfectly straightforward thing such as "Nice day, isn't it?" What does it mean that *this* should be a casual form of greeting? What does that tell us about this subculture as opposed to others that might have different phatic forms or habits? What Eco calls *overinterpretation* may in fact be a practice of asking precisely those questions that are *not* necessary for normal communication but that enable us to reflect on its functioning.

Eco conceives of the intention of the text, *intentio operis*, as the interpretation produced by the model reader postulated by the text. Actual readers make conjectures about the text's intention, and since "a text is a device conceived in order to produce its model reader," these are conjectures about how the model reader implied by the text would read it (*IO*, 64). We thus have a sophisticated version of the hermeneutic circle. Sometimes what Eco calls overinterpretation seems to be, as in the case of Rossetti, interpretation that posits an *intentio operis* and a model reader on scant evidence. At other times, though, overinterpretation seems to be interpretation that breaks out of that circle.

In fact, I think that both this problem in general and the specific problems Eco wants to address are better captured by an opposition Wayne Booth formulates in his *Critical Understanding*: instead of *interpretation* and *overinterpretation* Booth contrasts *understanding* and *overstanding*. *Understanding* he conceives as Eco does, in terms of something like Eco's model reader. Understanding is asking the questions and finding the answers that the text insists on. "Once upon a time there were three little pigs" demands that we ask "So what happened?" and not "Why three?" or "What is the concrete historical context?" for instance. *Overstanding*, by contrast, consists of pursuing questions that the text does not pose to its model reader. One advantage of Booth's opposition over Eco's is that it makes it easier to see the role and importance of overstanding than when this sort of practice is tendentiously called overinterpretation.

As Booth recognizes, it can be very important and productive to ask questions the text does *not* encourage one to ask about it. To illustrate the pursuit of overstanding, he asks,

What do you have to say, you seemingly innocent child's tale of three little pigs and a wicked wolf, about the culture that preserves and responds to you? About the unconscious dreams of the author or folk that created you? About the history of narrative suspense? About the relations of the lighter and the darker races? About big people and little people, hairy and bald, lean and fat? About triadic patterns in human history? About the Trinity? About laziness and industry, family structure, domestic architecture, dietary practice, standards of justice and revenge? About the history of manipulations of narrative point of view for the creation of sympathy? Is it good for a child to read you or hear you recited, night after night? Will stories like you—*should* stories like you—be allowed when we have produced our ideal socialist state? What are the sexual implications of that chimney—or of this strictly male world in which sex is never mentioned? What about all that huffing and puffing?[8]

Much better questions than "what happens next?" All this overstanding would doubtless count as overinterpretation. If interpretation is reconstruction of the intention of the text, *intentio operis*, then these are questions that do not lead that way; they are about what the text does and how: how it relates to other texts and to other practices, what it conceals or represses, what it advances or is complicitous with. Many of the most interesting forms of modern criticism ask not what the work has in mind but what it forgets; not what it says but what it takes for granted.

To take the elucidation of the text's intention as the goal of literary studies is what Northrop Frye in his *Anatomy of Criticism* called the Little Jack Horner view of criticism: the idea that the literary work is like a pie into which the author "has diligently stuffed a specific number of beauties or effects," which the critic, like Little Jack Horner, complacently pulls out one by one, saying, "O what a good boy am I." Frye, in a rare fit of petulance, called this idea "One of the many slovenly illiteracies that the absence of systematic criticism has allowed to grow up."[9]

8. Wayne Booth, *Literary Understanding: The Power and Limits of Pluralism* (Chicago: University of Chicago Press, 1979), 243.

9. Northrop Frye, *Anatomy of Criticism: Four Essays* (Princeton, NJ: Princeton University Press, 1957), 17.

The alternative for Frye, and I hope for us, is a poetics that attempts to describe the conventions and strategies by which literary works achieve the effects they do. Many works of literary criticism are interpretations in that they focus on particular works, but their aim may be less to reconstruct the meaning of those works than to explore the mechanisms or structures by which they function and thus to illuminate general problems about literature, narrative, figurative language, theme, and so on.

Works that do this are often criticized for overinterpretation or for distorting the works they treat by emphasizing one aspect to the neglect of others. So Toni Morrison's brilliant *Playing in the Dark: Whiteness and the Literary Imagination* contains interpretations of a number of literary works, from Willa Cather's *Sapphira and the Slave Girl* and Twain's *Huckleberry Finn* to Ernest Hemingway's *The Garden of Eden*. Taken in isolation, some of these interpretations may indeed seem extreme.

The Garden of Eden, for instance, is the story of a newly married couple, Catherine and David, who move around in the South of France: he writes in the morning, she sunbathes; they swim in the afternoon and eat well and make love a lot. Morrison emphasizes "the Africanist field in which the drama is played out," so that Catherine's devotion to tanning, her desire to become ever darker, is linked to "the specter of black sexuality," while her new husband, David, writes stories about hunting with his father in Africa (which Catherine eventually burns because they are not about her). "Africa, imagined as innocent and under white control, is the inner story," writes Morrison. "Africanism, imagined as evil, chaotic, impenetrable, is the outer story."[10] Though this is certainly a possible reading of Hemingway's novel, it neglects what most strikes readers: Catherine's determination to transform her intense sexual relationship with her new husband into incestuous androgyny—a different form of darkness and "devil things" not obviously marked by race. She strives to make the two of them look alike, cutting her long hair short like his and then bringing him to her hairdresser to have his hair lightened and cut like hers. She calls him "girl": "Let me feel your hair, girl. It's cut so full and has so much body and it's the same as mine. Let me kiss you girl."[11] David thinks, "She

10. Toni Morrison, *Playing in the Dark: Whiteness and the Literary Imagination* (Cambridge, MA: Harvard University Press, 1992), 88–89; hereafter abbreviated *PD* and cited parenthetically in the text.

11. Ernest Hemingway, *The Garden of Eden* (New York: Scribner's, 1986), 86; hereafter cited parenthetically in the text as Garden.

changes from a girl into a boy and back to a girl ceaselessly and beautifully" (*Garden*, 31). "Can I be a boy again?" she asks. "I'd like to be again in
bed at night if it isn't bad for you. . . . I'll only be a boy at night and won't
embarrass you?" (*Garden*, 56). And eventually she recruits another girl to
join their party, with whom she can have a lesbian affair and who can be a
woman for David. What starts as an obsession with tanning, a desire to be
ever darker, and for them both to be dark—"I want every part of me dark
and it's getting that way, and you'll be darker than an Indian and that takes
us further away from other people" (*Garden*, 30)—becomes an intense exploration of possible perversions, where the diabolical is scarcely African.

Morrison's Africanist focus seems an overinterpretation, especially
since Catherine sees darkness as Indian as well as African: "you'll be darker than an Indian," or "I wish I had some Indian blood. I'm going to be
so dark you won't be able to stand it" (*Garden*, 31). But Morrison's treatment of this story occurs in the context of a strong thesis about the constitutive role of blackness and slavery for the American literary imagination,
a brilliant account of how the distinctive characteristics of American literature have as their condition of possibility what she terms the Africanist
presence—the four-hundred-year-old presence of Africans in the United
States. "The imaginative and historical terrain upon which early American
writers journeyed," she writes, "is in large measure shaped by the presence
of the racial other" (*PD*, 46). Such concerns as autonomy, authority, new-
ness and difference, absolute power, which "become the major themes and
presumptions of American literature," are "made possible by, shaped by,
activated by, a complex awareness of a constituted Africanism. It was this
Africanism, deployed as rawness and savagery, that provided the staging
ground and arena for the elaboration of the quintessential American identity" (*PD*, 44). Thus, for instance, "the concept of freedom did not emerge
in a vacuum. Nothing highlighted freedom—if it did not in fact create
it—like slavery" (*PD*, 38). The celebration of freedom relies on an Africanist presence even in novels where there is no mention of slaves or slavery.

This is a speculative account of a framework for the explanation of
literary productions—but when in this enterprise one writes about particular works, it will seem like interpretation. If it is the case that the thematic
concerns of American literature are the product of the presence of an Africanist other, then this is true even for those works that conceal it best, but
to write about one of these works in this context is to give the impression

of saying that this hidden Africanism is what the work is "really about." Our preference for interpretation over poetics, our assumption that the payoff of critical work should be the interpretation of individual works, leads us to interpret critical writing as making such claims, but readers are scarcely to blame here, since even critics who maintain that they are not offering an interpretation are likely to end up suggesting that the structures they have identified are what the work is really about.[12] If the Africanist presence marks darkening the skin as dangerous and sexually charged for American literature, then the fact that this is disguised in various ways in Hemingway's plot is noteworthy, important for thinking about American literature, but to stress the Africanist presence when it is displaced is likely to seem an excessive, interested overinterpretation of the work.

If poetics is to literature as linguistics is to language, one should not take descriptions of literary works, produced in a theoretical framework, as interpretations. Since linguistics does not seek to interpret the sentences of a language but to reconstruct the system of its rules, linguistic descriptions are not thought to be proposing new meanings of a sentence. Often what seems a biased critical interpretation giving excessive weight to some factors and or structures and neglecting others should be seen, rather, as an attempt to understand the system of possibilities of literature, the general mechanisms of narrative, of figuration, of ideology, and so on.

In "The Pragmatist's Progress," a response to Eco's lectures, Richard Rorty resists the distinction between interpretation and overinterpretation, seeing it as a version of the distinction between interpreting a text and using it for your own purposes. "This, of course, is a distinction we pragmatists do not wish to make. On our view, all anybody ever does with anything is use it" (*IO*, 93). There is no difference between using a text for your own purposes and interpreting it as carefully as you can—both of these are just ways of putting the text to use. I will return to this disagree-

12. A remarkable case in point is Roland Barthes, who claims in *S/Z*, the step-by-step analysis of a novella by Balzac, that he is not trying to assign a meaning to this text but to identify the different codes that make possible its intelligibility, but he ends by asserting that "it is fatal, the text says, to remove the paradigmatic slash mark which permits meaning to function (the wall of Antithesis), life to reproduce (the opposition of the sexes) and property to be protected (the rule of contract)" (Roland Barthes, *S/Z* [New York: Farrar, Strauss, 1974], 215). The text inexorably comes to be about the signifying mechanisms that are revealed.

ment between Eco and Rorty in a moment. More crucial to my mind than this substitution of a monism for a dualism is Rorty's claim that we should abandon our search for codes, our attempt to identify structural mechanisms, and simply enjoy "dinosaurs, peaches, babies, symbols and metaphors without needing to cut into their smooth flanks in search of hidden armatures" (*IO*, 91). At the end of his response he returns to this claim, arguing that there is no need for us to bother trying to find out how texts work. "I see the idea that you can learn about 'how the text works' by using semiotics to analyze its operations as like spelling out certain word-processing subroutines in BASIC: you can do it if you want to, but it is not clear why, for most of the purposes which motivate literary critics, you should bother" (*IO*, 104). We should just use texts as we use word-processing programs, in an attempt to say something interesting.

But in this claim we do find a distinction between using a word-processing program and analyzing it, understanding it, and if we shift the analogy from the word-processing program that we might want to analyze only in order to improve or adapt it to, say, a natural language, then we might adduce the possibility that understanding how it works could be a legitimate pursuit, even an essential one. Rorty's own appeal to this distinction between using your word-processing program and analyzing it might be taken to refute his claim that all anyone ever does with a text is to use it, or at least to indicate that there are significant differences among ways of using a text. Granting Rorty's argument that for most purposes it is not important to find out how computer programs or natural languages or literary discourses work, we could argue that the purpose for which this is important is precisely the academic study of these subjects—computer science, linguistics, and literary criticism and theory. The fact that people can speak English perfectly well without worrying about its structure does not mean that the attempt to describe its structure is pointless, only that the goal of linguistics is not to make people speak English better. Similarly, the goal of poetics is neither to enable people to write better poems, plays, and stories or to produce new interpretations of individual literary works, though of course writers will often profit from learning how works they particularly admire have been structured. For the study of computer science or literature it is essential to try to understand how these systems work, what enables them to function as they do, and under what circumstances they might function differently.

What is confusing in literary studies is that when people write about literature, it may often seem, as Rorty might put it, that they are just using literary works to tell stories about the myriad problems of human existence. But sometimes they are in fact attempting to analyze aspects of the language, the system, the subroutines of literature, if you will, while presenting what they are doing as an interpretation of the literary works. The attempt to understand how literature works is not of interest to everyone—like the attempt to understand the structure of natural languages or the properties of computer programs. But the idea of literary study as a discipline is precisely the attempt to develop a systematic understanding of the semiotic mechanisms of literature, the various strategies of its forms.

What is missing from Rorty's response, therefore, is any sense that literary studies might consist of more than loving and responding to characters and themes in literary works. He can imagine people using literature to learn about themselves—certainly a major use of literature—but not, it seems, learning something about literature. It is surprising that a philosophical movement that styles itself "Pragmatism" should neglect this eminently practical activity of learning more about the functioning of important human creations, such as literature; for whatever epistemological problems might be posed by the idea of "knowledge" of literature, it is clear that practically, in studying literature, people do not just develop interpretations (uses) of particular works but also acquire a general understanding of how literature operates—its range of possibilities and characteristic structures.

But more than this neglect of institutional realities of knowledge, what is particularly disquieting about contemporary American Pragmatism—of Rorty and Stanley Fish, for example—is that people who attained their positions of professional eminence by engaging in spirited debate with other members of an academic field, such as philosophy or literary studies, by identifying the difficulties and inconsistencies of their elders' conceptions of the field and by proposing alternative procedures and goals, have, once they attain professional eminence, suddenly turned and rejected the idea of a system of procedures and body of knowledge where argument is possible and presented the field as simply a group of people reading books and trying to say interesting things about them. In effect, they would systematically destroy the structure through which they attained their positions and which would enable others to challenge them in their turn. Stanley Fish, for instance, established himself by offering theoretical arguments about the nature of literary meaning and the role of the reading process and claiming that his predecessors who had pronounced on this topic were wrong.[13] Once he had reached a position of eminence, however, he turned around and said something like, "Actually, there isn't anything here one could be right or wrong about; there isn't such a thing as the nature of literature or of reading; there are only groups of readers and critics with certain beliefs who do whatever it is that they do. And there is no way in which other readers can challenge what I do because there is no position outside belief from which the validity of a set of beliefs could be adjudicated." This is a less-happy version of what Rorty, in his response, calls the narrative of "pragmatist's progress," in which one gets beyond questions of truth and "all descriptions are evaluated according to their efficacy as instruments for purposes, rather than by their fidelity to the object described" (*IO*, 92).

Richard Rorty's own *Philosophy and the Mirror of Nature* is a powerful work of philosophical analysis precisely because it grasps the philosophical enterprise as a system with a structure and shows the contradictory relations between various parts of that structure—relations that put in question the foundational character of that enterprise.[14] To tell people they should give up attempting to identify underlying structures and systems but just use texts for their own purposes is to attempt to block other people from doing work like that for which he gained recognition. Similarly, it is all very well to say that students of literature should not bother trying to understand how literature works but should just enjoy it or read on in the hope of finding books that will change their lives. Such a vision of literary study, though, by denying any public structure of argument in which the young or marginalized could challenge the views of their eminent elders, helps make their positions unassailable and in effect confirms a structure in place by denying that there is a structure. Ultimately the crucial issue in Rorty's thinking here is not so much the distinction (or lack thereof) between interpretation and use but the claim that we should not

13. See in particular Stanley Fish, *Surprised by Sin: The Reader in "Paradise Lost"* (Berkeley: University of California Press, 1967).

14. Richard Rorty, *Philosophy and the Mirror of Nature* (Princeton, NJ: Princeton University Press, 1979).

bother to understand how texts work any more than we should seek to understand how computers work because we can use them perfectly well without such knowledge. Literary studies should be the attempt to gain such knowledge.

But to return to the disagreement between Eco and Rorty about interpretation. One thing Rorty and Eco share is a desire to dismiss deconstruction, which shared desire suggests that, contrary to popular report, deconstruction is alive and well. Curiously, however, Eco and Rorty give very nearly opposing descriptions of deconstruction. Eco seems to take it as "a radical reader-oriented theory of interpretation," as if it said that a text means anything a reader takes it to mean (*IO*, 25). Rorty, on the other hand, faults deconstruction—Paul de Man and Hillis Miller in particular—for refusing to give up the idea that structures are truly in the text and that deconstructive readings are "coerced by the texts themselves" (*IO*, 102–3). Rorty faults deconstruction for maintaining that there are basic textual structures or mechanisms and that one can find out things about how a text works. Deconstruction, in his view, is wrong because of its failure to accept that readers just have different ways of using texts, none of which tell you something "more basic" about the text. He thus faults deconstruction for failing to be what Eco thinks it is.

In this disagreement—does deconstruction say that a text means what a reader wants it to mean, or does it say that it has structures that have to be discovered?—Rorty is more nearly right than Eco. His account, at least, helps to explain how deconstruction could claim that a text might undermine categories or disrupt expectations. Eco has doubtless been misled by his concern with limits or boundaries. His theory of interpretation leads him to say that texts give a great deal of scope to readers but that there are limits. His Tanner lectures, when they are not happily expounding aberrant interpretations, try to draw lines, hoping to find some limits.

But what if this is the wrong way of conceiving the situation? Rorty, more sensibly, does not imagine that there are limits to interpretation but supposes, rather, that if I want to have a chance of convincing others, a chance of making my interpretation plausible, I will have to do various things, such as account for as much of the text as possible rather than just focus on one or two lines, and so on. There is no boundary surrounding proper interpretation and separating it from overinterpretation or aberrant interpretation; rather, there are discursive practices that can establish relevance and persuade others. Here deconstruction is with Rorty rather than with Eco. Deconstructive readings find that meaning is context bound—a function of relations within or between texts—but that context itself is boundless: there will always be new contextual possibilities that can be adduced, so the one thing we *cannot* do is set limits. Generally, of course, we do imagine that there are limits. Wittgenstein asks, "Can I say 'Bububu' and mean, if it does not rain I shall go out for a walk?" And he replies, "[I]t is only in a language that one can mean something by something."[15] This aphorism may appear to establish limits, suggesting that "Bububu" could never mean this, unless the language were different; but in fact the way in which language works, especially literary language, prevents this establishment of a limit or boundary. Once Wittgenstein has produced this positing of a limit, it becomes possible in certain contexts—in the corridor of a philosophy department, for example—to say "Bububu" and at least allude to the possibility that if it does not rain, one might go for a walk. But this lack of limits to semiosis does not mean, as Eco seems to fear, that meaning is the free creation of the reader. It shows, rather, that describable semiotic mechanisms function in recursive ways, the limits of which cannot be identified in advance.

In his critique of deconstruction for its failure to become a happy pragmatics, Rorty suggests that de Man believes philosophy "can lay down guidelines for literary interpretation" (*IO*, 102). This is a misconception that should be corrected: de Man's engagement with philosophical texts is always critical and, in a sense, literary—attuned to their rhetorical strategies; he does not draw from them anything like a *method* for literary interpretation. But it is certainly true that he does not believe that philosophy and philosophical questions can be left behind, as Rorty seems to. Deconstructive readings characteristically show how the problems posed by traditional philosophical distinctions prove ubiquitous, turning up repeatedly even in the most "literary" of works. It is this continuing engagement with the hierarchical oppositions that structure Western thought, and the recognition that the belief one has overcome them once and for all is likely to be a facile delusion, that give deconstruction a critical edge. These hierarchical oppositions structure concepts of identity and the fabric of social and political life, and to believe one has gone beyond them is to risk complacently abandoning the enterprise of critique, including the critique of ideology. The pragmatist's conviction that all the old problems and dis-

15. Ludwig Wittgenstein, *Philosophical Investigations* (Oxford, UK: Blackwell, 1963), 18.

tinctions can be swept away, installing us in a happy monism, where, as Rorty puts it, "all anybody ever does with anything is use it," has the virtue of simplicity but the difficulty of neglecting the sorts of problems with which Eco and many others have wrestled, including the question of how a text can challenge the conceptual framework with which one attempts to interpret it. These are problems that will not disappear with the pragmatist's injunction not to worry but simply to enjoy interpretation.

Roland Barthes, who was congenitally given to hesitating between poetics and interpretation, once wrote that those who do not reread condemn themselves to read the same story everywhere.[16] They recognize what they already think or know. Barthes' claim was, in effect, that some sort of method for "overinterpretation"—for instance, an arbitrary procedure that divided the text up into sequences and required that each be examined closely and its effects spelled out, even if it did not seem to pose interpretive problems—was a way to make discoveries: discoveries about the text and about the codes and practices that enable one to play the role of reader. A method that compels people to puzzle over not just those elements that might seem to resist the totalization of meaning but also those about which there might initially seem to be nothing to say has a better chance of producing discoveries—though like everything else in life there is no guarantee here—than a procedure that seeks only to answer those questions that a text asks its model reader.

At the beginning of his second lecture Umberto Eco links overinterpretation to what he called an "excess of wonder," an excessive propensity to treat as significant elements that might be simply fortuitous (*IO*, 50). Barthes' step-by-step analysis of lexemes of Balzac's story, however unimportant they may seem, might be one version of this propensity. Excess of wonder can masquerade as diligent systematicity. This propensity to puzzle over elements in a text, which Eco regards as a bad thing, a *déformation professionnelle*, seems to me, on the contrary, the best source of the insights into language and literature that we seek, a quality to be cultivated rather than shunned. It would be sad indeed if fear of overinterpretation should lead us to avoid or repress the state of wonder at the play of texts and interpretation, which seems to me all too rare today, though admirably represented in the novels or semiotic explorations of Umberto Eco.

16. Barthes, *S/Z*, 16.

8

Omniscience

"Omniscience" is a notion I have used in discussing narrative, without giving it much thought, but also without much conviction that "the omniscient narrator" is a well-grounded concept or really helps account for narrative effects. Looking into the matter, I find this is not untypical. Critics refer to the notion all the time, but few express much confidence in it. The idea of omniscience has not received much critical scrutiny.[1]

Recently I have spent time working on this problem, in a return

An early version of this chapter was written for the 2003 conference of the Society for the Study of Narrative Literature in Berkeley, California. I am grateful to Dorothy Hale for the invitation to speak at the conference, and to the audience and fellow keynote speakers, Mary Poovey and Elaine Scarry, for their responses to the paper. I have also profited from discussion with audiences at the School of Criticism and Theory, Cornell, and at the Universities of Torino and Siena, and at the 2005 Narrative conference in Louisville. I would like to thank Marlon Kuzmick for research and advice on the tradition of theological debates about omniscience and Harry Shaw, Audrey Wasser, and Jim Phelan for comments on drafts.

1. Notable exceptions are Audrey Jaffe, *Vanishing Points: Dickens, Narrative, and the Subject of Omniscience* (Berkeley: University of California Press, 1991); Richard Maxwell, "Dickens' Omniscience," *ELH* 46 (1979): 290–313; Meir Sternberg, *The Poetics of Biblical Narrative* (Bloomington: Indiana University Press, 1985); Meir Sternberg, *Expositional Modes and Temporal Ordering in Fiction* (Bloomington: Indiana University Press, 1978); and recently, Nicholas Royle, *The Uncanny* (New York: Routledge, 2003).

to narratological matters, which I had rather neglected for a number of years. Studying omniscience while observing a president who espouses Total Information Awareness, manifestly thinks he has nothing to learn from anyone, and is convinced of the infallibility of his judgment of evil in its accordance with God's, I have tried to keep my rising repugnance from attaching to the concept of omniscience in narrative poetics. I have endeavored to separate the concept of narrative omniscience from current political fantasy, and I hope I have succeeded. I am reminded, though, of Virginia Woolf's comment in a letter to her sister after receiving a visit from T. S. Eliot, who talked of his religious conversion: "I mean there's something obscene in a living person sitting by the fire and believing in God."[2]

I do not think the idea of omniscience is obscene, but I *have* reached the conclusion that it is not a useful concept for the study of narration, that it conflates and confuses several different factors that should be separated if they are to be well understood—that it obfuscates the various phenomena that provoke us to posit the idea. Wallace Martin writes that "'omniscient narration' becomes a kind of dumping ground filled with a wide range of distinct narrative techniques."[3] I believe that we should try to recover and recycle what we have dumped there. In one of the alternatives I have seen, Nicholas Royle proposes in *The Uncanny* to replace *omniscience* with *telepathy*—an idea about which I will say more later.[4] *Telepathy* does have certain advantages, especially that of estrangement. *Omniscience* may have become too familiar for us to think shrewdly about it.

The basis of omniscience appears to be the frequently articulated analogy between God and the author: the author creates the world of the novel as God created our world, and just as the world holds no secrets for God, so the novelist knows everything that is to be known about the world

2. Woolf to Vanessa Bell, Feb. 11, 1928. Virginia Woolf, *The Letters of Virginia Woolf*, ed. Nigel Nicholson and Joanne Trautmann, 6 vols. (New York: Harcourt Brace, 1975–80), 3:457–58.

3. Wallace Martin, *Recent Theories of Narrative* (Ithaca, NY: Cornell University Press, 1986), 146.

4. I am greatly indebted to Nicholas Royle for sending me a draft of a chapter of this book, "The 'Telepathy Effect': Notes Toward a Reconsideration of Narrative Fiction," which, in juxtaposing my own unthinking use of the term *omniscience* with my call for literary studies to take a critical attitude to religious themes and presuppositions, prompted me to take up this topic.

of the novel. This is all very well, but if, for instance, we do not believe in an omniscient and omnipotent God, then we cannot draw on what we know of God to illuminate properties of narrative. Even if we believe in God, there is precious little knowledge about him on which to rely. If you look into theological discussions of omniscience, you will quickly be dissuaded of any idea that God's omniscience could serve as a useful model for omniscience in narration, for discussions of divine omniscience are generally based on what is called "Perfect Being Theology." God is by definition perfect, and since to lack knowledge of any kind would be to fall short of perfection, God must be all-knowing. The main problem for theological discussions of omniscience, then, becomes whether the perfection of divine omniscience is compatible with free will, both of which are taken for granted as necessary and desirable. Since criticism need not presuppose either the perfection of the author or the freedom of characters, it seems unlikely that criticism can learn much from these theological debates.

The fundamental point is that since we do not know whether there is a God and what he or she might know, divine omniscience is not a model that helps us think about authors or about literary narration. On the contrary, one could say that the force of the analogy works the other way: the example of the novelist, who creates his or her world, peopling it with creatures who come to seem to us autonomous and have interesting adventures, helps us to imagine the possibility of a creator, a god, a sentient being, as invisible to us as the novelist would be to the characters who exist in the universe of the text this god created. Indeed, theologians can draw on the analogy between the author and God to help explain God. For instance, "What it means to say God's knowledge is the cause of something is that God's thinking has the power to make things exist, rather like Shakespeare's thinking has the power to make Hamlet exist."[5]

One of the few critics who wholeheartedly approve of the concept of omniscient narration and one who offers an explicit account and defense of it is Meir Sternberg. In *Expositional Modes and Temporal Ordering in Fiction* he maintains that the author or implied author is omniscient by definition: "Within the limits of the microcosm of the universe he has himself created, the author is invariably, divinely omniscient; the common phrase 'the omniscient author' forms, as a matter of fact, a self-implicative attri-

5. Katherine Rodgers, *Perfect Being Theology* (Edinburgh: Edinburgh University Press, 2000), 76.

bution, in which the modifier is logically redundant."[6] This sounds plausible, and the expression is common, but in fact it is hard to work out what this means. Does the author know only the facts stipulated in the novel, or does he or she by definition know the color of the eyes of each character in the novel, even if this is never mentioned? That seems the sort of thing that omniscience ought to involve: a vast store of knowledge, in excess of what might be expressed. Does the author know the complete histories of minor characters? Some authors, notoriously, can tell you much more about their characters than is recorded in the novel, but is this an aspect of authorial omniscience? Jane Austen apparently confided to her nephew that "Mr. Woodhouse survived his daughter's marriage and kept Emma and Mr. Knightley from settling at Donwell about two years,"[7] but would we count this as knowledge of *Emma*? It seems more like ancillary anecdote than the sort of certain knowledge to which *omniscience* points. Do we want to say that the novelist necessarily knows about the lives of the children that the heroine may or may not have had, as she lived happily ever after, after the wedding that concludes the novel? An omniscient God would presumably know whether an Emma Woodhouse and Mr. Knightley had children and what became of them, and their children, but novelists are not omniscient in this sense, about aspects of the lives of characters not touched on in the book.

In fact, what the omniscience of the novelist probably means is that no one else can know more about the world of the novel than the novelist (a debatable proposition, if you think about fanatical Janeites), and it means especially that what the novelist chooses to have be true of the novel's world *will* be true. But "omniscience" is scarcely a good gloss for "no one else knows more about this," and the power to decide what will be the case in this world is a product of a conventional performative power of language, or, at best, omnipotence, not omniscience. When the novelist writes that Mr. Knightley came to dinner, she cannot be wrong, but that is a power of invention, of incontrovertible stipulation, not a matter of knowledge. The novelist can simply declare what will be the case in this world. To call this "omniscience" is extraordinarily misleading.

Sternberg maintains that the necessarily omniscient author may or may not invest the narrator with omniscience.[8] Omniscient narrators dif-

6. Sternberg, *Expositional Modes*, 255.
7. Jane Austen, *Emma*, ed. Stephen Parrish (New York: Norton, 1972), 335n.

fer greatly from one another, not in knowledge but in their readiness to share their unlimited knowledge with the reader.[9] Sternberg distinguishes, for instance, the "omnicommunicative narrators" of Trollope, who do not withhold any important information, from the "deliberately suppressive narrator" of Fielding, who withholds information he indicates that he possesses in order to create suspense and produce surprise. Sternberg goes a step further to argue—a highly original claim fully consonant with the presumption of originary omniscience with which he begins—that accounts of narrators with limited knowledge confuse what the narrator chooses to tell with what the narrator knows. He rejects what he calls the presumption that when the narrator "fails to communicate something, it necessarily follows that he doesn't know it."[10] Claims of partial omniscience

fail to take into account that omniscience, being a superhuman privilege, is logically not a quantitative but a qualitative and indivisible attribute; if a narrator authoritatively shows himself to be able to penetrate the mind of one of his characters and report all his secret activities—something none of us can do in daily life—then he has thus decisively established his ability to do so as regards the others as well.[11]

This is a radical claim: an author or narrator who reports the thoughts of one character must by definition be treated as knowing those of the others. You can't have selective omniscience, only selective communicativeness.

But why not say, then, that *all* narrators are omniscient and that some of them just choose to tell the story from various limited perspectives? Sternberg does not himself seem to take this line, but his model of omniscience and its separation of what is known from the evidence of what is told opens the door for it. For instance, one partisan of omniscience, Barbara Olsen, argues that Hemingway's "The Killers," which is often cited as the very model of a limited, camera-eye narrative, has an omniscient narrator; it "actually features Hemingway's omniscient narrator at his most reticent."[12] This narrator *could* tell all but prefers not to. She cites Sternberg to refute the "all too common error" of assuming that "what the narrator does not say is what he does not and cannot know." So one critic

8. Sternberg, *Expositional Modes*, 255.

9. Ibid., 258.

10. Ibid., 282.

11. Ibid.

12. Barbara K. Olsen, *Authorial Divinity in the Twentieth Century* (Lewisburg, PA: Associated University Press, 1997), 42.

notes that the narrator does not know the killers' names until he has over-heard them. "She does not realize," Olsen rejoins, "that this narrator only delays disclosing their names; he would make us feel with the other charac-ters the strange namelessness and universality of evil's threat. . . . He knows that 'Al' and 'Max' are only aliases for these intruders."[13] Olsen does admit that the fact that the narrator uses the term *nigger* does "at first glance seem to bespeak human limitations in judgment." But she argues that this "may be the narrator's way of suggesting that the name-calling and otherwise co-ercive treatment temporarily reduced Sam in his own eyes to the demean-ing status that the term suggests."[14]

This is an extreme case, but it perfectly illustrates, I think, the prob-lems to which the idea of the omniscient narrator gives rise: since omni-science is said quite logically to be indivisible, even the slimmest indication of unusual knowledge provokes the idea of a narrator who knows every-thing, and then the critic finds herself obliged to explain why the omni-scient narrator declines to tell us all the relevant things he or she must know—including the real names and full past histories of Al and Max. Imagining motivations for this refusal yields strange contortions, because such choices are properly explained as choices made by the author, for ar-tistic reasons. They are decisions about how to craft the text, not choices of which bits of prior knowledge to relate. Obviously the author could have chosen to include more information about Al and Max but chose this cam-era's-eye strategy to achieve the literary effects that have made this story notorious. The presumption of omniscience gives us, instead of Heming-way deciding whether to invent pasts for Al and Max, a scenario of an imagined narrator knowing all about them and deciding whether to reveal their pasts. The artistic choices are obfuscated by being transformed into decisions of an imagined narrator.

Rejecting Olsen's view that all narrators are omniscient but variously keep quiet about what they know, we might turn to the more usual model, exemplified by Sternberg. Here we might wonder why there are there only two possible conditions of knowledge: ordinary human limitations or else omniscience. Why nothing in between? No doubt this is because Stern-berg, like other theorists, assumes narrators to be persons, and he has only two possible models: mortal persons and a divine person. Narrators may

13. Ibid., 42–43.
14. Ibid., 43.

be human characters, or they may be divinely omniscient. He writes, "Not being one of the fictive agents, such a narrator may safely share the infallible awareness of the all-knowing immortals, in terms of whose superior nature alone his superhuman attributes can indeed be conceived at all."[15]

To assume that the only alternative to the knowledge permitted ordinary persons is the infallible awareness of a god is to treat the omniscience of a god as something given and known. But since we have only rumor and speculation to go on, no reliable knowledge of the "immortals"—a strange expression for a devoted analyst of the Hebrew Bible to use—and since it is we who posit whatever knowingness a god might have, we can imagine many versions of superior knowingness, from the ability infallibly to predict the weather to the capacity to read the minds of animals to telepathic sympathy for the old and infirm. One could have knowledge of all past actions but not of anyone's thoughts; one could know the future as well as the past or only the future. Why not imagine a narrator who can authoritatively describe the thoughts of men but not of women? We can also imagine all sorts of recording or reporting devices, from the camera's eye to the tape recorder to the "radio receiver" of Salman Rushdie's *Midnight's Children*, Saleem Sinai, whose head is full of voices. The only justification of the claim that a narrator who can report the thoughts of one character must have full omniscience is the unjustifiable belief that an omniscient God is the only alternative to a human's partial knowledge.

Sternberg, in his later book, *The Poetics of Biblical Narrative*, which analyzes biblical narrative as a special case, the true model of omniscient narration, significantly revises the views that I have quoted. Instead of citing as a known quantity "the infallible awareness of the all-knowing immortals," he writes:

It is curious that literary scholars should refer to a superhuman viewpoint as an "Olympian narrator," for the model of omniscient narration they have in mind is actually patterned on the Hebraic rather than the Homeric model of divinity. Homer's gods, like the corresponding Near Eastern pantheons, certainly have access to a wider range of information than the normal run of humanity, but their knowledge still falls well short of omniscience, concerning the past as well as the future.[16]

15. Sternberg, *Expositional Modes*, 295.
16. Sternberg, *Poetics of Biblical Narrative*, 88.

What happened to the idea that superhuman knowledge of any sort entails full omniscience? But the later Sternberg is right: the Greek gods display various sorts of special knowledge; one cannot assume that they really know everything but choose not to reveal it or act on it. Perhaps, if only to break with the Judeo-Christian concept of omniscience, narratology should call on the Greek gods to embody the myriad sorts of uncanny knowledge that narratives deploy.

But rather than substitute one pantheon for another, we should approach the matter from the other direction by asking what are the effects people have sought to describe through the dubious notion of omniscience and whether it is apposite or helpful in these cases. There are four sorts of phenomena that are important: (1) the performative authoritativeness of many narrative declarations, which seem to bring into being what they describe; (2) the reporting of innermost thoughts and feelings, such as are usually inaccessible to human observers; (3) authorial narration, where the narrator flaunts his or her godlike ability to determine how things turn out; and (4) the synoptic impersonal narration of the realist tradition. Let me take these up in turn.

(1) One thing that contributes to the ascription of omniscience is the incontrovertible narrative declaration. "Emma Woodhouse, handsome, clever, and rich, with a comfortable home and happy disposition, seemed to unite some of the best blessings of existence; and had lived nearly twenty-one years in the world with very little to distress or vex her."[17] Critics are inclined to say that the narrator knows these things. Since we cannot dispute them, arguing that probably Emma was really older and not handsome at all, we might think that we are dealing with special, superhuman knowledge. But in fact it is not a question of knowledge. You could know this about a friend—it would be a permissible sort of generalization—but in the novel the claim has a different status: by convention we accept the statement as truth, as a given of the narrative world.

In this respect narrative fiction differs radically from nonfictional narrative. The basic convention of literature is that narrative sentences not produced by characters are true, whereas in nonfiction similar statements would have a different status. Consider this: "The job he had his eye on now was Secretary of the Navy, and when in October 1942, the man in that job, Frank Knox, was away from Washington on an inspection tour for the

17. Austen, *Emma*, 1.

President, Johnson planted with Walter Winchell, Drew Pearson and other friendly columnists, the rumor that Knox was about to resign and that he himself was in line for the post."[18]

In a novel this would simply be a statement about the actions of a character that we would accept as given and true, and the question of exactly how the narrator knew this would not arise (unless the narrator were a character). It is not a matter of omniscience but of the constitutive convention of fiction. In Robert Caro's biography of Lyndon Johnson it has a different status: we may wonder exactly how the author, Caro, knows this and whether it is true that Johnson was himself the source of these rumors. "In narrative that is specifically literary," though, as Felix Martinez-Bonati writes, "the validity attributed to the narrator's mimetic discourse is maximal, absolute."[19] (When doubts arise, the narrator turns into a character whose different claims we must evaluate—which illustrates the constitutive force of the presumption of truthfulness.) The truth of the heterodiegetic narrator's discourse is, in Kantian terms, a transcendental principle of the comprehension or experience of literary narration. What Martinez-Bonati calls "the ironic acceptance of the absolute truth of the narrator's mimetic apophansis" is a condition of possibility of literature.[20] The case of first-person narrative is different: there readers may certainly wonder whether the narrator is telling the truth, but for so-called third-person narrative, which is where the ascription of omniscience occurs, the truth of the narrative's "mimetic discourse" is a convention of fiction.

But all narrative assertions in the novel do not benefit from this convention, as they would have to if the narrator were indeed omniscient. Martinez-Bonati distinguishes the mimetic discourse or mimetic content of the narratorial sentences from affirmations that are not narrative or descriptive: generalizations, aphorisms, opinions, moral views—which by convention are *not* taken as constitutive of the world of the novel and may receive varying degrees of acceptance from readers. Thus, in *Emma*

18. Robert A. Caro, *Means of Ascent*, vol. 2 of *The Years of Lyndon Johnson* (New York: Random House, 1990), 72.

19. Felix Martinez-Bonati, *Fictive Discourse and the Structures of Literature* (Ithaca, NY: Cornell University Press, 1986), 34.

20. "Ironic" in that we accept statements as truth within a universe we take to be fictional. *Apophansis* is Martinez-Bonati's term for the mimetic representations asserted as true by definition in this novelistic world. Martinez-Bonati, *Fictive Discourse*, 35.

when Isabella resists her father's urging to stay at Highbury with him but proposes to return with her husband to London, we hear that Mr. Woodhouse "was obliged to see the whole party set off and return to his lamentations over the destiny of poor Isabella—which poor Isabella, passing her life with those she doted on, full of their merits, blind to their faults, and always innocently busy, might have been a model of right feminine happiness."[21]

Although we must accept as true the claim that Isabella departed and Mr. Woodhouse lamented this as an unhappy destiny, we are not obliged to accept that she is the model of right feminine happiness. If we were dealing with something modeled on divine omniscience, both claims would have to be true, as would all the other value judgments in the novel.[22] Consider the opening of *Anna Karenina*: "All happy families are alike, but each unhappy family is unhappy after its own fashion." This may be wise; it may be insightful; but it is not true by definition, as it would be if the narrator were really omniscient. We certainly do not take it as a necessary truth about families in the world of this novel. In fact, it is only because we do *not* take it as by definition true of the world of the novel that we are able to consider it as a possible insight into the human condition.

Critics who use the term *omniscience* presume that the narrator is omniscient only about the world of the novel, but fiction of the realist tradition, where the term is most used, is full of general claims that we assess as generalizations about a larger world that extends into our own. *Omniscience* is precisely the wrong term for such statements, which are different from those that describe the characters specific to the novel.

21. Austen, *Emma*, 95.

22. It might be argued that in the world of Austen's novel it is true that Isabella is the model of right feminine happiness, and our dissent amounts to saying we do not believe this is the case in our world. If this were a science fiction novel, then the narrator would be free to stipulate what counts as happiness in this special world, just as the narrator can stipulate that Isabella is Emma's sister, but in the realist novel judgments do not carry the same stipulative authority of descriptive statements. We can say that the narrator "believes" this is the right model of happiness but can be wrong, whereas it makes no sense to say that the narrator "believes" that Isabella is Emma's sister but can be wrong (unless, of course, the narrator is a character). The two sorts of statements have a different status. And the effect of wisdom projected by the narrator depends on the fact that the judgments and assessments are not true by definition but are open to appraisal.

The conventionally authoritative statements of narrators vary widely, from swift summaries of antecedent history to claims about feelings of which characters are not conscious. At one extreme we have traditional folk narration: "The king was exceedingly pleased but his greed for gold was still not satisfied, so he called in his daughter, the most beauteous young woman in the land, and said . . . " At the other we have the authoritative statements of the psychological novel. Once we recognize that their authority comes not, as it would in historical narrative, from the fact that someone knows these things but from a conventional performativity of narrative stipulation, we lose much of the impetus to postulate omniscience.

(2) A second set of cases involves inside knowledge of others that empirical individuals cannot attain. Dorrit Cohn has argued that this is one of the major features that distinguish fiction from nonfictional narrative: if a story starts reporting a character's thoughts, expect it to be fiction.[23] By Sternberg's logic, as we have seen, access to the thought of any character entails an omniscient narrator, but critics have seldom in fact followed this logic. Wayne Booth notes "a curious ambiguity in the term 'omniscience.' Many modern works that we usually classify as narrated dramatically, with everything relayed to us through the limited views of the characters, postulate fully as much omniscience in the silent author as Fielding claims for himself. The roving visitation into the minds of sixteen characters" in *As I Lay Dying* is usually not associated with omniscient narrative, "but this method is omniscience with teeth in it."[24]

When we are given access to the thought of one character principally, as in the focalized narratives practiced by Henry James and celebrated by Percy Lubbock and others, we speak not of "omniscience" but of "limited point of view." I suspect this is because the underlying motivation for the postulation of omniscience is our inclination to recuperate textual details or effects by attaching them to the consciousness of a person, who becomes their source. If there is a consciousness somewhere about, as there is in focalized narratives, we feel less need to invent another person who knows what goes on in the first character's head. It is above all when there is no

23. Dorrit Cohn, *The Distinction of Fiction* (Baltimore: Johns Hopkins University Press, 1999), 21–29.

24. Wayne Booth, *The Rhetoric of Fiction*, 2nd ed. (Chicago: University of Chicago Press, 1987), 161.

primary character through whom narration is focalized that our proclivity leads us astray: we invent a person to be the source of textual details, but since this knowledge is not that which an ordinary person could have, we must imagine this invented person to be godlike, omniscient.[25] We posit a narrator so as to frame the story as something known by someone rather than imagined by an author, and then since the story contains things that no one could know—internal states of others—we treat this knower as superhuman, omniscient. But there are more accurate ways to describe these effects—particularly the presentation of characters' thought.

Consider the following extract from James Joyce's "The Boarding House," which gives us representations of two consciousnesses:

> Nearly the half-hour! She stood up and surveyed herself in the pier-glass. The decisive expression of her great florid face satisfied her and she thought of some mothers she knew who could not get their daughters off their hands.
>
> Mr. Doran was very anxious indeed this Sunday morning. He had made two attempts to shave but his hand had been so unsteady that he had been obliged to desist. Three days' reddish beard fringed his jaws and every two or three minutes a mist gathered on his glasses so that he had to take them off and polish them with his pocket-handkerchief. The recollection of his confession of the night before was a cause of acute pain to him; the priest had drawn out every ridiculous detail of the affair and in the end had so magnified his sin that he was almost thankful at being afforded a loophole of reparation. The harm was done. What could he do now but marry her or run away? He could not brazen it out. The affair would be sure to be talked of and his employer would be certain to hear of it. Dublin is such a small city: everyone knows everyone else's business.[26]

What is especially interesting about this story, in which a boarder has become involved with the landlady's daughter and now is going to have to marry her, is that readers are privy to the boarder's thoughts and to the mother's—the first paragraph is hers—but not to the daughter's, so we don't know to what extent she has been complicitously working to achieve this end. Again, *omniscience* is quite specifically not the right term for what

25. This inclination may be compounded, James Phelan suggests, by the fact that narrators characteristically know how the story turns out. Combined with special knowledge of characters' thoughts, this may provoke the ascription of omniscience.

26. James Joyce, "The Boarding House," in *Dubliners* (New York: Viking, 1968), 165–66.

happens here. It is pointless to wonder whether the narrator knows the daughter's thoughts and does not tell or does not know, for it is not a matter of knowledge.

A more perplexing situation arises in *À la recherche du temps perdu*, where we encounter a homodiegetic or character narrator with unusual knowledge. Marcel is the narrator, and many stretches of this enormous narrative can be read as focalized through him—either what he might have observed at the time or what he may later, with his insatiable curiosity, have come to learn. But there is information, such as the thoughts of Bergotte on his deathbed, which cannot have been reported to Marcel because no one had access to them. Or consider the scene of Marcel watching Vinteuil's daughter from outside her window at Montjouvain, in which there is rigorous focalization through Marcel with respect to what is seen and heard (he is hiding outside, looking through a lighted window) but which is focalized through Mlle Vinteuil for thoughts and feelings. "She felt that she had been indiscreet, her sensitive heart took flight etc."[27] Gérard Genette hesitates about how to describe such cases. On the one hand, he calls them moments "we must indeed attribute to the 'omniscient' novelist,"[28] with quotation marks around "omniscient" that seem to indicate doubts about this traditional way of talking about special knowledge; but he also speaks of "double focalization," involving feelings "which only an omniscient narrator, capable like God himself of seeing beyond actions and of sounding body and soul, can reveal."[29]

The novel itself, though, offers by way of explanation of such effects an evocation of a technical device: while lying in bed Marcel thinks of his childhood in Combray and of

what many years after leaving this little town, I had learned about a love affair in which Swann had been involved before I was born, with that precision of details easier to obtain sometimes about lives of people dead for centuries than about those of our most intimate friends; a thing which seems impossible, just as it used to seem impossible to converse from one town to another—before we learned of the device by which that impossibility has been overcome.[30]

27. Marcel Proust, *À la recherche du temps perdu*, 3 vols. (Paris: Gallimard, 1954), 1:159–65.

28. Gérard Genette, *Narrative Discourse: An Essay in Method* (Ithaca, NY: Cornell University Press, 1980), 208.

29. Ibid., 209.

30. Proust, *À la recherche du temps perdu*, 1:186.

The analogy of the telephone suggests an unnamed device permitting imaginative recuperation of details of inner and outer lives of the characters. As long as the narrator is imaginative and resourceful, he need not be hindered by physical limitations.[31] Is "telepathy" a way of describing what happens here and elsewhere? Nicholas Royle writes, "'Telepathy' opens possibilities of a humbler, more precise, less religiously freighted conceptuality than does omniscience for thinking about the uncanniness of what is going on in narrative fiction."[32] In particular, the notion of telepathy helps capture the fact that in cases of reports of characters' thoughts, we are not dealing with narrators who know everything all at once but rather with narrative instances reporting now on this consciousness, now on that, often relaying, transposing, or translating thought into the intermediate discourse of free indirect speech, for example. Telepathy seems especially apposite—much more so than omniscience—for cases where an extradiegetic homodiegetic narrator displays special knowledge. Supplementing Marcel with an omniscient narrator would miss the point that these sentiments are supposed to have become known to Marcel the narrator, impossible as this seems. Genette finds himself hesitating between two options he rightly regards as unsatisfactory: positing an extra narrator (omniscient) who produces some of the clauses of apparently seamless paragraphs while Marcel produces the others, or else ascribing knowledge to the author, who of course does not know anything but invents, ascribes, declares the feelings of Mlle Vinteuil or Bergotte or Swann to be such and such. The massive tale of Swann's love, which includes both details that the hypercurious Marcel, obsessed with Swann, might well have learned, and Swann's most intimate thoughts, which it is impossible to imagine making their way to Marcel without telepathic transmission, beautifully instantiates the problem. The narrative effect here, as Marcel laboriously teases out this story like a spider spinning the web that supports it, depends on Marcel's imaginative, telepathic retailing of information that the novelist invented (just as he invented Marcel and Marcel's account of himself). Recourse to omniscience would obscure the specificity of this effect.

Richard Walsh, in an important article, has argued for dispensing

31. Robert Scholes and Robert Kellogg, *The Nature of Narrative* (New York: Oxford University Press, 1966), 260.

32. Royle, *The Uncanny*, 261.

with narrators who are not characters: either a narrator is identifiable as a character, such as Marlow or Marcel, or we do not need this fiction.[33] This is, of course, an ongoing argument, which has previously been carried out on linguistic grounds, by Ann Banfield, for instance, and which I lack the space or expertise to explore.[34] Walsh claims that we do not need to postulate a narrator to account for instances of omniscience, since what is in question is not something that a person can know anyway. Rather than translate novels into stories that are reported by someone, we should, I suggest, try to work with other alternatives—whether telepathic transmission, a reporting instance, or some similar device—that allow us to focus on the art with which these details have been imagined.

Seymour Chatman once explored the possibility that heterodiegetic, extradiegetic narration with what Genette calls zero focalization should not lead to the imagination of a narrator, but in *Coming to Terms* he proposed a compromise: by definition every narrative has a narrator, in the sense of an agent of narration, but this agent can be nonhuman, a *presenter* of the signs, just as film can present a narrative without a human narrator.[35] So *As I Lay Dying* would not have an omniscient narrator but only a recorder, a presenter of signs, a transmission device. Such an approach is more satisfactory than the positing of a knower for any information presented.

(3) The third case of effects that provoke ascription of omniscience is what is called "authorial narration": a narrator who identifies him- or herself as the author, the shaper if not outright inventor of the tale. There are those who, like the narrator of Diderot's *Jacques le fataliste*, flaunt their power to determine the course of the story:

> You see, reader, that I am well on my way, and that it is completely up to me whether I shall make you wait one year, two years, or three years for the story of Jacques' loves by separating him from his master and having each of them go through the vicissitudes that I please. What's to prevent my marrying off the mas-

33. Richard Walsh, "Who Is the Narrator?" *Poetics Today* 18, no. 4 (1997): 495–513.

34. See Ann Banfield, *Unspeakable Sentences: Narration and Representation in the Language of Fiction* (Boston: Routledge and Kegan Paul, 1982).

35. Seymour Chatman, *Coming to Terms: The Rhetoric of Narrative in Fiction and Film* (Ithaca, NY: Cornell University Press, 1990), 116.

ter and making him a cuckold? Shipping Jacques off to the islands?[36]

Fielding's narrator in *Tom Jones* combines the roles of *histor*, bard, and, for instance, maker, when he wonders how he can rescue Tom Jones from jail and still not violate modern standards of probability.[37] Susan Lanser's exploration of the forms of authorial narration has emphasized the trade-offs between the establishment of authority and the highlighting of authorial presence through the interventions, digressions, and evaluations that establish a distinctive voice.[38] The greater the presence, the less "omniscience," one might imagine. This is a complex subject; authorial narration covers a considerable range of possibilities that call for careful discrimination, and I will observe only that although one might expect that flaunting of the power to determine the course of the tale would be inversely related to the "reality" of the story, as something that has already happened, in fact narrators who claim to be able to determine what happens may simultaneously suggest the independence of aspects of the story. Narrators thrusting themselves forward may, for instance, comment on their ignorance of certain matters; by making the narrator more of a character, this helps to preserve at one level the illusion of realism that is being undermined at another. In any event the assertion of ignorance and the occasional flaunting of omnipotence, as well as the self-consciousness and playfulness of this mode, suggest that *omniscience* is not a good label for this sort of narration.

(4) What is left, then, as a field for omniscience? Finally, the examples where the best case could be made for the notion are those nineteenth-century novels, from George Eliot to Anthony Trollope, with extradiegetic-heterodiegetic narrators who present themselves as *histors*: spokespersons of authority who judiciously sift and present information, know the innermost secrets of characters, reveal what they would keep hidden, and offer sage reflections on the foibles of humankind. But even here, where the idea of omniscience might actually seem appropriate, it is not clear that it helps to elucidate the stakes and the effects. The opening chapter of George El-

36. Jacques's refrain that his captain said that whatever we do for good or ill is "écrit là-haut" [written on high] only adds piquancy to the authorial narrator's claim to be able to determine what we will hear. Denis Diderot, *Jacques le fataliste*, in *Œuvres romanesques* (Paris: Garnier, 1962), 495.

37. Henry Fielding, *Tom Jones* (New York: Norton, 1973), 347.

38. Susan S. Lanser, *Fictions of Authority: Women Writers and Narrative Voice* (Ithaca, NY: Cornell University Press, 1992), 16–22.

iot's *Middlemarch* presents the heroine, Dorothea Brooke, in a fashion that is scarcely unusual in the great realist novels:

Miss Brooke had that kind of beauty which seems to be thrown into relief by poor dress. Her hand and wrist were so finely formed that she could wear sleeves not less bare of style than those in which the Blessed Virgin appeared to Italian painters; and her profile as well as her stature and bearing seemed to gain the more dignity from her plain garments, which by the side of provincial fashion gave her the impressiveness of a fine quotation from the Bible,—or from one of our elder poets,—in a paragraph of to-day's newspaper. She was usually spoken of as being remarkably clever, with the addition that her sister Celia had more common-sense.[39]

This opening appeals to community standards ("that kind of beauty," "the impressiveness of a fine quotation from the Bible") and to cultural knowledge presumed shared ("Italian painters," "elder poets"). It displays a concern with seeming—how one appears, how one is thought of—that is not contrasted with being. The analogy with a quotation in "to-day's newspaper" suggests an interest in communal perceptions and effects—how we seem to each other in society.

"We belated historians," declares the narrator of *Middlemarch*, distinguishing this mode from Fielding's, "must not linger after his example. . . . I at least have so much to do in unraveling certain human lots, and seeing how they were woven and interwoven, that all the light I can command must be concentrated on this particular web and not dispersed over the tempting range of relevancies called the universe."[40] Unraveling and exploring are not the actions of the omniscient. They are the operations of the historian, who can investigate and capaciously survey. Such narrators engage in reflection and link such wisdom as they offer to the process of judicious rumination, while an omniscient God should not need to reflect at all: he or she simply knows. For another thing, those reflections, which embody the wisdom distilled from observation of the characters whose doings are reported, are themselves not necessarily true, as they would be if proffered by an omniscient being, but are offered for our consideration and assent, in a mode of persuasion. Finally, as a number of crit-

39. George Eliot, *Middlemarch* (Oxford: Oxford University Press, 1950), 1.
40. Ibid., book 2, chap. 15, 147–48.

ics have argued, these novels may embody not a judgment of the universe from without, from a position of divine authority, but something like an instantiation of social consensus. J. Hillis Miller and Betsy Ermath suggest that what is often called omniscient narration in the nineteenth-century novel is in fact misnamed, that it is rather the voice of a collective subject. Ermath speaks of "the narrator as nobody," a narrating instance, a "collective result, a specifier of consensus, and as such . . . really not intelligible as an individual." The convention that an invariant world exists "means that consciousness is always potentially interchangeable among individuals because it is consciousness of the same thing."[41] This recalls Benedict Anderson's argument, discussed in Chapter 2, that the "old-fashioned novel," with its reporting of what happens at the same time in different places, to characters who do not know one another, makes possible the imagined community of a nation. Anderson speaks of the "omniscient reader" who sees A telephoning C, B shopping, and D playing pool, but clearly omniscience is the wrong term for this effect, which does not require access to the consciousness of individuals but merely the presentation of more strands of simultaneous action than an individual could observe.

Hillis Miller notes that the notion of the "omniscient narrator has tended to obscure clear understanding of the narrative voice in Victorian fiction." Narrators tend to have pervasive presence rather than transcendent vision, and to write is to identify with the general consciousness of a community, a collective mind.[42] What saves the narrator from the limitation of viewpoint, argues Ermath, "is not omniscience, personalized in the author as surrogate God, but the extension to infinity provided by narrative consensus."[43]

I do not feel competent to assess these claims about a large corpus of very long novels. Harry Shaw has argued, against the ascription of omniscience, that the rhetoric of such novels depends on our thinking that we are being addressed by a narrator modeled on a human being.[44] I certainly confess to some skepticism about the idea of consensus and am more at-

41. Elizabeth Ermath, *Realism and Consensus in the English Novel* (Princeton, NJ: Princeton University Press, 1983), 65–66.

42. J. Hillis Miller, *The Form of Victorian Fiction* (South Bend, IN: Notre Dame University Press, 1968), 63–67.

43. Ermath, *Realism and Consensus*, 76.

44. Harry Shaw, *Narrating Reality: Austen, Scott, Eliot* (Ithaca, NY: Cornell University Press, 1999), 236–39.

tracted to the argument of Richard Maxwell, in "Dickens' Omniscience," that what appears to be omniscience is not transcendent vision but more like the work of a sharp operator who gets around and knows a lot: what each character is doing or thinking. There is accumulation, certainly, but not the synthesis of omniscience. The ability to grasp the city all at once is rarely attained.[45] It is in the effects of these central works of the realist tradition that the best case for the pertinence of omniscience could be made, but I expect that it will fail.

In sum, my claim is that four rather different phenomena—the conventional establishment of narrative authority, the imaginative or telepathic translation of inner thoughts, the playful and self-reflexive foregrounding of creative actions, and the production of wisdom through the multiplication of perspectives and the teasing out of intricacies in human affairs—are what have provoked the ascription of omniscience, the postulation of omniscient narrators, and have thereby not only obscured the distinctiveness or salience of these practices but have repeatedly obfuscated them so that we fail to see what is going on.

Omniscient narration has often had bad press, as the literary agent of panoptic discipline and control, linked to the policing power of narrative and thus diverting narrative fiction from its inherent dialogism to a dubious monologism.[46] But in fact, I would argue, it is the *idea* of omniscient narrative rather than the diverse practices to which the name applies that should sadden or outrage us. Our habit of naturalizing the strange details and practices of narrative by making the consciousness of an individual their source, and then imagining a quasi-divine omniscient consciousness when human consciousnesses cannot fill that role, generates a fantasy of omniscience, which we then find oppressive. Since this fantasy oppresses at the same time that it obfuscates the narrative effects that lead us to posit it, we should abandon this critical vocabulary that does no service to us or to narrative. It's time to remove the blinders and explore alternative vocabularies better attuned to the strange effects of literature.

45. Maxwell, "Dickens' Omniscience," 290.

46. See, e.g., D. A. Miller, *The Novel and the Police* (Berkeley: University of California Press, 1988); and John Bender, *Imagining the Penitentiary: Fiction and Architecture of Mind in Eighteenth-Century England* (Chicago: University of Chicago Press, 1987). Audrey Jaffe speaks, appropriately, of omniscience as "a fantasy" (Jaffe, *Vanishing Points*, 6, 19).

CRITICAL PRACTICES

9

Bad Writing and Good Philosophy

I began work on this topic for a conference at the University of London on style in philosophy. The organizers asked me to address the question of what it is for a piece of philosophy to be badly written—no doubt thinking that as a reader of French philosophy I would have special expertise on this question, or at least a lot of relevant experience.

In fact, I was happy to take up this question because I have been intrigued by claims made in the world of Anglophone philosophy about bad writing. The journal *Philosophy and Literature*, edited by an analytical philosopher, Denis Dutton, had for several years announced a Bad Writing Award, and since this award had been conferred on a sentence by Judith Butler that appeared in *Diacritics* during my stint as editor, I had a personal interest in the concept of bad writing in philosophy and the criteria of selection. What counts as bad writing for this journal? What were the parameters of their Bad Writing Contest?

This contest was conducted for four years, and the prize was always awarded to someone well known (no surprise, this)—never to analytical philosophers but always to someone involved with Marxist, feminist, or postcolonial theory: Fredric Jameson, Roy Bhaskar, Homi Bhabha, Judith Butler. The contest attempted, the journal announced, "to locate the ugliest, most stylistically awful passage found in a scholarly book or article published in the last few years." In an article in the *Wall Street Journal* Denis Dutton explains: "The rules were simple: Entries should be a sentence or two from an actual published scholarly book or journal article. No translations into English allowed, and the entries had to be nonironic."[1] I was surprised to learn that the editor asked only to see a sentence or two. When the *New York Times* phoned me for my reaction to Butler's having received the award, I said that it seemed to me a matter of bad faith to take a single sentence out of context and charge it with obfuscation; I hadn't realized that this was actually the basis of the contest.[2] What if, for example, the sentence uses jargon that has just been explained?

I confess that it had never occurred to me that one ought to be able to understand every sentence of a work of philosophy in isolation, that every sentence should be clear *in and of itself,* that ugliness and impenetrability can be assessed independently of what comes before. I wondered whether only theorists of a continental persuasion produced sentences that failed this test, and I thought I would take a look, in a negative version of *sortes vergilianae.*

The first book I took down from the shelf was one with a good reputation—one of those books I had always meant to read—Robert Nozick's *Philosophical Explanations.* Though Nozick sometimes writes highly technical philosophy, he has achieved a broad audience, and this book takes on large questions of interest to many people (its chapters are "The Identity of the Self," "Why Is There Something Rather Than Nothing," "Knowledge and Skepticism," "Free Will," "Foundations of Ethics," and "Philosophy and the Meaning of Life"). But the first page to which I opened, in the opening chapter on the identity of the self, contained this sentence:

We have said that W is a whole relative to parts $p_1, \ldots, p_n$ when the closest continuer of W need not be the sum of the closest continuers of the parts p_i, when (a) it is possible that the closest continuer of W exists yet does not contain as a part some existing closest continuer of one of the p_i's; or (b) it is possible that the closest continuer of W exists and contains some part q that is not a closest continuer of any of the p_i (nor a sum or other odd carving up of these); or (c) it is possible that at some later time no continuer of W is close enough to be it, even though each of the p_i then has a continuer close enough to be it—the parts exist at the later time but the whole does not.[3]

1. Denis Dutton, "Language Crimes," *Wall Street Journal,* Feb. 5, 1999, W11.

2. I understand that the contest has now been abandoned, perhaps because Dutton realized that this was not a good basis for judgment.

3. Robert Nozick, *Philosophical Explanations* (Cambridge, MA: Harvard University Press, 1981), 101.

This is certainly ugly, awkward, and hard to follow (a potential prizewinner, I should have thought!), but one *can* follow it if one is interested in the project of trying, with elaborate invented examples, to work out what logically would have to be the case for some *y* to count as a continuation of *x* and all the conceivable configurations that might complicate such ascriptions of identity. Having found enough sentences like this to assure myself that analytic philosophy is not necessarily more graceful, witty, and comprehensible than other sorts, and that looking for sentences that by themselves are ugly and opaque is not a very good way of evaluating philosophy, I happened to glance at the opening page of Nozick's book, to see if he said anything about the kind of writing he was doing, and here is what I found. The book begins:

I, too, seek an unreadable book: urgent thoughts to grapple with in agitation and excitement, revelations to be transformed by or to transform, a book incapable of being read straight through, a book even to bring reading to a stop. I have not found that book, or attempted it. Still, I wrote and thought in awareness of it, in the hope that this book would bask in its light.[4]

Prose that basks in the light of the hope of unreadability. That this might be the goal of an eminent analytic philosopher warns us not to take ease of assimilation and transparency as the hallmarks of good writing in philosophy or difficulty as the necessary sign of bad writing.

With this idea in mind let me turn to the winner of the 1999 Bad Writing Award—a sentence from a brief essay by Judith Butler called "Further Reflections on Conversations of Our Time." This essay introduced a conversation between Butler and Ernesto Laclau, whose book, *New Reflections on the Revolutions of Our Time*, provides the basis for Butler's title. Here is the sentence.

The move from a structuralist account in which capital is understood to structure social relations in relatively homogeneous ways, to a view of hegemony in which power relations are subject to repetition, convergence, and rearticulation, brought the question of temporality into the thinking of structure, and marked a shift from a form of Althusserian theory that takes structural totalities as theoretical objects to one in which the insights into the contingent possibilities of structure inaugurate a renewed conception of hegemony bound up with the contingent sites and strategies of the rearticulation of power.[5]

4. Ibid., 1.

5. Judith Butler, "Further Reflections on Conversations of Our Time," *Diacritics* 27, no. 1 (spring 1997): 13.

This is not an easy sentence, certainly. Here is what Denis Dutton says about it in commenting on the award. "Kitsch theorists mimic the effects of rigor and profundity without actually doing serious intellectual work. Their jargon-laden prose always suggests but never delivers genuine insight."[6] Then comes Butler's sentence. Dutton continues: "To ask what this means is to miss the point. This sentence beats readers into submission and instructs them that they are in the presence of a great and deep mind. Actual communication has nothing to do with it."

I think this is complete rubbish, actually. I wonder *who* it is who has failed to do serious intellectual work—such as read Butler's three-page article. Her sentence summarizes, in the third paragraph of the article, why she has taken an interest in Laclau and Mouffe's writing. She first became interested when she realized "that I had found a set of Marxist thinkers for whom discourse was not merely a representation of pre-existing social and historical realities, but was also constitutive of the field of the social and of history."[7] Then she saw that

central to their notion of articulation, appropriated from Gramsci, was the notion of rearticulation. As a temporally dynamic and relatively unpredictable play of forces, hegemony had been cast by Laclau and Mouffe as an alternative to the static forms of structuralism that tend to construe contemporary social forms as timeless totalities. I read in Laclau and Mouffe the political transcription of Derrida's "Structure, Sign and Play": a structure gains its status as a structure, its structurality, only through repeated reinstatements. The dependency of that structure on its reinstatement means that the very possibility of structure depends on a reiteration that is in no sense determined fully in advance, that for structure and social structure as a result to become possible, there must first be a contingent repetition as its basis.

This is important, as she explains later, because if what is dominant in a society depends for its dominance on constant repetition and rearticulation, there may be sites and strategies for altering that repetition and effecting change. In these opening paragraphs Butler identifies sources of concepts and introduces key terms such as *hegemony* and *rearticulation*, noting that for Laclau and Mouffe hegemony is something dynamic, depending on repetition and rearticulation, which keep it going. Then

6. Dutton, "Language Crimes," 11.
7. Butler, "Further Reflections," 13.

comes the prizewinning sentence summing up why she found their work important:

The move from a structuralist account in which capital is understood to structure social relations in relatively homogeneous ways, to a view of hegemony in which power relations are subject to repetition, convergence, and rearticulation, brought the question of temporality into the thinking of structure, and marked a shift from a form of Althusserian theory that takes structural totalities as theoretical objects to one in which the insights into the contingent possibilities of structure inaugurate a renewed conception of hegemony bound up with the contingent sites and strategies of the rearticulation of power.

Hegemony is a term that seems to provoke strong reactions, and when it appears twice in a sentence, that may seem the height of obfuscation; but this sentence has been well prepared, and it is not hard to explain, though of course it would help to have some specific examples involving contingent sites and strategies of power. But we are still on page 1. Butler goes on, on page 2, to establish a link between Laclau's work and her own writing on a particular aspect of hegemony: the dominant conceptions of gender in society. "Gender is not an inner core or static essence but a reiterated enactment of norms, ones which produce, retroactively, the appearance of gender as an abiding interior depth."[8] She stresses two points that mirror what Laclau and Mouffe are doing in their theorization of hegemonic politics:

(1) that the term that claims to represent a prior reality produces retroactively that priority as an effect of its own operation and (2) that every determined structure gains its determination by a repetition and hence, a contingency that puts at risk the determined character of that structure. For feminism, that means that gender does not represent an interior depth but produces that interiority and depth performatively as the effect of its own operation. And it means that "patriarchy" or "systems" of masculine domination are not systemic totalities bound to keep women in positions of oppression but, rather, hegemonic forms of power that expose their own frailty in the very operation of their iterability. The strategic task for feminism is to exploit these occasions of frailty as they emerge. (14)

This is difficult writing, certainly, though not excessively difficult once one understands a few key terms and has in mind some particular illustrations of the processes at stake. My undergraduate students quickly

8. Ibid., 14.

become able to handle it. In fact, despite the high level of abstraction, it is quite pedagogic writing. Key points are rephrased and repeated so that if readers don't catch on the first time around, they have another chance when the terms come by again. Butler has a distinctive style, determined in part by the counterintuitive processes she is describing: there is not a set of given entities that produce certain effects, but, rather, what we take to be the entities are the performative effects of repetition. Since English leads us to assume that the nouns we use have preexisting referents, sentences arguing that these entities are themselves produced through repetition turn back on themselves in ways that may make them hard to read. Thus: "gender does not represent an interior depth but produces that interiority and depth performatively as the effect of its own operation." This is clear once you grasp the structure.

Denis Dutton maintains, "When Kant or Aristotle or Wittgenstein are most obscure, it is because they are honestly grappling with the most complex and difficult problems that the human mind can encounter. How different from the desperate incantations of the Bad Writing Contest Winners, who hope to persuade their readers not by argument but by obscurity that they too are the great minds of the age."[9] I do not find helpful the distinction between honest grappling and the desperate production of obscurity, but Butler is certainly grappling with difficult problems.

Dutton's comment indicates, though, the ease with which—depending on whether or not one sympathizes with the philosophical mode—one can praise difficult writing as a heroic struggle with the antinomies of thought or else condemn it as pretentious vacuousness. There is bad writing everywhere, but public complaints about bad writing in philosophy generally seem complaints about a philosophical mode: a mode of thought one finds uncongenial, concerns whose pertinence one fails to see, so that the writing seems pointless and pretentious in its flaunting of specialized language (as I found the Nozick passages).

In the hope of avoiding the issue of sympathy with or antipathy to a philosophical mode, I want to approach the problem of philosophical style and bad writing not through texts outside the analytic tradition but through a very interesting and enigmatical figure, Stanley Cavell. A student of J. L. Austin and admirer of Wittgenstein, Cavell is known for his

9. Dutton, "Language Crimes," 11.

distinctive writing. What is happening philosophically in Cavell's stylish writing?

The reviews suggest that if we wanted a famous philosopher who could be charged with bad writing, Cavell would be an obvious choice. The *Times Literary Supplement*'s review of his most famous book, *The Claim of Reason*, speaks of Cavell's "self-indulgent" style, especially the penchant for gratuitous qualifications and parenthetical interruptions, and concludes that despite "Cavell's philosophical and literary gifts, his book is a misshapen, undisciplined amalgam of ill-sorted parts."[10] Mark Glouberman in the *Review of Metaphysics* calls his style "inexcusable."[11] Dan Ducker writes in the *International Philosophical Quarterly*, "the pattern of withholding judgment, of putting off closure, builds certain frustrations in the reader. There are moments in Cavell's book where one wants to scream, 'Good God, come to the point!'"[12] Even admirers have harsh words for his style. At the beginning of *Stanley Cavell: Philosophy's Recounting of the Ordinary*, Stephen Mulhall notes "a feature of his writing which has become increasingly prominent over time, a feature one might call its 'lack of momentum'—a sense that there is no necessity to continue beyond the end of any given sentence."[13] Richard Fleming, in another book-length study, speaks of "the inertia of the many voices expressed in [Cavell's writing] and its constant self-reflections and pondering about self-knowledge. . . . It is certainly true that Cavell's way of writing has kept him outside of mainstream philosophy—if only because it has kept him from being read."[14] Bad writing? Without further ado, here is the opening sentence of Cavell's most famous book, *The Claim of Reason*:

If not at the beginning of Wittgenstein's later philosophy, since what starts phi-

10. Anthony Kenny, "Clouds of Not Knowing," review of *The Claim of Reason*, *TLS*, April 18, 1980, 449.

11. Mark Glouberman, *Review of Metaphysics* 32 (June 1979): 913.

12. Dan Ducker, *International Philosophical Quarterly* 21 (March 1981): 109–11.

13. Stephen Mulhall, *Stanley Cavell: Philosophy's Recounting of the Ordinary* (Oxford, UK: Clarendon Press, 1994), xii.

14. Richard Fleming, *The State of Philosophy: An Invitation to a Reading in Three Parts of Stanley Cavell's "The Claim of Reason"* (Lewisburg, PA: Bucknell University Press, 1993), 10–11. One should note that *The Claim of Reason* is in its seventh printing, but possibly many purchasers quickly stop reading.

losophy is no more to be known at the outset than how to make an end of it; and if not at the opening of *Philosophical Investigations*, since its opening is not to be confused with the starting of the philosophy it expresses, and since the terms in which that opening might be understood can hardly be given along with the opening itself; and if we acknowledge from the commencement, anyway leave open at the opening, that the way this work is written is internal to what it teaches, which means that we cannot understand the matter (call it the method) before we understand its work; and if we do not look to our history, since placing this book historically can hardly happen earlier than placing it philosophically; nor look to Wittgenstein's past, since then we are likely to suppose that the *Investigations* is written in criticism of the *Tractatus*, which is not so much wrong as empty, both because to know what constitutes its criticism would be to know what constitutes its philosophy, and because it is more to the present point to see how the *Investigations* is written in criticism of itself; then where and how are we to approach this text?[15]

And the first paragraph concludes: "How shall we let this book teach us, this or anything?"

Is it necessary to say that this is deliberate? I imagine that an editor at Oxford University Press might have red-penciled this sentence and been told to let it stand. It would certainly have been easy to make it easier for the reader. For example: "How should we approach Wittgenstein's *Philosophical Investigations*? We could start on page 1, but the terms for understanding the beginning of the text aren't given with the text itself; nor is the beginning of the text the beginning of the philosophy. Moreover, the beginning of the philosophy is not something we can know at the outset." And so on. The difficulty here is the difficulty of beginning philosophy, where there is in principle nothing that can be taken for granted. This is the difficulty Hegel confronts in the preface to the *Phenomenology* (where there are points similar to Cavell's about the ways in which particular contextual approaches mislead). Hegel's confrontation produces a text thought to be hard to read, though not harder, I think, than this sentence of Cavell's, which seeks not to expound the difficulties but to confuse the reader. The two "if not at . . . " clauses presuppose objections, and the "since . . . " clauses may be taken to embody those objections, but

15. Stanley Cavell, *The Claim of Reason: Wittgenstein, Skepticism, Morality, and Tragedy* (New York: Oxford University Press, 1979), 3; hereafter abbreviated *Claim* and cited parenthetically in the text.

since we do not, until after two hundred words have past, get the question "where and how to approach?" to which the supposed answers are being rejected, the reader could not understand the sentence until the very end, and by then, the structure of the sentence has been obscured by the shift halfway through from the negative, "if not at . . . since" structure (which would have been comprehensible), to the positive "if we acknowledge at the opening, anyway leave open . . . that," which doesn't talk about a *place* to start or not start, and thus leaves readers more at sea. If good writing is that which considers the reader and gives him or her what is needed to follow, this is bad writing, especially since no virtues of elegance or aphoristic élan compensate for the befuddlement generated.

Richard Fleming, who wrote an entire book about Cavell's book, claims that the first sentence shows "the care and high respect that he has for the reader. He writes to someone who has been and continues to be engaged at a sophisticated level by Wittgenstein's struggle with the state of philosophy."[16] I think that is wrong. The sentence is not any clearer to a sophisticated Wittgensteinian. The explanation lies in a different direction— one indicated by the epigraph to *The Claim of Reason*, from Emerson: "truly speaking, it is not instruction but provocation that I can receive from another soul." The opening sentence provokes—and thus can, arguably, serve its function of alerting us to the fact that philosophy as Cavell conceives it is not something systematic or even expoundable. The sentence can work this way even if it also makes reviewers write that his style is inexcusable: it makes readers experience what it might *be* for nothing to be given and thus, in a minor way, to live the impossibility of deciding what comes first and how to go about thinking. "A philosophical question has the form: 'I don't know my way about,'" writes Wittgenstein.[17] I imagine this aphorism lurks somewhere in the murk from which Cavell's monstrous sentence arises.

After this sentence Cavell continues: "I will say first, by way of introducing myself and saying why I insist, as I will throughout the following pages, upon the *Investigations* as a philosophical text, that I have wished to understand philosophy not as a set of problems but as a set of texts" (3). Not "I understand philosophy," but "I have wished to understand." This is the sort of thing that prompts people to call his writing precious or self-

16. Fleming, *The State of Philosophy*, 22.

17. Ludwig Wittgenstein, *Philosophical Investigations*, 3rd ed., trans. G. E. Anscombe (New York: Macmillan, 1968), # 123, 49.

indulgent. But that is an interesting charge: "self-indulgent." What does that mean? How is the self being indulged? By contrast with the epistemic standpoint of "I understand . . . " or the impersonality of "Philosophy is better understood as a collection of texts," "I *have wished* to understand" does gesture toward a self with desires and a history. But Cavell's writing is rarely autobiographical, and here, when he might easily take the opportunity of introducing the self, with some substantial remarks about its past and its experiences, such as might determine the wish mentioned here, we get only the slim reference to a wished-for understanding of philosophy.[18] He does not seek to explain his views by evoking a past history. "I have wished to understand" marks the fact that an understanding, perhaps especially in philosophy, is not something that can be treated as unproblematically given but consists of inclinations, temptations, possibilities that have been attempted, ways of proceeding. To understand philosophy as a set of texts would be—what?—to try to write in ways that treat philosophy as different practices of writing (not easy to do).

But Cavell makes life hard for those who, like me, seek to justify his style: after this sentence he immediately asks whether this remark about texts is itself to be understood as a text, produces a two-page excursus on the different sorts or lengths of texts, and then continues: "But I was supposed to be saying more, having said something first, by way of introducing myself, and concerning how we should approach Wittgenstein's text. Accordingly, I will say, second, that there is no approach to it, anyway I have none" (*Claim*, 6).

This is writing that, first and foremost, calls attention to itself as writing. These sentences do that, with a coyness one can certainly find irritating—as in the gratuitous "second" here. Is this not coyness more than self-scrutiny, or at best, parody of the idea of steps or method?[19] Why would

18. Elsewhere Cavell does, I admit, seem to spend more time than other philosophers telling us about the genealogy of his writings—how what we are reading relates to his past writings—and this can certainly seem a form of self-indulgence designed to focus attention on the career and corpus of this self, but I think that what we are dealing with in this passage is different.

19. Cavell writes, "If I could set every word down and question the very setting of that word down as I set it down, I would do that to the point of self-excruciation" (James Conant, "Interview with Stanley Cavell," in *The Senses of Stanley Cavell*, ed. Richard Fleming and Michael Payne [Lewisburg, PA: Bucknell University Press, 1989], 59.) His critics would say this self-excruciation is excruciating to readers.

philosophy call attention to itself as writing? Philosophy is writing because that is the form in which we generally encounter it, but most important because the fundamental philosophical question, for Cavell, is how we understand each other and ourselves. Philosophy and philosophical writing need to seek, and to question in seeking, that understanding. Thus philosophy cannot be a matter of attempted proofs and well-wrought arguments but rather of working to find common ground through words that others will feel carry weight, that will capture what has remained elusive:

If you give up something like formal argument as a route to conviction in philosophy, and you give up the idea that either scientific persuasion or poetic persuasion is the way to philosophical conviction, then the question of what achieves philosophical conviction must at all times be on your mind. The obvious answer to me is that it must lie in the writing itself. But in *what* about the writing? It isn't that there's a rhetorical form, any more than there is an emotional form, in which I expect conviction to happen. But the sense that nothing other than this prose just here, as it's passing before our eyes, can carry conviction, is one of the thoughts that drives the shape of what I do.[20]

Cavell does not answer the question of what in writing might carry conviction. Obviously, there is no recipe for it. But what is involved here? How is what Cavell does—write philosophy—shaped by the need to write so as to give conviction a chance to happen? And since Wittgenstein's is the philosophical writing with which he is most concerned, how is Wittgenstein's writing shaped by this end?

The Claim of Reason is a book focused on the *Philosophical Investigations*, which Cavell thinks has been approached wrongly, as if, for instance, it contained a philosophy of language to be teased out. "Wittgenstein has no philosophy of language at all," he writes. Wittgenstein is interested in matters of language because "they are topics in which the soul interests and manifests itself, so the soul's investigation of itself, in person or in others, will have to investigate these topics and those interests as and where they ordinarily manifest themselves" (*Claim*, 15). Cavell spends a lot of time on the question of the nature of criteria, where his two philosophical mentors and models, J. L. Austin and Wittgenstein, are at odds. The appeal to what we say and the search for criteria "are claims to community. And the claim to community is always a search for the basis on which it can be or has been established" (*Claim*, 20). Appeals to criteria expose the fragile

20. Conant, "Interview," 59.

agreements on which our relations with others are based. In the exploration of how such appeals are conducted and of their entanglement with the stream of life, Cavell's Wittgenstein is not seeking to refute skepticism but to explore the problem of the other, of other minds, which philosophy has been too inclined to treat as a special problem, whereas in fact it is central to most aspects of life, including doing philosophy, which is writing that must find ways to engage the other.

When he began to study the *Investigations*, Cavell writes, he was struck by the play of skeptical voices and answering voices. "I knew reasonably soon thereafter and reasonably well that my fascination with the *Investigations* had to do with my response to it as a feat of writing. It was some years before I understood it as what I came to think of as the discovery for philosophy of the problem of the other; and further years before these issues looked to me like functions of one another" (*Claim*, xiii). Here again we have that spare form of self-indulgence, a style shaped by the reference to the temporality of a self but where the content is not other than philosophical—that is, Cavell is not trying to ground, justify, or explain a philosophical position by reference to some other sort of life experience.

This might better be seen as confession—impersonal confession: recounting your thoughts in a way that invites readers to consider the possibility of trying out the relation that is narrated. This is different from writing, "I intend to show that the text as a feat of writing is a version of the problem of the other." Is the implication that there is no other way to show this than to invite the reader to repeat the passage from one to the other?

Wittgenstein and Cavell write stylish philosophy but in very different ways. Wittgenstein is accused of being maddeningly enigmatical or unforthcoming but never, I think, of writing badly. He is spare, aphoristic, enigmatical, paratactic. Cavell is orotund, expansive, digressive, fussy, hypotactic. But since Cavell regards the *Investigations* as, more than any other text, "paradigmatic of philosophy for me" (*Claim*, xv) and has sought to discover "ways of writing I could regard as philosophical and could recognize as sometimes extensions—hence sometimes denials—of Wittgenstein's" (*Claim*, xv), one might ask whether there are things that Cavell's and Wittgenstein's ways of writing share. What does Cavell point us to in Wittgenstein's writing?

Neither claims to advance philosophical theses, for instance. I quoted earlier a passage suggesting that Cavell had no pretension to formal argument or poetic persuasion. He remarks, even more strikingly, on Wittgenstein's writing:

There is exhortation, ("Do not say: 'there *must* be something common' . . . but *look* and *see* . . . ") not to belief but to self-scrutiny. And that is why there is virtually nothing in the *Investigations* which we should ordinarily call reasoning; Wittgenstein asserts nothing which could be proved, for what he asserts is either obvious—whether true or false—or else concerned with what conviction, whether by proof or evidence or authority would consist in. Otherwise there are questions, jokes, parables, and propositions so striking that they stun belief. (Are we asked to believe that "if a lion could talk we could not understand him")? Belief is not enough. Either the suggestion penetrates past assessment and becomes part of the sensibility from which assessment proceeds, or it is philosophically useless.[21]

This strikes me as a very significant and acute passage. It is also, of course, a very strong contention: that what does not penetrate past assessment is philosophically useless. That sets high standards for philosophical utility. The goal of penetrating past assessment to become part of the sensibility from which assessment proceeds is a daunting one, a real challenge for philosophical style. But it is clear also that skillful writing is what it calls for: writing that appeals to the other, not to persuade but to find an echo and ultimately to receive acknowledgment.

Wittgenstein's writing works out methods for attaining self-knowledge that aspires also to be knowledge of others: posing questions where readers must try out their responses to an imagined situation, seeing what might be said and meant. He makes very heavy use of questions, for example (as does Judith Butler, I might mention); and he goes to much trouble, Cavell writes, "to give them a rhetorical air," as in "What gives the impression that we want to deny anything?" which certainly seems to suggest that he is not denying anything.[22] "He wants to leave that way of taking them open to us, to make it hard to see that they needn't be taken rhetorically, that instead the question is one he is genuinely asking, asking himself, and asking us to ask ourselves. The implication of this literary procedure here

21. Stanley Cavell, "The Availability of Wittgenstein's Later Philosophy," in *Must We Mean What We Say? A Book of Essays* (Cambridge, UK: Cambridge University Press, 1976), 71.

22. Wittgenstein, *Investigations*, 102.

is that it is difficult to see that such a question genuinely needs asking, difficult to ask it genuinely" (*Claim*, 103). This claim—about the function of making something difficult so that the reader may need aggressively to make an effort to ask a question seriously—may provide clues to some of Cavell's own writing decisions.

Cavell sees the *Investigations* as engaging in the mode of the confession—not because it offers personal information but because in confessing what you would or would not say, what you are tempted to say or resist saying, "you do not explain or justify, but describe how it is with you. And confession, unlike dogma, is not to be believed but tested, and accepted or rejected."[23] The *Investigations* is convincing because its questions and suppositions play out a desire, a willingness to resist the temptations of habitual misunderstandings. Wittgenstein's talk of what "we say" or would not say adduces his linguistic intuitions, his sense of our ways of talking and thinking. "And the fact is," Cavell writes, "so much of what he shows to be true of his consciousness is true of ours (of mine). This is perhaps the fact of his writing to be most impressed by; it may be the fact that he is most impressed by—that it can be done at all" (*Claim*, 20). Elsewhere Cavell notes that "skepticism about our knowledge of others is frequently accompanied by complacency about our knowledge of ourselves" but that those who historically have been capable of the deepest personal confession (such as Augustine, Rousseau, Thoreau, Kierkegaard, and Freud) have been those "most convinced that they were speaking from the most hidden knowledge of others" (*Claim*, 109). In such cases, of course, the universal bearing of the confession is inextricable from the skill of writers. To write convincingly about the self is to write about others as well.

In Cavell and Wittgenstein the attempt to make suggestions that may have a chance to penetrate past assessment also generates language that attempts to get attention, to stop you, even to make itself memorable, as in Wittgenstein's famous aphorisms: "Why can't a dog tell a lie? Is it because he is too honest?" But Cavell does not attempt aphorism. He is concerned to spell out, inviting participation and recognition, once he has secured attention; his mode is capacious, exfoliating, running to parentheses and qualification. The larger part of *The Claim of Reason* engages in very laborious examination of Wittgensteinian problems, with Cavell imagining questions and questioners, offering discriminations about pre-

23. Cavell, *Must We Mean What We Say?* 71.

cisely what concerns him here and what does not, reflecting on the meaning of the various terms we might or might not offer in connection with such dialogues. This is prose that flows on continuously, with passages that go on and on—at the opposite remove, it might seem, from the paratactic paragraphs of the *Investigations*. Yet, in the end, in one way the effect is surprisingly similar. Just as you can't read Wittgenstein straight through but must stop and become involved in the little dramas of questioning and self-questioning his fragments stage, so with Cavell, I find, you cannot read straight through to find out what he is saying but have to break the text into short chunks (four or five pages at a time is my limit) and allow yourself to get engaged in puzzling over these matters. You must forget or at least set aside the fact that there are more than five hundred pages to this book and read as if it were a series of short scenarios.[24]

Cavell does not, to my knowledge, talk about what might count as bad style in philosophy, but he is critical of philosophy's habit of proceeding by charging other philosophers with mistakes, nonsense, blindness, contradiction, circularity, what have you. Nozick, for instance, reports in *Philosophical Explanation* that he "usually reads works of philosophy with all defenses up, with a view to finding out where the author has gone wrong."[25] This leads to the situation Cavell regrets, where any graduate student can rehearse "how Descartes was mistaken about dreams, or Locke about truth or Berkeley about God or Kant about things in themselves or moral worth, or Hegel about logic, and so forth."[26] But what if philosophers, following Austin's analysis of what is involved in doing something by accident or by mistake (his analysis and not his own conduct in charging other philosophers with mistakes), were to "grant to other philosophers the ordinary rights of language and vision that Austin grants all other men: to ask them, in his spirit, why they should say what they say where and when they say it, and to give the full story before claiming satisfaction."[27] Then just as ordinary language philosophy ties understanding to the elucidation of underlying consistencies or acknowledgment of commonality, so philosophy might become less of an esoteric battle and

24. My own preference, therefore, is for the shorter essays of *Must We Mean What We Say?*

25. Nozick, *Philosophical Explanations*, 6.

26. Cavell, "Austin at Criticism," in *Must We Mean What We Say?* 111.

27. Ibid.

more of an enterprise of understanding. Cavell recommends, at least, that philosophy treat criticisms it feels "phenomenologically, as temptations or feelings; in a word, as data not answers" (110). In sum, the goal should be not to find mistakes in other philosophers but to understand from within, in the hope of reaching, if not understanding and agreement, recognition and acknowledgment.

In something of this spirit, in a fine essay, "Aesthetic Problems of Modern Philosophy," Cavell takes up an issue in philosophy where it is hard to imagine reconciliation. Kant distinguishes the judgment that something is pleasant (canary wine is pleasant—which means "pleasant to me") from the judgment that an aesthetic object is beautiful (it would be "laughable," he says, to justify oneself by saying it is "beautiful to me"). The latter judgment demands or claims or imputes general validity. There is thus supposed to be a difference of kind in the judgments involved. "One hardly knows," writes Cavell, "whether to call this a metaphysical or a logical difference. Kant called it a transcendental difference; Wittgenstein would call it a grammatical difference. But how can psychological differences like finding something laughable or foolish (which perhaps not *every* person would) be thought to betray such potent, or anyway different, differences?"[28] Cavell continues:

Here we hit upon what is to my mind the most sensitive index of misunderstanding and bitterness between the positivist and the post-positivist components of analytical philosophy: the positivist grits his teeth when he hears an analysis given out as the logical one which is so painfully remote from formality, so obviously a question of how you happen to feel at the moment, so "psychological"; the philosopher who proceeds from everyday language stares back helplessly, asking, "Don't you feel the difference? Listen, you *must* see it?" Surely both know what the other knows and each thinks the other is perverse, or irrelevant, or worse.[29]

He sets out to describe why philosophers like him want to call such differences logical, in responding to the element of necessity felt in them, together with a sense of the ways such judgments are supported and conviction produced—by recurrent patterns of support. And he goes on to argue

28. Cavell, "Aesthetic Problems of Modern Philosophy," in *Must We Mean What We Say?* 90.
29. Ibid.

that Kant's aesthetic judgments, with their "universal" character that does not depend on empirical evidence about assent, are similar to philosophers' claims about "what we say." If you disagree you do not try to collect data but try to determine why, and if you cannot explain the disagreement, you try to find an explanation for that, with different examples.

"The philosopher appealing to everyday language," he writes, "turns to the reader not to convince him without proof but to get him to prove something, test something, against himself. He is saying: look and find out whether you can see what I see, wish to say what I wish to say. . . . [Finally] all the philosopher, this kind of philosopher, can do is express, as fully as he can, his world and attract our undivided attention to our own."[30]

The reader may well be put off or be preoccupied with other things, but language that gets one's attention may also, unpredictably, give conviction a chance to happen. Or rather—since Cavell says that unless suggestion penetrates past assessment, it is philosophically useless—we might speak of the reader "getting the hang of it": coming to participate in a way of thinking that feels right, as something he or she can now do.

It is to give this unpredictable possibility a chance that Cavell writes this stylish, mannered prose designed to capture attention. If it aspires to provocation rather than instruction, it nevertheless instructs, if you take it in small enough chunks that its *longueurs* become occasions for reflection—leading you to see something for yourself—rather than for irritation. It can be remarkable philosophy, even though its parts, such as the opening sentence of *The Claim of Reason*, could win any bad writing contest.

30. Ibid., 96.

10

Writing Criticism

To discuss writing criticism these days is a daunting task. Literature professors write about the text of *Piers Plowman*, breast-feeding in the
French Revolution, the image of cigarettes in modern literature and culture. How to talk about writing criticism without being hopelessly plural-
istic or excessively polemical? One ought in principle to be able to analyze
one's discipline as a discursive practice, where knowledge is produced by
its ways of writing, and in principle one ought to be able to characterize
changes in the discipline as changes in modes of writing; but the prospect
of examining crucial moments in the history of literary studies and especially influential texts that have shaped it seems too vast a project.[1] One
way to make it more manageable is to discuss the history of my own in-
volvement with the discipline: what sort of writing first engaged me and
how my sense of the most attractive disciplinary practices and possibilities
has changed over the years, in response to particular instances of critical
writing. I can thus treat criticism as a practice of writing by analyzing some
essays that have been important for me, that embody significant shifts in
the discipline, and that involve distinctive ways of writing criticism. After
all, one's sense of what it is to work in a particular field derives from possibilities enacted in key texts.

    1. In his invitation to tackle this topic for a lecture series titled "Writing the
Disciplines," Jonathan Monroe suggested that contributors might take as their
model Eric Auerbach's *Mimesis*—which of course did not reassure us about the
feasibility of the project.

I first gained a sense of literary study as a discipline based on principles of criticism in my first year as an undergraduate, when my graduate-student tutor assigned a comparison of essays by Cleanth Brooks and Douglas Bush. In 1962 this exchange was already ten years old, but it helps define a shift in the practice of criticism after World War II. Brooks, a leader among the so-called New Critics, had published an essay on Andrew Marvell's "Horatian Ode," to which Douglas Bush, a literary historian, replied.[2]

Marvell wrote "An Horatian Ode upon Cromwell's Return from Ireland" after Oliver Cromwell, who had previously led the Parliament to victory in the English Civil War and brought about the execution of Charles I, had, with an English army, ruthlessly put down an Irish rebellion. Here is a problematical passage in the poem, about which Bush and Brooks argue.

And now the Irish are asham'd
To see themselves in one Year tam'd:
  So much one Man can do,
  That does both act and know.
They can affirm his Praises best,
And have, though overcome confest
  How good he is, how just,
  And fit for highest trust.

Is this jokey, facetious, sardonic, ironic, or a serious claim about the Irish? Brooks argues that if the poem is any good, this passage must make sense *dramatically*. As a straightforward claim—that the defeated Irish confess how good Cromwell is, how just—it would be foolish, a blemish on the poem as a whole, which Brooks sees as a complex, balanced portrait full of judicious but often double-edged praise of Cromwell. Brooks hears a grim irony in these lines: the Irish who have been crushed can tell just how just he is (with a sword at their throat, they confess how good he is . . .).

2. Cleanth Brooks, "Literary Criticism," in *English Institute Essays* (New York: Columbia University Press, 1946), 127–58; Douglas Bush, "Marvell's Horatian Ode," *Sewanee Review* 60 (1952): 363–76; Cleanth Brooks, "A Note on the Limits of 'History' and the Limits of 'Criticism,'" *Sewanee Review* 61 (1953): 129–35. The exchange is collected in *Seventeenth Century English Poetry: Modern Essays in Criticism*, ed. W. R. Keast (Oxford, UK: Oxford University Press, 1962), 321–58. References to this edition will be abbreviated *SCEP* and cited parenthetically in the text.

Bush calls this a "desperate solution." Nothing in the wording carries "the faintest trace of irony; it is as straightforward a statement as we
could have, however little we like it" (*SCEP*, 349). He is not worried about
how it fits into the poem or whether it is a blemish: "we really must accept
the unpalatable fact that Marvell wrote as an Englishman of 1650; and, in
regard to what seems to us a strange assertion, we must say he is indulging in some wishful thinking—Cromwell is so great a conqueror that even
the Irish must share English sentiment and accept the course of history"
(*SCEP*, 349). But note that even Bush cannot stomach the literal claim of
these lines—that the Irish have "confessed how good he is, how just"—and
he paraphrases this as "accept the course of history." Here, as often, writing
criticism is a matter of seeking a paraphrase or reformulation that bears a
plausible relation to the text while fitting an argument. And critical debate
at the microlevel bears on the supposed distortions accomplished by others' paraphrases.

At stake in this disagreement are several principles. First, Brooks insists that, considering the poem as a critic, one must focus on whether its
elements contribute to an artistic unity—a matter that does not bother the
literary historian. "If we unify the poem," Brooks writes, "by saying that it
reflects the uncertainties and contradictions of a man who was uncertain
and self-contradictory, and sometimes foolish, . . . then we may have a useful historical document but I am not sure that we have a poem" (*SCEP*,
356). The fact that he worries about how to read these lines as contributing to the whole, whereas Bush does not, shows, Brooks says, how different their aims are.

Second, whereas Bush in his response focuses on what historical evidence can tell us about what Marvell thought at the time when he wrote
the ode, for Brooks this is a "coarse method" that will not tell us what the
poem says because (1) even if we knew what Marvell the man thought of
Cromwell at the moment he was writing the poem, the man is not the
same as the poet (who is, for instance, composing a Horatian Ode); and
(2) even if we knew what Marvell the poet intended to say in his poem,
this would not prove that the poem actually said this. Brooks writes, "there
is surely a sense in which anyone must agree that a poem has a life of its
own. . . . [T]he poet sometimes writes better than he knows" (*SCEP*, 322).
We are trying to read the poem and thus appeal "to the full context of

the poem itself," not to Marvell's mind. For Brooks, what determines the meaning of these lines is how they function in the context of the poem as a whole, not what we imagine Marvell the man thought at the time. It is a problem of poetic organization not of biography or history.

Bush disputes what he calls "such an arbitrary doctrine of criticism" (*SCEP*, 341). He quarrels with Brooks's identification of ironies and ambiguities, casting himself as a historian for whom the text means what it says (given historical knowledge), and he accuses Brooks of forcing the poem to fit the prejudices of a good modern liberal, for whom it goes without saying that a smart sensitive fellow like Marvell could not have admired a crude, ruthless man of action like Cromwell, who must have been something like a Puritan Stalin (*SCEP*, 342). Brooks replies, "The title *liberal* alas, is one that I am scarcely entitled to claim. I am more often called a reactionary, and I have been called a proto-fascist" (*SCEP*, 354). This particular point shows the difficulty of relating what a text says to the opinions of its historical author: Bush's incorrect inference from Brooks's text to the supposedly liberal opinions of its historical author, Cleanth Brooks, shows that one cannot presume continuity between what the text says and what the historical individual believes.

What is at stake here for writing criticism? First, the principle, central to the New Criticism, of separating what the text says from what the empirical author may have thought, instead of assuming that the way to determine what a text means is to investigate the historical experience of the author. The reasons for driving a wedge between what is in the author's mind and what is on the page are two: writing a poem is different from, say, recording one's thoughts, and poets may not in any event accomplish what they intend. This separation of the meaning of the text from the historical experience of the author retains considerable critical importance today. In a post–New Critical age it gives new interest to biographical criticism, which, in taking for granted this separation, can then work on the relation between the historical intentions of authors and what their works actually achieve. For instance, Jacques Derrida in his reading of Rousseau contrasts what Rousseau wants to say and what his text ends up doing.[3]

Second, the New Critical separation between thinking of the poem

3. See, e.g., Jacques Derrida, *Of Grammatology* (Baltimore: Johns Hopkins University Press, 1976), 141–64.

as a work of art and thinking of it as a historical document has in our day
made possible a new historicist criticism that returns to that scene, not,
like the old historicism, to equate the meaning of the work with what
Marvell the historical author thought but to contrast the work's aesthetic
purpose and unity with its status as a historical act. As a historical event its
relations to other discourses of the day give it a particular ideological function. The separation permits a better historicism than one that must claim
that what it investigates is the meaning of the work.

Brooks claimed in 1943 that the New Criticism had almost no influence in universities; by 1962 it was still contested—it was a distinctly mi-
nority position at Harvard, for instance, which added to its appeal for me.
An orthodox New Criticism never became hegemonic, but one respect in
which it undoubtedly did triumph was in establishing the assumption,
which still holds sway, that in general the test of any critical activity is
whether it helps us produce new, richer, more compelling interpretations
of particular literary works. One effect of this assumption is the creation of
a new type of knowledge: previously, to put it crudely, what had counted
as knowledge was historical and philological information; now to produce
interpretations of poems is to make a contribution to knowledge, and this
knowledge is a form of writing, something that must be written, not just
written up. Historical or philological investigations may achieve a positive
result—a demonstration that Marvell did serve in the Civil War or that a
poem falsely attributed to others is really his; but interpretative criticism
yields not a result that can be summed up but a text that tries to render explicit the structure of meaning and implication woven through a poem.

Let us consider a few more lines of this writing. Bush quotes the lines
that immediately follow the passage about the Irish:

> How good he is, how just,
>   And fit for highest trust,
> Nor yet grown stiffer with command,
> But still in the Republic's hand.

Bush writes,

Says Mr. Brooks: "Does the emphasis on 'still' mean that the speaker is surprised
that Cromwell has continued to play homage to the republic? Does he imply that
Cromwell may not always do so? Perhaps not: the emphasis is upon the fact that

he need not obey and yet does. Yet the compliment derives its full force from the fact that the homage is not forced but voluntary and even somewhat unexpected. And a recognition of the point implies the recognition of the possibility that Cromwell will not always so defer to the commonwealth." But such darker connotations are quite gratuitous. "Still" here—as later in "Still keep thy sword erect"—has its normal seventeenth-century meaning, "always." (*SCEP*, 350)

Bush is rejecting what he calls illegitimate ambiguities that Brooks detects, such as the possibility that "still" implies that he may not always defer.

Brooks writes the quoted paragraph to argue that Marvell's praise of Cromwell at this point is ambiguous, but notice how obliquely Brooks puts it: "Does he imply . . . ? Perhaps not." He is bending over backward to fit into a critical consensus, to avoid appearing to deny anything that other critics might think about the meaning of the poem, while nevertheless opening the possibility of a slight ambiguity that he hopes others will find plausible. Recall the passage from Brooks I quoted earlier: "surely everyone would agree that there is a sense in which a poem has a life of its own." There seems a presumption that there will be a critical consensus, that one must be careful not to say something blatant that might seem extreme, so that others will be brought along with you by virtue of your very reasonableness. Interpretation has to be new (otherwise why write it) but acceptable, convincing to those who had previously read things differently. It is as if that ability to enter the consensus one seeks mildly to expand were the test of critical writing. But note that this is a *convention* of critical writing rather than a reality of critical debate, as we see from the fact that Douglas Bush is not seduced or deceived: he takes Brooks, for all his modest reasonableness, to be making a strong claim—one that he disputes. In this mode of writing, "Surely . . . " or "we would all agree that . . . " becomes a sign that something contestable is being said. Brooks's method of writing criticism works to suggest the ambiguity, plant the seed, so that the reader will find it plausible, as something he or she now sees in the poem. That is how this sort of knowledge is written.

Another striking feature of this passage is that neither critic even alludes to what is likely to leap off the page to a modern reader in "Nor yet grown stiffer with Command, / But still in the republic's hand"—lines that seem to cast Cromwell as a phallus that might grow stiff by itself in the thrill of command but may also be a tool in the republic's hand, whereby it experiences its potency and pleasures itself. (The poem proceeds to declare that it is wonderful for England to have a Caesar who will conquer new empires for it.) Today, critics might feel it necessary at least to acknowledge the possibility of some such line of reflection so as not to be thought obtuse about the suggestiveness of words or blinkered by conventional thinking. The age of Monica Lewinsky and *Sex and the City* knows different standards of what can be entertained.

Such texts as Brooks's encouraged me to adopt a resolutely New Critical attitude in my college years. The critical task was to show how the various parts of a poem fit together, to track as closely and sensitively as possible the stances, tones, attitudes of a poem, treating it as the act of a speaker (not to be equated with the biographical author) whose shifting affects and tones were to be captured in a work of writing: a response that explains and espouses the poem. If critical writing shows that the work is more complicated, ironical, and self-reflexive than others had thought, all the better.

The New Critical task is not one of which you can ever feel master: trying to translate the experience of the poem into knowledge, to analyze poetry in prose, you find that there always remain puzzling elements in the poem or a tone that is hard to identify or assess. It is a continuing challenge for writing, for the imagination. But the parameters of the task seemed well known—work out what is being said with what affect, demonstrate the subtlety, complexity, and unity of the work as a whole—and debates like the Brooks/Bush exchange made it clear that the rules could be challenged. By the end of my undergraduate years I felt ready to question both conventions of the interpretive project (such as treating the poem as, in effect, a dramatic monologue) and the project itself, the presuppositions of criticism. I began to study philosophy, linguistics, and literary theory, not to leave criticism but to reflect on its presuppositions.

Many texts could illustrate this sort of trajectory. Let me offer a slim example by Roland Barthes. As the leading French structuralist in the field of literary studies, Barthes was of great importance to me (in 1979 Wayne Booth even called him "the man who may well be the strongest influence on American criticism today"—though I think that was above all a complaint about people like me).[4] In a little paper from 1968 called

4. Wayne Booth, *Critical Understanding: The Power and Limits of Pluralism* (Chicago: University of Chicago Press, 1979), 69.

"L'effet de réel" [The Reality Effect] Barthes begins with a sentence from Flaubert's "Un cœur simple." Describing a room, the narrator tells us that "an old piano supported, beneath a barometer, a pyramidal heap of boxes and cartons."

For Brooks the task of critical writing is to show how every detail of a text contributes to the organic effect of the whole, but what of descriptive details like these? Barthes writes,

if it is possible to see in the notation of the piano an indication of its owner's bourgeois standing and in that of the cartons a sign of disorder and a kind of lapse in status likely to connote the atmosphere of the Aubain household, no purpose seems to justify a reference to the barometer, an object neither incongruous nor significant, and therefore not participating, at first glance, in the order of the *notable*.[5]

Barthes concludes that in modern literature there is an opposition between meaning or function on the one hand and reality on the other. There is an assumption, deeply ingrained in Western culture, that the world—reality—is what is simply there, prior to our perception of it or interpretation of it. What does not bear meaning or is not being interpreted may thus stand for the real. When there occur items that have no role in the plot and do not tell us anything about the character, this very absence of meaning enables them to anchor the story in the real but, Barthes emphasizes, not by denoting reality but by connoting it. "It is the category of the real which is then signified."[6] The more meaningless the details, Barthes concludes, the more vigorously they signify, "we are the real."

What is different in this kind of criticism is, most obviously, the goal, which is not to produce a new and improved interpretation of Flaubert's story. Barthes is working to advance a theoretical understanding of literary discourse. This is poetics rather than hermeneutics. That is a distinction made clear by an analogy with linguistics, which offered a model for literary studies in the structuralist ambiance of the late 1960s and 1970s. Linguistics does not produce new interpretations of English sentences but attempts to make explicit the underlying set of rules—the grammar of a language—that enables these sequences of sounds to have the meanings

5. Roland Barthes, "The Reality Effect," in *The Rustle of Language* (Berkeley: University of California Press, 1989), 142.
6. Ibid., 148.

they do for speakers of the language. So a poetics modeled on linguistics seeks not to provide new interpretations of literary works but to understand the conventions and techniques that enable them to have the effects they do (what makes this passage ironic? why is the ending of a poem ambiguous? and so forth).

My *Structuralist Poetics* argued that literary studies should abandon hermeneutics for poetics.[7] We have plenty of interpretations of literary works, and people will certainly go on interpreting in any event, yet we still don't understand very well how literature works. But this attempt to change the paradigm did not succeed, and critics and theorists in America were incredibly swift to embrace the idea of *post*structuralism so that they could believe that the systematic projects of structuralism were passé and so we could happily go on interpreting, though in a new, decentered way.

Why should this have happened? First, there are good reasons for doubting the possibility of achieving a comprehensive poetics, for as soon as any convention is recognized as such, literary works seek to outplay it. But the main reason for resisting poetics is the lure of interpretation, which is extraordinarily powerful in literary studies. If people study works of literature, it is generally because they think these works have important things to tell them and they want to know what those things are. Moreover, it is easy enough to convince oneself that the payoff for investigating some aspect of narrative or of literary discourse generally should be the ability to understand better the works that interest you. What tends to happen, then, is that interesting work in poetics is mistaken for or converted into an interpretive claim. Thus, the payoff of Barthes' identification of the "reality effect" is the possibility of reinterpreting "Un cœur simple," for instance as "really about" (as we say in the business) the problematic relation between reality and signification. At the same time that I was writing *Structuralist Poetics* I wrote a book on Flaubert in which I argued that what these novels are really about is the exposure of the contingent and conventional nature of human attempts to make sense of experience and thus the ultimate vanity (though inescapable necessity) of the attempt to impose meaning on things.[8]

7. Jonathan Culler, *Structuralist Poetics: Structuralism, Linguistics, and the Study of Literature* (London: Routledge, 1975).

8. Jonathan Culler, *Flaubert: The Uses of Uncertainty* (Ithaca, NY: Cornell University Press, 1974).

This propensity in literary studies to convert poetics into hermeneutics applies not just to formal investigations like Barthes' but to all sorts of claims about conditions of possibility of literary effects. For instance, as I mentioned in Chapter 7, Toni Morrison's *Playing in the Dark: Whiteness and the American Literary Imagination* offers a brilliant account of how the most distinctive characteristics of American literature—the thematic focus on freedom, autonomy, authority, and absolute power—have as their condition of possibility what she terms America's Africanist presence—the centuries-old presence in the United States of African slaves and then, after emancipation, of the memory and the social consequences of slavery. The Africanist presence provides the grounds for the elaboration of American identity, with the emphasis on the quest for freedom and autonomy. Thus, for instance, "the concept of freedom did not emerge in a vacuum. Nothing highlighted freedom—if it did not in fact create it—like slavery."[9]

This is poetics, in the form of a speculative account of a framework for accounting for the effects of literary works, especially the distinctive qualities of American literature; but it becomes available as a resource for interpretation, so after Morrison one can write about the hidden (occulted) Africanist presence in a given work. (Indeed, if the Africanist presence is a condition of possibility, then the fact that there are not overt traces of it in a given work—that it is repressed—is all the more noteworthy.) This situation can give rise to interpretations that seem extreme, strained, partial—a familiar experience in reading contemporary critical writing, where what has been posited as an important aspect of literary discourse of a period or in general is transformed, by the conversion of poetics into hermeneutics, into what the work at some level is *really about*. Let me stress that if it is true that the thematic concerns of American literature are the product of the presence of an Africanist other, then this is true even for those works where there is no mention of slaves, slavery, or Africa. But it does not follow that interpretation of those works should focus on a concealed Africanism. Hermeneutics is not poetics. The assumption that the payoff of critical work should be the interpretation of individual works is what can lead from powerful theoretical investigations to what are perceived as partial or strained interpretations.

Many of the so-called schools of modern criticism derive from the-

9. Toni Morrison, *Playing in the Dark: Whiteness and the American Literary Imagination* (Cambridge, MA: Harvard University Press, 1992), 38.

oretical accounts of what is held to be most important in language, culture, and society, but when converted to hermeneutic enterprises, these schools give rise to particular interpretations, easily satirized as what each predictably takes the literary work to be ultimately about: the class struggle (Marxism), the Oedipal conflict (psychoanalysis), the containment of subversive energies (New Historicism), the self-deconstructive nature of the text (deconstruction), the asymmetry of gender relations (feminism), imperialism and the hybridities it generates (postcolonial theory). It is the persistence of the notion of interpretation as the task and goal of literary study that generates this result.

But I have leaped ahead of my autobiographical narrative. A way to gauge the shifts in conventions of writing interpretive criticism in recent years is to juxtapose an essay by Cleanth Brooks with Paul de Man's reflections on the same text, W. B. Yeats's poem "Among School Children." In *The Well-Wrought Urn* Brooks devotes a chapter to this poem, exploring its dramatic structure and its complex attitudes by following the movement of the poetic speaker's mind. De Man, on the other hand, is not interested in the speaker, his tone, or the complexity of his attitude toward love, mortality, his past, and the "presences" that break hearts but in the relation between grammatical structure and rhetorical figure in the concluding stanza:

O chestnut-tree, great-rooted blossomer,
Are you the leaf, the blossom, or the bole?
O body swayed to music, o brightening glance,
How can we know the dancer from the dance?

Critics read these sentences as rhetorical questions asserting the impossibility of telling the dancer from the dance or the inappropriateness of trying to divide a living unity into its constituents. Brooks writes, with a characteristic twist of turning the poem on itself, "Certainly, we ought to do no less here than apply Yeats's doctrine to his own poem. The poem, like the 'great-rooted blossomer' that it celebrates, is not to be isolated in the 'statement' made by Stanza V or by Stanza VII, or by Stanza VIII." We must not mistake a part of the poem or tree for the whole, investigating "the root system (the study of literary sources) or sniffing the blossoms (impressionism) or . . . questioning the quondam dancer about her life history (the

study of the poet's biography)."[10] We must experience the dramatic structure of the whole.

Brooks confidently takes the apostrophes to the chestnut tree and
the body swayed to music as rhetorical questions: obviously the tree is not
to be equated with one of its parts or the dancer distinguished from the
dance. But "it is equally possible," de Man writes, "to read the last line lit-
erally rather than figuratively, as asking with some urgency the question
. . . how can we possibly make the distinctions that would shelter us from
the error of identifying what cannot be identified? . . . The figural reading,
which assumes the question to be rhetorical, is perhaps naïve, whereas the
literal reading leads to greater complication of theme and statement."[11]

Now the normal standard of critical judgment would be to ask which
interpretation—literal question or rhetorical question—better accords
with the rest of the poem. But de Man goes out of his way to note that
the figural reading can yield a coherent interpretation, and he sketches the
alternative (literal) line of interpretation in a most offhand fashion without attempting to convince. He is not trying to produce a more complete
or convincing interpretation. In fact, what is at issue is precisely the critical principle of using notions of unity and thematic coherence to exclude
possibilities awakened by structures of the language. The literal reading of
Yeats's question, as urgently asking how we can make the distinction so as
not to be misled, cannot be dismissed as irrelevant. "The two readings,"
de Man writes, "have to engage each other in direct confrontation, for the
one reading is precisely the error denounced by the other and has to be
undone by it." We cannot justifiably choose one and reject the other, but
we are compelled to choose: "the authority of the meaning engendered by
the grammatical structure is fully obscured by the duplicity of a figure that
cries out for the differentiation that it conceals."[12]

How to explain this sentence that twists around itself? The rhetorical question here is a duplicitous figure that conceals a differentiation (between dancer and dance) while demanding or relying on or crying out for

10. Cleanth Brooks, *The Well-Wrought Urn* (New York: Harcourt Brace,
1947), 185, 191.

11. Paul de Man, "Semiology and Rhetoric," in *Allegories of Reading: Figural
Language in Rousseau, Nietzsche, Rilke, and Proust* (New Haven, CT: Yale University Press, 1979), 11.

12. Ibid., 12.

a version of the same differentiation (between entity and performance). To take Yeats's question as a rhetorical question is to assume that we *cannot* tell the difference between the dancer and the dance—say an entity and its performance. On the other hand, the very idea of a rhetorical question depends on the general possibility of distinguishing a form or grammatical structure on the one hand from its rhetorical performance on the other. How can we simultaneously distinguish the grammatical question from its rhetorical performance and take it for granted that we *cannot distinguish* the dancer from the dance? The claim that Brooks and others have interpreted the poem as making—the affirmation of fusion or continuity (the impossibility of making a distinction)—is subverted by the discontinuity (between the interrogative grammatical structure and the noninterrogative figure of the rhetorical question) that has to be assumed in order to infer the claim of continuity.

The contrast between de Man's and Brooks's essays gives us a number of differences. Most obviously, perhaps, de Man's key sentences, whose twistedness is an emblem of the complexities of a thought interrogating the relations between levels of discourse, are engaged in a different activity from Brooks's conciliatory appeals to a critical consensus that they attempt to enrich. De Man is not alerting us to a new possibility we might want to consider but identifying what he claims is an ineluctable necessity, whether or not we see it. Though he is not here attempting to put forward a new interpretation of the poem, his emphasis on the necessity of choosing an interpretation without valid grounds for choice—what he elsewhere calls an "aporia"—could itself be a type of interpretation, and de Man usually undertakes powerful and detailed interpretations of texts or portions thereof in pursuing a theoretical issue.

The unity of the poem (Brooks's watchword) has not vanished, but it is no longer conceived as an organic unity—harmonious balance and continuous functionality, with every part contributing to the effect of the whole. It is the *presumption* of unity, though, that highlights dissonance or self-division, as here between what has to be assumed to infer the figural meaning and the implications of the meaning inferred. A most striking contrast here is the different understandings of the self-reflexivity of literature. For the New Criticism, poems are ultimately about poetry or sense-making, and a strategy of critical writing is to work out what the poem says about poetry and interpretation (Brooks, you recall, asks us to apply Yeats's doctrine to his own poem). In effect, self-referentiality closes off interpretation, which is how it came to be associated with a poem's organic unity. But for de Man the self-referentiality of the text is what ruins any organic unity: the poem fails to practice what it preaches; self-reference opens a gap, as in the notorious logical paradox of the Cretan liar (if his claim that all Cretans are liars is true, then he is a liar, but if he lies, then his claim is the more true). In general, self-referentiality does not create a self-enclosed organic unity but paradoxical relations between what is said and how it is said and inaugurates an impossible and therefore open-ended process of self-framing.

Finally, note that de Man does not focus on the posture and stance of the speaker as Brooks does. No longer unified as the act of a posited speaker (separated from the poet him- or herself), the poem is a rhetorical construction, subject to comparison with other sorts of discourses, in an investigation of aspects of language. (In de Man's previous example in the essay, Archie Bunker dismissively replies, "What's the difference?" to Edith's question of whether he wants his bowling shoes laced under or laced over. To understand his utterance as denying difference, one must, as in the Yeats example, differentiate the grammatical form from rhetorical performance.)

But de Man's powerful text is itself now more than twenty years old. Let me, like Auerbach, leap another couple of decades to my last text—an instance of the critical writing I particularly admire today. Since difference from Cleanth Brooks seems my principle of selection, I turn to an essay that starts from Keats's "Ode on a Grecian Urn," the poem that furnishes the title of Brooks's *The Well-Wrought Urn*. This is Barbara Johnson's "Muteness Envy," in her book *The Feminist Difference*.

This exemplary piece, which highlights the importance of cultural studies in the field of literary criticism, reads Keats's ode, with its "still unravished bride of quietness," against Jane Campion's film *The Piano* and the critical reception of the film in order to explore the cultural construction and aestheticization of female muteness as a repository of feminine value. (Johnson notes that "it's no accident that every actress who has been nominated for playing the part of a mute woman—Jane Wyman, Patty Duke, Marlee Matlin, and Holly Hunter—has won an Oscar"—an astonishing fact).[13]

The feminine urn of Keats's ode—"Thou still unravished bride of quietness"—is celebrated for its mute tales and melodies, sweeter than poetry or audible music. Do male poets celebrating mute speech suffer from "muteness envy," as women are said to suffer from penis envy—envying that thing they cannot by definition have if they are to be poets? Jacques Lacan, notoriously, treats feminine jouissance as something about which women remain mute—"we've been begging them on our knees to tell us about it—well, not a word!"—and he looks to Bernini's silent statue of St. Teresa for information. With Keats's ode, Johnson writes,

> the question of feminine *jouissance* (or lack of it) is very much at issue. By calling the urn a "still unravished bride," Keats implies that the urn's destiny is to become a *ravished* bride. The word "ravished" can mean either "raped" or "sent into ecstasy." Both possibilities are readable in the scenes depicted on the urn:

> > What men or gods are these? What maidens loth?
> > What mad pursuit? What struggle to escape?
> > What pipes and timbrels? What wild ecstasy?

> The privileged aesthetic moment is a freeze frame just prior to ravishment. But how does pressing the pause button here make us sublate the scene of male sexual violence into a scene of general ecstasy? How does the maiden's struggle to escape congeal into aesthetic triumph? (*FD*, 134–35)

The tradition provides similar scenarios: when Daphne turns into a laurel tree in order to escape rape at the hands of Apollo, he gets to pluck a laurel branch as sign of an aesthetic triumph that elides sexual violence. Glancing at some other examples, Johnson concludes that the work performed by the idealization of women's silence is that "it helps culture not to be able to tell the difference between their pleasure and their violation" (*FD*, 137).

Johnson turns to Jane Campion's *The Piano*, with its mute heroine, Ada, where the question of violence or pleasure arises. "What is the movie saying about the muteness that articulates and confuses women's oppression and women's desire?" Reactions to the film by readers and critics have

13. Barbara Johnson, *The Feminist Difference: Literature, Psychoanalysis, Race, and Gender* (Cambridge, MA: Harvard University Press, 1998), 150; hereafter abbreviated *FD* and cited parenthetically in the text.

been remarkably varied. "Like the aesthetic tradition on which it implicitly comments, *The Piano* seems to be about telling, or not telling, the difference between women's violation and women's pleasure" (*FD*, 147). Those who view it as a love story concentrate on the characters: from this point of view Ada's muteness is not passivity but a form of resistance and subjecthood; she is a vital character. But the *framework* within which the film places her makes her an object of male bargains and violence. The frame of the movie "says that women can find the way of their desire within a structure in which they are traded between men" (*FD*, 147).

Interestingly, the viewers intent on proving that Ada is not a victim, that her muteness is not silence, seem determined to produce a silenced woman elsewhere, castigating the *Boston Globe* for allowing its female reviewer to object to the film. And the question of muteness does not stop there. *Newsweek* reports that men who had felt silenced by the hoopla surrounding the film are finally daring to utter their dislike ("Slowly, timidly the naysayers are gathering courage to speak . . . ") (*FD*, 150). The whole thing, Johnson writes, "becomes a political game of muteness, muteness, who's got the muteness" (*FD*, 150).

Why, she asks, are so many white men—from Petrarchan poets to today's self-proclaimed victims of political correctness—"so eager to claim a share in the victimhood sweepstakes? . . . To speak about female victimization is to imply that there is a model of male power and authority that is other than victimization," but perhaps this is not so. After all, the men in this movie are both depicted as in some sense powerless. "It is in this male two-step—the axe wielder plus the manipulative sufferer, *both* of whom see themselves as powerless—that patriarchal power lies." Victimhood, she suggests, may be the most effective "*model* for authority, particularly literary and cultural authority. . . . The most highly valued speaker gets to claim victimhood" (*FD*, 153).

Several features of this essay are salient for me. First, in contrast with Brooks it marks the remarkable insights and the concomitant changes that feminism has brought to criticism and theory. But for Johnson it is not a matter of condemning the works of the literary tradition, much less of declining to read them, but of examining the gendered scenarios that they deploy and that can be exposed by critical readings drawing on the textual resources of these works. If we were reading Keats alone, her analysis might sound like simple condemnation, but that the "Ode on a Grecian

Urn" shares many of these structures with a work of a contemporary feminist filmmaker suggests that the situation is not a simple one—certainly not one where we can easily or pertinently separate the virtuous productions from the compromised.

Second—in contrast with Bush's essay on Marvell with which I began—this reading does not use nonliterary materials as documents to shed light on or to explain for us the literary work. Whether we are talking about movies, reviews and critical articles, or letters to the editor, these are all texts that have to be read, with the same kinds of techniques and attention—texts that share many of the same structures. This is in part because, as Johnson shows, reading or interpretation involves not so much judgment from a position of exteriority to the work being read as a repetition and displacement of the scenarios that structure the work and through which it draws in its readers. Thus the question of "muteness, muteness, who's got the muteness," as Johnson puts it, moves through the dramas of our culture.

Third, I want to note Johnson's development of what in de Man we encountered as the aporia of the rhetorical question, where it was structurally impossible to opt for one reading or the other because to generate one reading, one had to assume a principle that the reading denied. Here we have a similar case of structural undecidability, between violation and pleasure, but it is even more evident that we have to choose one or another: readers cannot just remain neutral. The undecidability here stems from the possibility of focusing on the subjectivity of the characters or on the objectivity of the framework: any attempt to sustain one interpretation will encounter compelling objections from the other perspective. What in de Man seems to appear as a property of language emerges here more as a feature of the relations between levels of the work and of readers' necessary interpretive investments.

Finally, I want to single out what is for me the most powerfully seductive feature of this mode of writing criticism. I would love to write like Barbara Johnson but cannot manage it. She is the supreme master of the short critical essay, able to go straight to the heart of the matter with a telling example, and then jump to another example that confirms but neatly, elegantly advances the argument—like the brief turn to Lacan. Even when, with little space, I tell myself that I must try to write like Johnson,

I find I can't do it. I always feel I have to give more background (explain who Cromwell is, what Marvell's "Horatian Ode" is about, for instance) or try to argue that the example I am offering is representative and not special pleading—an issue that bothers her not at all. She skips all the background, the filling, the justifications, judging (rightly, I think) that if readers do not find her example telling, a paragraph claiming its representativeness will not help.

And she achieves great economy by using questions—"How does the maiden's struggle to escape congeal into an aesthetic triumph?"—letting the reader try to answer rather than herself laboriously filling all this in. There is a spareness and incisiveness to this writing that leaps daringly from the single example to the general proposition. That structure of argumentation—nothing could be farther from the idea of heaping up evidence until you have proved your point—marks this criticism as speculative and as theory, though it works by reading little bits of texts, always key texts that bring some interesting twist to the argument. Can this be a paradigm for the future of criticism? Since it's damnably hard to imitate it, probably not, but it alerts us to changes in what might be demanded in the discipline and provides a horizon toward which one might aspire in writing criticism.

11

Doing Cultural Studies

Cultural studies has become established as a category in bookstores and publishing in the United States and thus has come to count as a field—at least in American publishing and intellectual life.[1] It is worth reflecting for a moment on what makes something count as a field, for cultural studies does not yet have much of an existence in institutional structures. There are very few departments of cultural studies and not many institutions where it is possible to take a BA or a PhD in cultural studies.[2] But

1. See, e.g., the argument of the editor-in-chief at Routledge, William P. Germano, "Why Interdisciplinarity Isn't Enough," in *The Practice of Cultural Analysis*, ed. Mieke Bal (Stanford, CA: Stanford University Press, 1999), 326–34.

2. New York University has inaugurated a Department of Social and Cultural Analysis,

which will explore the range of relationships between human collectivities, on the one hand, and institutions and structures of power, on the other. In large measure, then, it will take up issues rendered salient within 'cultural studies,' pursuing them with a degree of analytical rigor that reaches beyond prior achievements in that field. Specifically, the Department will combine theoretical insights from feminism, critical race theory, and social geography with research methods derived from the social sciences and the humanities. To be included among its objects of study are consumer culture, industrial production, urban life, mass media representations, artistic expressions, oppositional subcultures, and aspects of everyday life in their economic, material, political, and historical contexts. ("Proposal for New Department of Social and Cultural Analysis," New York University, Faculty of Arts and Science, 2005, 1)

This department will serve as an umbrella organization for already-existing programs in Africana Studies, American Studies, Asian/Pacific/American Studies, Gender and Sexuality Studies, Latino Studies, and Metropolitan Studies.

for scholars, as for publishers, it counts as a field. Fields may have an institutional reality, but they have above all an imaginary existence, as phantasmic objects with which people identify. Bookstores, journals, and especially publishers play a role here. By publishing and displaying engaging books under the rubric of cultural studies, they create the desire and the identifications that make the field a force to be reckoned with, even if it is not realized in educational institutions. These same cultural agents helped to make "theory" a significant field, even though there remain to this day very few programs in theory or degrees in theory.

It is understandable that publishers would be attracted to the idea of cultural studies since this category, born of an impatience with disciplinary boundaries, enables them to avoid deciding whether a work should be placed under the heading of sociology or film theory or women's studies or literary criticism, or all of the above, and to hope that it will appeal to students from many departments. But despite the shelves in bookstores and the recent proliferation of introductions and anthologies, it is surprisingly difficult to work out what "cultural studies" means. Routledge's classic *Cultural Studies*, edited by Larry Grossberg, Cary Nelson, and Paula Treichler, begins by declaring that cultural studies is neither a field or a method, for culture includes everything and can be studied by a vast range of methods. Cultural studies is "an interdisciplinary, transdisciplinary, and sometimes counterdisciplinary field that operates in the tension between its tendencies to embrace both a broad, anthropological and a more narrowly humanistic conception of culture."[3] This is a rather strange, grammatically convoluted statement: notice that it declines to say "the tension between the broad conception and the narrow conception," or even "the tension between the tendency to embrace the broad conception and the tendency to embrace the narrow conception," although that is what the sentence must mean. It avoids this, I dare say, because that would seem too much like a binary opposition, a situation of either/or. Eschewing a structure that would present the possibility of choice, the statement locates the field "in the tension between its tendencies to embrace both . . . "

"Cultural Studies," the introduction continues, "is thus committed to the study of the entire range of a society's arts, beliefs, institutions, and

3. Larry Grossberg, Cary Nelson, and Paula Treichler, eds., *Cultural Studies* (New York: Routledge, 1992), 4.

communicative practices."[4] No question of choosing here. Often the point of cultural studies seems to be to resist any exclusion that definition might involve. Its defining principle is to resist exclusion on principle, as a matter of principle. As a result, it often seems as if the only positive claim is that whatever is studied and by whatever method, cultural studies should aim to make a political difference. "Cultural studies thus believes," the editors write, "that its own intellectual work is supposed to—can—make a difference."[5] Once again the ways this odd statement trips itself up may be revealing: cultural studies does not believe that its intellectual work *will* make a difference. That would be overweening, not to say naive. It believes that its work "is supposed to" make a difference. Perhaps sensing that this is scarcely a credo to energize a field—"I believe that my work is *supposed to* make a difference!"—the editors insert a parenthetical "can," but the distinguishing feature of cultural studies may well in fact be the conviction that its work is *supposed to* make a political difference. It is as though the redemptive goals that have often animated work in the humanities have been retained by cultural studies, but that the idea that this goal is linked either to a particular content (literature will make us whole again) or to a particular method (critique will demystify ideology and make change possible) has been abandoned. But a redemptive scenario that lacks either a distinctive content or a particular method for which claims could be made is scarcely plausible. A strange result indeed!

Culture is on the one hand the system of categories and assumptions that makes possible the activities and productions of a society and on the other hand the products themselves, so the reach of cultural studies is vast. But since meaning is based on difference, cultural studies in practice has gained its distinctiveness from the interest in popular or mass culture, as opposed to high cultural forms already being studied in universities—illogical as this may seem. In the United States identifying with cultural studies seems to mean resisting literary studies. Bill Germano, whose Routledge volumes did much to define the field, notes that to do cultural studies means not to study canonical writers.[6] Literary studies is one orthodoxy against which cultural studies defines itself.

In Britain, where cultural studies began, the idea of studying popular

4. Ibid.
5. Ibid., 6.
6. Germano, "Why Interdisciplinarity Isn't Enough," 331.

culture—the habits and pastimes of the working and lower-middle classes, for example—had a political charge. Cultural studies was the relay of proletarian experience. In Britain, where the national cultural identity was linked to monuments of high culture—Shakespeare and the tradition of English literature, for example—the very fact of studying popular culture was an act of resistance, in a way that it is not in the United States, where national identity has often been defined *against* high culture. Jackson Pollock could be hailed as the great American painter because he departed in so many ways from the image of high culture.[7] Perhaps *Huckleberry Finn* seems the great American novel—the work that does as much as any other to define Americanness—because at the end Huck lights out for the territories because Aunt Sally wants to "sivilize" him. He seeks to escape civilized culture. High culture has not been part of the definition of national identity in the United States. *Au contraire*, traditionally, the real American is the man on the run from culture. In the United States it is scarcely self-evident that shunning high culture to study popular culture is a politically radical or resistant gesture. On the contrary, it may involve the rendering academic of mass culture more than the radicalizing of academic studies. If this is so, then it is all the more important for cultural studies to retain its nonacademic connections and to continue to move back and forth across the boundaries of the university.[8]

The origins of cultural studies in Britain are associated particularly with Raymond Williams and Richard Hoggart, the latter the founder of the Birmingham Center for Cultural Studies. In 1980 Stuart Hall, Hoggart's successor at Birmingham, published an article, "Cultural Studies: Two Paradigms," contrasting the early model of Williams and Hoggart, which undertook to study popular culture as a vital expression of the working class, with a later model—of Marxist structuralism—which studies mass culture as meanings imposed on society, an oppressive ideological formation.[9] The tension between these two options continues to animate cultural studies today: on the one hand, the point of studying popular

7. See Griselda Pollock, "Killing Men and Dying Women: Gesture and Sexual Difference," in Bal, *The Practice of Cultural Analysis*, 86.

8. See Jon Cook, "The Techno-University and the Future of Knowledge: Thoughts After Lyotard," in Bal, *The Practice of Cultural Analysis*, 303–24.

9. Stuart Hall, "Cultural Studies: Two Paradigms," *Media, Culture, and Society* 2 (1980): 57–72.

culture is to get in touch with what is important for the lives of ordinary people—their culture—as opposed to what is important for aesthetes and professors; on the other hand, there is a strong impetus to show how people are being constructed and manipulated by cultural forms. There is considerable tension here—so much so that I find it tempting to define the field of cultural studies by this tension (more pertinent than the tension between the tendencies to embrace both the broad and narrow conceptions of culture that Grossberg and his colleagues mention). Cultural studies dwells in the tension between, on the one hand, the analyst's desire to analyze culture as a hegemonic imposition that alienates people from their interests and creates the desires that they come to have and, on the other hand, the analyst's wish to find in popular culture an authentic expression of value. If one takes this tension to define cultural studies, then the central strand of cultural studies would be that which finds a way of negotiating this tension, most often these days by showing that people are able to use the cultural materials foisted on them by capitalism and its media and entertainment industries to produce a culture of their own. Popular culture is made from mass culture. Popular culture is made from cultural resources that are opposed to it and thus is a culture of struggle, a culture whose creativity consists in using the products of mass culture. Defining cultural studies as the negotiation of this tension makes it a narrower and graspable project—so much so that it has the air of a project or particular line of argument rather than a field—but would make it a great deal easier to decide, if that seemed important, what is cultural studies and what is not: what belongs instead to sociology or film studies or literary criticism.

A narrow definition could, then, situate the field in the tension between the critique of mass culture as ideology and the celebration of popular culture as the resistance to the hegemony of capitalism, but if one resists such narrowing there remains the larger question of whether cultural studies is supposed to study all culture, of the past as well as present, high as well as low, or whether it focuses on the present and the popular, in contradistinction to traditional forms of study. There is, of course, a great deal of historical work that investigates the culture, broadly conceived, of past societies, to wit "the entire range of a society's arts, beliefs, institutions, and communicative practices."[10] It is hard to imagine any historical study that would not qualify as cultural studies by this definition, but clearly assimi-

10. Grossberg, Nelson, and Treichler, *Cultural Studies*, 4.

lation to the traditional domain of history is not what denizens of cultural studies have in mind, so there must be some crucial distinguishing factor. One version, which the Amsterdam School of Cultural Analysis calls "cultural analysis" rather than cultural studies, would make the distinguishing factor the reflection on the constitution of the past, the reflection on our own implication in the object of analysis.[11] There is also the key question of whether cultural studies is opposed to contemporary theory or, on the contrary, the concrete expression of contemporary theory. Some students who embrace cultural studies—particularly the study of historically marginalized cultures—see themselves as opposed to theory and as the champions of historical and cultural particularity. I am struck by the fact that Bill Germano accepts theory as one field and cultural studies as another, even though his description of the modes of cultural studies—work engaged with race, gender, postcoloniality, hybridity, feminism, queer theory, film, and cyberspace—adduces many theory-laden fields. And it is clear that, even if the proponents of cultural studies identify against "theory," the majority of work that presents itself as cultural studies is highly theorized—self-conscious about and involved with theoretical and methodological questions—and I suspect that the link with theory is where factors distinguishing cultural studies from historical studies might be found.

In fact, the notion of *text*, a theoretical concept articulated in French theory of the 1970s (as discussed in Chapter 4), was explicitly interdisciplinary and opened new possibilities of analysis for cultural objects and practices of all sorts, from Balinese cockfights to French films. As Fredric Jameson writes in *The Ideologies of Theory*, "Textuality may be rapidly described as a methodological hypothesis whereby the objects of study of the human sciences are considered to constitute so many texts that we *decipher* and *interpret*, as distinguished from older views of these objects as realities or existents or substances that we in one way or another attempt to *know*."[12] The theoretical concept of text brought to cultural studies the presumption that items under consideration cannot be taken as given— one must consider how they come to be produced, isolated, presented to attention—and that the analyst's methods and standpoint need to be considered in the process of treating the objects of study themselves.

11. See Mieke Bal, introduction to *The Practice of Cultural Analysis*, 12.

12. Fredric Jameson, "The Ideology of the Text," in *The Ideologies of Theory* (Minneapolis: University of Minnesota Press, 1987), 18.

When thinking about the relation between cultural studies and "high theory," as it is sometimes called, especially by the partisans of cultural studies who perhaps are seeking to distinguish themselves from theory in the hope that this, at least, will give their field an identity, I am struck by the idea that the difficulty of defining cultural studies is analogous to the difficulty of defining what we call just "theory" for short. What is theory? What goes by the nickname "theory" in the United States is sometimes called "literary theory" because of its links with departments of literature, but it is certainly not theory of literature in the traditional sense—accounts of the nature of literature, the distinctiveness of literary language, and so on. Much of what is central to theory—the historical and genealogical studies of Michel Foucault, the psychoanalytic theory of Jacques Lacan, the deconstructive readings of philosophical texts by Jacques Derrida—and so on, is only marginally concerned with literature. Like cultural studies, theory is broad, amorphous, interdisciplinary. You can imagine almost anything fitting in if it is done in an interesting way. It is difficult to say that any particular discourse is in principle excluded from theory because what makes something theory, as I have suggested, is that it is taken up as interesting and suggestive for people working outside the discipline within which it arises. So discussions of perspective or of madness, of rubbish or tourism or prostitution can all enter theory if they seem to have implications for people in other fields, for their thinking about signification and the constitution of subjects. Indeed, if we ask what so-called theory is the theory of, the answer can only be something like signifying practices in general, the constitution of human subjects, and so forth—in short, something like culture, in the sense that it is given in cultural studies. My second proposal, then, is that cultural studies is—or should be conceived as—the general name for the activities of which what we call "theory" for short is the theory. Cultural studies can be the study of anything whatsoever, when it is made theoretically interesting. There is therefore a need for a certain surprise, which is hard to theorize and, as the field grows older, hard to achieve.

If cultural studies is the practice of which what we call "theory" is the theory—and I think that this certainly makes sense—then the question becomes not one of the general relationship of cultural studies to theory but, rather, a question of the benefits and virtues of various theoretical discourses for the study of particular cultural practices and artifacts. I think that this would be a beneficial sort of debate, for too often these days in the United States, at least, argument about theoretical discourses or approaches is carried on not in relation to particular sorts of cultural practices but as an abstract evaluation that often appeals to general theoretical and especially political consequences. A certain theoretical orientation, it is claimed, does not grant enough agency to subjects, or that approach makes it difficult for people to convince themselves of the groundedness of their identities, and so on. And because this has been the focus of theoretical debate, there has been too little attention to whether particular theoretical orientations or discourses help to achieve convincing results in the analysis of cultural systems.

So far I have offered two hypotheses about what is cultural studies: the first, the narrow, is that cultural studies investigates how people make popular culture from mass culture; the second is that cultural studies is that practice of which what we call "theory," for short, is the theory. But when I think of my own work, a third hypothesis arises, to set alongside these other two. There are several instances in my book *Framing the Sign* where I am inclined to class what I have written as cultural studies rather than literary criticism or theory. The first is a chapter called "Literary Criticism and the American University," which attempts to analyze the imbrication of developments in criticism with the structures of professional life and to identify models that underlie and make possible this development.[13] Then there are essays on junk and rubbish and on tourism, which, although using some discussions of these topics in literary works, are not focused on literature but seek to identify structures that underlie the articulation of the social. For instance, in the chapter on rubbish I am interested in the mechanisms for the establishment of value, particularly the interplay between two incompatible systems, the system of transience (things that have value when new and gradually lose it) and the system of durables (things presumed to have stable or even increasing value). Junk or rubbish is analyzed as the point of intersection and exchange between these two systems.[14] In the discussion of tourism I focus on the intelligibility of the world that emerges through the agency of the generally denigrated figure of the tourist, who not only seeks in unusually explicit fashion

13. Jonathan Culler, *Framing the Sign* (Oxford, UK: Blackwell, 1988), 3–40.
14. Ibid., 168–82.

signs of Frenchness and so forth but also, in a dialectic crucial to modern life, tries to see something of the "real Italy," to get off the beaten track, as we say, and experience an authenticity defined in opposition to the explicitly touristic.[15]

Now when I ask what makes these essays seem to exemplify cultural studies rather than something else, I conclude that it is the attempt to identify underlying signifying structures, general semiotic mechanisms at work here. I am led to the hypothesis that cultural studies is (or should be) structuralism, that crucial enterprise that has been unfairly, in my view, shunted aside, especially in the United States, in that enthusiasm for the new that generates "poststructuralism." Since what we call "theory" is generally linked with *post*structuralism, one might imagine that the inclination of people in cultural studies to dissociate themselves from theory might be the displaced form of a return to the analytical projects of structuralism, which sought to help us understand the mechanisms that produce meaning in social and cultural life.

I should add here that if cultural studies is structuralism, it would be a structuralism crucially informed by the work of Michel Foucault. Foucault claimed not to be a structuralist, but this claim was belied by his work: to study the discourses (such as those of sexuality) that construct the categories they then treat as natural is a quintessentially structuralist project, constructed on the paradoxes of structuralism. (Language consists of signs but signs are the categories produced by languages, for example.) And the Foucauldian claim that power is not something one possesses but the name of a configuration of relations in a given state of society is a structuralist hypothesis of a classic sort.

I would also note that although poststructuralism caricatures structuralism as blindly scientistic, in fact structuralist works frequently foreground the move, which should be part of cultural studies, of recognizing that your analysis is conditioned by your own place in the present and is thus involved in that which it seeks to analyze. So Lévi-Strauss, the archstructuralist whom no one ever called poststructuralist, concedes that his massive *Mythologiques* is a myth of mythology.[16] Roland Barthes suggests that his breaking up of the text to identify five codes in *S/Z* is, finally, ar-

15. Ibid., 153–67.

16. Claude Lévi-Strauss, *Mythologiques*, vol. 1, *Le cru et le cuit* (Paris: Plon, 1964), 14.

bitrary, and he also declares that "la littérature c'est ce que s'enseigne. Un point. C'est tout" [Literature is what is taught, period].[17] Literature is not something existing out there that the critic proceeds to study; it is the product of that academic discursive practice in which he is himself engaged.

This, then, is my third hypothesis: cultural studies is really a disguised return to the uncompleted projects of structuralism, a return that highlights some aspects of structuralism that have been neglected. But I daresay that this hypothesis will be even less popular than the other two.

Why should cultural studies be a growth area in the humanities? In a sense its emergence, at least in the United States, seems a logical result of the extension of literary methods of analysis to a wide range of nonliterary objects and texts. But I want to conclude with a more general question about the emergence of cultural studies, developing some of the ideas of Bill Readings, a brilliant young critic who was tragically killed in a plane crash in the autumn of 1994. Readings had completed a book he called *The University Beyond Culture* but to which the publisher ultimately gave the more dramatic title, *The University in Ruins*.[18] He argues that cultural studies is made possible by a recent shift in the governing idea of the university. To put it most simply, Kant based the university on a single regulative principle, the principle of Reason. Humboldt and the German Idealists gave us the modern university by replacing the University of Reason with the University of Culture, an institution whose purpose was jointly teaching and research—an institution given its raison d'être by the production and inculcation of national self-knowledge, the formation of educated citizens imbued with a national culture. Here culture is the goal of the university: for instance, the reproduction of the man of culture instantiated in the professor—whence the possibility of such anecdotes as that of a dowager accosting an Oxford don during the first World War: "Young man, why aren't you in France fighting to defend civilization." "Madam," came the reply, "I *am* the civilization they are fighting to defend."

It was this notion of the university, the University of Culture, that

17. Roland Barthes, *S/Z* (Paris: Seuil, 1970), 20; and "Reflexions sur un manuel," in *L'Enseignement de la littérature*, ed. Serge Dubrovsky and Tzvetan Todorov (Paris: Plon, 1969), 170.

18. Bill Readings, *The University in Ruins* (Cambridge, MA: Harvard University Press, 1996).

gave literary studies the centrality that philosophy had enjoyed in the University of Reason. Cardinal Newman wrote in *The Idea of a University*, "[B]y great authors the many are drawn up into a unity, national character is fixed, a people speaks, the past and the future, the East and the West are brought into communication with one another."[19] The goal of the traditional university was not so much to promulgate the unity of knowledge (little promulgation of such unity took place) as to represent it: to represent it in its array of departments, in its degree courses, and so on.

With the globalization of capital, the importance of forming national subjects has diminished, the production of the cultured citizen, hitherto the goal of a liberal arts education, has become less central, and the University of Culture has given way, at least in the United States and the United Kingdom, to what Jon Cook calls the techno-university but what I, with Bill Readings, would prefer to call most simply the University of Excellence. The university has no particular goal, except to have its various parts functioning excellently—where excellence becomes a contentless measure permitting homogenization and bureaucratic control. All divisions of the university can be asked to demonstrate their excellence, and since this takes the form of ratings or rankings, they are all rendered comparable, even if they engage in radically different sorts of activities—advising students, maintaining buildings, raising funds, teaching history. The techno-university, as described by Jon Cook, appears to have some specific goals, such as processing the largest number of students. The University of Excellence need have no such specific or demeaning goals but is free to strive for excellence without defining it. In practice, excellence is connected with professionalization: you are judged by your peers, which means that excellence is determined by how you are rated by others.

When culture is no longer the goal or purpose of the university, it can become an object of study among others. As Readings claims, "the Human Sciences can do anything they like with culture, can do cultural studies, because culture no longer matters for the university."[20]

To flesh out this claim we might say that literature (and to a lesser extent history and art history) was previously the site where culture could be observed, assimilated, studied (and of course there were debates about

19. John Henry Newman, *The Idea of a University* (London: Longmans, Green, 1926), 193.
20. Readings, *The University in Ruins*, 91.

what precisely in literature was central to the production of cultured citizens). The rise of cultural studies is assisted by arguments that the notion of culture involved in taking literary study as the instrument of culture is elitist and by recent analyses of the nationalist projects of literary studies. These have helped fuel the move to cultural studies, but cultural studies will not replace literary studies at the center of the university's idea of itself because cultural studies is not based on a project of forming cultured citizens in a non-elitist way. Sometimes in the United States cultural studies *is* linked to the idea of forming a nonracist, nonhomophobic, multicultural citizenry, but generally this is not the impetus, both because the idea of forming a citizenry seems nationalist and totalizing and because practitioners of cultural studies think that their political intervention will occur at some other level or through some agency other than that of their students (they may believe "that their work is supposed to—can—make a difference" in other ways). The formation of citizens is no longer the project of the university. A few conservatives pretend to argue for the return to the cultivation of traditional subjects, but even they have given up the idea of a national culture as community and are willing to settle for something like what E. D. Hirsch called "cultural literacy," common information.[21] It is not that people need to have read certain works in order to be educated citizens: they must recognize their titles and other cultural references so that they can be the audience addressed by newspapers and the media. Culture as common information reinforces administrative authority (of those who select, transmit, and test this information), whereas culture as shared texts might actually encourage possibilities of thought—at least in the sense of challenging what those texts are usually taken to mean.

Now that the goal of the production of national subjects is no longer central, it is perfectly all right for academics in universities to analyze and to teach all sorts of cultural materials and practices. This is not necessarily subversive. It feeds right into the culture industry and even constitutes something like its exotic arm. The American press is amused by cultural studies and likes to run stories about academics writing about Madonna, *Star Wars*, or cereal boxes. Cultural studies can thus be a continuation of journalism that contributes to the general disdain for academics, who are thought to make a complicated fuss about things that really should simply be consumed.

21. E. D. Hirsch, *Cultural Literacy: What Every American Needs to Know* (Boston: Houghton Mifflin, 1987).

It seems desirable to imagine, therefore, a version of cultural studies that would not define itself against literary studies or against so-called high theory. The term used in the Amsterdam School for Cultural Analysis and the NYU Department of Social and Cultural Analysis—"cultural analysis"—seems a good one.[22] Cultural analysis is not engaged in a battle against literary studies. It is not focused primarily on popular culture or on the present. But cultural analysis therefore needs something else to give it definition, and it finds this in a particular sort of theoretical engagement: its reflection on the way in which its own disciplinary and methodological standpoints shape the objects that it analyzes.

But rather than introduce a new term, *cultural analysis*, while leaving *cultural studies* alone, it seems more desirable to try to argue for a cultural studies that is not defined by commitment to popular rather than high culture or to the present rather than the past. After all, every discipline should reflect on itself and how it constructs its objects of analysis, so this should not become a way of differentiating a rigorous, self-conscious cultural analysis from cultural studies.

Barbara Johnson's "Muteness Envy," discussed in Chapter 10, is a prime example of a cultural studies that is not opposed to literary studies (the most canonical of literary works, Keats's "Ode on a Grecian Urn" provides the point of departure and constant point of reference for Johnson's investigation of a pervasive cultural structure) but that also reads nonliterary cultural practices, such as film and journalism. The goal of Johnson's analysis is an understanding of this trope of female muteness and of general structures of victimhood as sources of political and cultural power, so it is certainly analysis that is supposed to—can—make a difference. It seems to me exemplary, not only of the possibilities of literary criticism today, as I argued in Chapter 10, but also of a cultural studies that does not think it necessary to define itself against high culture and that can draw freely on the discourses of so-called high theory in its explorations of foundational cultural structures.

A second suggestion is offered by Mieke Bal in *The Practice of Cultural Analysis*. Focusing especially on the construction of cultural objects, Bal proposes that the practice of museums might be taken as a general

22. See Bal, *The Practice of Cultural Analysis*; and Mieke Bal, *Double Exposures: The Subject of Cultural Analysis* (New York: Routledge, 1996).

model for cultural analysis. One virtue of this suggestion is that it displaces the potentially paralyzing gesture of self-reflexivity into a feasible research project: the investigation of one's analytic activity as a social, institutional practice and as a form of exposition and presentation. This socializes the act of self-reflection, making some progress possible, though of course it does not avoid the final impossibility of accounting for oneself, of fully analyzing oneself analyzing. But instead of attempting to look inward and anxiously to seize one's assumptions, beliefs, and unspoken commitments as they flit past, one can attempt to examine the social practice in which one is participating.

There seems to me much to recommend the idea of taking the museum as paradigm and analyzing "apodeictic" discourse, as Bal calls it: the reflection on the historicity of one's discipline and standpoint, apodeictic practice should be part of every discipline, not something distinguishing cultural analysis from cultural studies generally. Literary studies, art history, sociology, and especially philosophy ought to do this too. But cultural studies, as the questioning of disciplinary identities and boundaries, seems particularly well placed to engage in the reflexivity that ought to characterize all disciplines.

Such an orientation would give cultural studies a contingent historical identity, related to the particular structures of academic disciplines in a changing university, allowing it to become something else, as it surely will, if it communicates its self-reflexivity to other disciplines. In the meantime, effecting a focusing of self-reflexivity certainly can create lively modes of analysis so that cultural studies can function as a site for imagination and perhaps, more specifically, as a rendering permeable of the boundaries of the university—whether it is the University of Culture or the University of Excellence, or something in between, or a university not yet imagined.

12

Comparative Literature, at Last

Like the linguistic sign, disciplines and departments have a differential identity: as Ferdinand de Saussure put it, "their most precise characteristic is that they are what the others are not."[1] Once upon a time, comparative literature focused on the study of sources and influence, bringing together works where there seemed a direct link of transmission that subtended and served to justify comparison. But then comparative literature liberated itself from the study of sources and influence and acceded to a broader regime of intertextual studies—broader but less well-defined, except differentially. In its recent history in the American academy comparative literature has been differentiated from other modes of literary study because it did not take for granted—as did the departments of English, French, Spanish, Italian, Chinese—that a national literature in its historical evolution was the natural and appropriate unit of literary study. Since comparative literature could not avoid the question, as the national literature departments could, of what sorts of units were most pertinent—genres? periods? themes?—comparative literature also became the site of literary theory, while national literature departments frequently resisted, or at least remained indifferent to, the sorts of theory that did not emanate from their own cultural spheres. Comparative literature was thus distinguished by its interest in addressing theoretical issues, as well as knowledgeably importing and exploring "foreign" theoretical discourses. It was where

1. Ferdinand de Saussure, *Course in General Linguistics*, trans. Wade Baskin (London: Peter Owen, 1974), 117.

those questions about the nature and methods of literary study begged in other literature departments were taken up, argued about, even made the focus of teaching and research.

If neither of these features suffices any longer to distinguish comparative literature, it is because so many people in other departments have jumped on these bandwagons, or gradually come around to the views of comparatists. Even the study of American literature, once committed to exceptionalism and totalization (Americanists had to have a theory about the nature and distinctiveness of American literature), is now in the process of reconfiguring itself as comparative American literatures. The question of comparative literature has become everybody's question or, in Haun Saussy's formulation, comparatists have become "universal donors."[2]

Whatever the reasons for the spread of these formerly distinctive features, comparative literature has triumphed, and one might therefore expect a triumphal tone to the 2004 report on the state of comparative literature.[3] But of course the spread of what once distinguished the field leads to a lack of distinctiveness and thus a crisis of identity, and the tone of Saussy's magisterial review of the history of the discipline is scarcely a triumphant one. For good reason: departments or programs of comparative literature have not reaped the benefits of this success. (Saussy fantasizes that people in national literature departments should have to pay a small tax to comparative literature each time they cite de Man, Said, Spivak, Auerbach, and so on, which would do wonders for the field.) Programs in compara-

2. Haun Saussy, "Exquisite Corpses Stitched from Fresh Nightmares: Of Memes, Hives, and Selfish Genes," in *Comparative Literature in an Age of Globalization*, ed. H. Saussy (Baltimore: Johns Hopkins University Press, 2006), 4. Saussy's title seems designed to prevent anyone from taking his essay as an authoritative report, though it is the core of the American Comparative Literature Association's 2004 Report on the State of the Discipline.

3. The by-laws of the American Comparative Literature Association mandate that a report be prepared every ten years. The 1993 report, "Comparative Literature at the Turn of the Century," was a collective document (though largely written by Charles Bernheimer) and published with sixteen responses or position statements as *Comparative Literature in the Age of Multiculturalism*, ed. Charles Bernheimer (Baltimore: Johns Hopkins University Press, 1995). The 2004 report, *Comparative Literature in an Age of Globalization*, avoids the appearance of consensus: the central portion written by Saussy alone is one of a dozen essays on aspects or problems of the field, published with various responses.

tive literature are still small or struggling, and we have to tell the very smart and interesting graduate students we admit, "Welcome to comparative literature, where we do not believe that the national literature is the logical basis of literary study, but be warned that while doing comp. lit. you also need to act as if you were in a national literature department so as to make yourself competitive for a job in one." Though comparative literature has triumphed, and many others are comparatists now, the jobs are still in the national language and literature departments.

If one took an intellectual rather than an institutional view, one should be pleased at this result. And it is worth noting that the triumph of comparative literature is similar to other triumphs that do not give cause for celebration. Theory has triumphed, in that it is everywhere these days—one need only sit on a hiring committee to see how far candidates have been influenced by theory, in the questions they are posing, in the references that are expected of them, even as people write books and articles declaring the passing of theory. Feminism, too, alleged to be dead, can be said to have triumphed in the academy, in that much of what feminist critics and theorists struggled for now goes without saying. Gail Finney notes that women students take for granted the equality sought by feminism. "They reject the label 'feminist' but have internalized the goals of the ideology."[4] This is an outcome, like the triumph of theory and the triumph of comparative literature, that one cannot *not* wish to have happened, though one still would rather that such triumphs gave more cause for joy and were not so easy to identify with the death of what has triumphed.

There is little joy in this ACLA report, though it is too disparate and dispersed for one to speak of any consistent tone or take. But for thinking about the state of the discipline or field of comparative literature, it is instructive to identify some contrasts with the previous ACLA report of 1993, "Comparative Literature at the Turn of the Century," which promotes two courses of action, each of which has a good deal to recommend it. On the one hand, it urges comparative literature to abandon its traditional Eurocentrism and turn global—an injunction entirely justified, both as a reflection of contemporary cultural realities and as a response to the growing understanding of how Western cultures have been determined by their relations to non-Western others. On the other hand, the 1993 report recom-

4. Gail Finney, "What's Happened to Feminism?" in Saussy, *Comparative Literature in an Era of Globalization*, 123.

mends that comparative literature turn from a concentration on literature to the study of cultural productions or discourses of all sorts. This, too, is a course for which a good case can be made. Scholars of literature have discovered that their analytical skills can shed light on the structures and the functioning of the wide range of discursive practices that form individuals and cultures; and comparatists' contribution to the study of philosophical, psychoanalytical, political, medical, and other discourses, not to mention film, conduct books, and popular culture, has been so valuable that no one could wish to restrict literature faculties to the study of literature alone. Treating literature as one discourse among others, as the report recommends, seems an effective strategy.

Each of these turns, then, can be amply justified, but the result of both moves together, going global and going cultural, is a discipline of such overwhelming scope that it no longer sounds like an academic field at all: the study of discourses and cultural productions of all sorts throughout the entire world. If one were creating a university from scratch, one could doubtless construct a large department of comparative literature charged with global cultural studies, but then the question of differential identity raises its head: would there be any other departments in the humanities to contrast with comparative literature? Would there be a need for music and art and literature and philosophy departments or departments to study different areas of the world, or would comparative literature in this new dispensation cover everything in the humanities and much of the social sciences?

As soon as one tries to think about the place of the new global and cultural comparative literature in the university, one wonders whether the 1993 report is less a proposal for the reform of a particular department or discipline than a recommendation for how literary and cultural studies in general should proceed. In fact, isn't this how things ought to be? Shouldn't a report on comparative literature project a future for the humanities? Comparative literature has functioned as a vanguard discipline in the humanities, open not only to various national traditions and their theoretical texts—Marx, Kierkegaard, Hegel, Nietzsche, Saussure, Freud, Durkheim, Wittgenstein—but also to experimentation with modes of critical engagement and critical writing, since there was no presumption that understanding a national literary tradition in its historical evolution was the overriding goal. Comparative literature has been where critical and theoretical interdisciplinary projects could be freely tried, with results that are exemplary for others and thus affect the direction of literary and cultural studies at large. But this success of comparative literature brings a loss of identity.

The most controversial topic in the Bernheimer report and the associated position papers was the role of literature in a comparative literature that was simultaneously going global and going cultural. In that report and the responses to it those of us who defended literature, or opined that the study of literature ought to retain a central place in comparative literature, were treated as retrograde by Charlie Bernheimer—who, in a fashion typical of him, disregarded everyone's comments to write just what he wished. Defenders of literature were treated as old fogies who were inexplicably resisting getting with the program. Close reading of literary texts in the original languages manifestly seemed dispensable to Bernheimer—not a necessary part of the new dispensation.

In my own response to the Bernheimer report I argued that as national literature departments have increasingly given a role to theory or, perhaps more accurately, allowed literary and cultural studies to reorganize themselves around questions that have emerged from theoretical debates rather than the conventional literary-historical periods, and as these departments have increasingly brought a wider range of cultural productions into their purview—not just film and popular culture but discourses of sexuality, the construction of the body, and the formation of national and cultural identities, for instance—they have become in effect departments of national cultural studies: English and American Studies, French Studies, German Studies, Hispanic Studies. The turn to culture makes sense for national literature departments: the division of literature by national or linguistic boundaries was always rather dubious, but such divisions are a very reasonable way of organizing the study of culture. Perhaps, as German literature departments turn to German cultural studies, French literature departments to French studies, the national names will finally represent fields that are more intellectually coherent. And as the national literature departments turn to culture, they will leave comparative literature with a distinctive role. If, having in large measure made possible the expansion of literary studies into cultural studies, comparative literature does not insist on claiming that field for its own, it might find itself with a new identity, as the site of literary study in its broadest dimensions—the study of literature as a transnational phenomenon. The devolution of other fields would have left it with a distinctive and valuable identity at last.[5] Comparative literature, as the site of the study of literature in general, would provide a home for poetics.

This does not mean that members of comparative literature departments should be discouraged from studying literature in relation to other cultural practices or even pursuing projects to which literature is only marginally related—far from it. As always, comparatists will participate in the most interesting methodological and theoretical developments in the humanities, wherever these take them. Since literature is not a natural kind but a historical construct, the study of literature in relation to other discourses is not only inevitable but necessary, but, as opposed to the other departments of the humanities, comparative literature would have as its central responsibility the study of literature, which could be approached in the most diverse ways.

My argument that comparative literature should accept the differential possibility that the evolution of literary and cultural studies has created, as the site for the study of literature as a transnational phenomenon, did not gain many adherents, and the question of what comparative literature should be has remained as much in dispute as ever, except insofar as we agree that it is the nature of comparative literature to be the site at which the most diverse options of the humanities contend—not just a discipline in crisis but by its very nature a site of crisis. It is striking, though, that since 1994 the sense of literature as under siege has somewhat abated. While the question of the role of literature in comparative literature was central to the 1993 report, in the 2004 report the place of literature no longer seems such a contentious issue. This might of course be because the proponents of cultural studies have won and so no longer need raise the issue, but then you would expect the partisans of literary study to be complaining that literature has been forced out of comparative literature, and that seems not to have happened. Haun Saussy, speaking of comparative

5. My comments are published in Bernheimer, *Comparative Literature in the Age of Multiculturalism*, 117–21.

literature as "comparisons with literature," presumes the centrality of literature, in the sense that comparative literature involves reading texts of diverse sorts but "reading literarily."[6]

One could say that while the legitimacy of comparative literature projects that do not involve literature has become established, the centrality of literature is not in question as it formerly was—if only by a swing back of the pendulum. This conclusion drawn from the 2004 report seems to me confirmed by observation: for instance, there is in the humanities manifestly an increasing interest in aesthetics, which for a while was a dirty word. In running a very broad search in comparative literature, which attracted applications from many candidates working in postcolonial studies, I was struck by the extent to which even dissertations that focus on social and political issues and would not need to address literature at all seem to include several chapters on Anglophone novelists—demonstrating that there has come into being a new hypercanon of Anglophone writers: Rushdie, Achebe, Walcott, Coetze, and others.[7] The role of literature in comparative literature seems very robust these days, even if literary works are frequently read symptomatically.

In fact, if there is an issue that emerges from the disparate essays that make up the 2004 report, it is not whether literary or cultural studies should predominate but how comparative literature should deal with "world literature." I emphasize that term, for the question is not whether we should study all the literatures of the world but about the stakes in the construction by comparative literature departments of "world literature," as displayed most concretely in world literature courses.

This returns us to the problem of comparability, to which the fate of comparative literature seems inexorably tied—testimony to the power of a name. As comparative literature liberated itself from a comparability based on attested relations of contact, thus on sources and influence, and acceded to a broader regime of intertextual studies where in principle anything could be compared with anything else, we began to hear talk of a "crisis of comparative literature," no doubt because of the difficulty of explaining the nature of the new comparability that served to structure and, in principle, to justify comparative literature as a discipline. This problem of

6. Saussy, "Exquisite Corpses," 23.

7. See David Damrosch, "World Literature in a Postcanonical, Hypercanonical Age," in Saussy, *Comparative Literature in an Era of Globalization*, 48.

the nature of comparability is certainly rendered more acute by the shift of comparative literature from a Eurocentric to a global discipline, though in some respects this has been concealed from us. There has been a phase, one might say, where the problem of comparability might apparently be set aside because a good deal of new work has focused on cross-cultural contacts and hybridity within postcolonial societies and within the literatures of colonizing powers. A lot of exciting work has, in effect, been a sophisticated modernized version of the study of sources and influences: insofar as comparative study addresses the diverse literary and cultural influences at work in Derek Walcott's *Omeros*, or Salman Rushdie's *The Satanic Verses*, or Ousmane Sembène's *Les bouts de bois de Dieu*, or Rodolpho Gonzalez's *Yo soy Joaquin*, comparison is based on direct cultural contacts and traceable influences. But in principle the problem of comparability remains unsolved and more acute than ever. What, in this newly globalized space, justifies bringing texts together?

World literature courses that bring together the great books from around the world seem to base comparability on a notion of excellence that resonates, for me at least, with Bill Readings's brilliant analysis of the "University of Excellence" in *The University in Ruins*, which I discussed briefly in Chapter 11. Kant gave us the model of the modern university organized by a single regulatory ideal, the principle of Reason. Humboldt and the German Idealists replaced the notion of Reason with that of Culture, centering the university on the dual task of research and teaching, the production and inculcation of national self-knowledge. But now the model of the University of Culture, the university whose task was to produce cultured individuals, citizens imbued with a national culture, has in the West given way. Today, says Readings, "No one of us can seriously imagine himself or herself as the hero of the story of the University, as the instantiation of the cultured individual that the entire great machine labors day and night to produce. . . . The grand narrative of the university centered on the production of a liberal, reasoning subject, is no longer readily available to us."[8] Similarly, whereas once we might have imagined the study of comparative literature as leading to the production of the immensely cultured individual—a Curtius or an Auerbach—who had mastered the literatures of Europe, now the subject is so large and so diversely specialized that no

8. Bill Readings, *The University in Ruins* (Cambridge, MA: Harvard University Press, 1996), 9.

such exemplar can exist. The best we can imagine are accomplished comparatists with very different interests and ranges of knowledge, who would all be excellent in their own ways. Thus, the University of Culture gives way to the "University of Excellence."

I am interested in the relation between the comparability of comparative literature and the "excellence" that serves as a standard of comparison in the University of Excellence. The crucial thing about excellence, Readings points out, is that it has no content (there need be no agreement about what is excellent).[9] In that sense it is like the cash nexus. It has no content and thus serves to introduce comparability and bureaucratic control. As Readings explains, "[I]ts very lack of reference allows excellence to function as a principle of translatability between radically different idioms."[10] The idea of excellence enables us to make comparable entities that have little in common as to structure or function, input or output. But that is only half of its bureaucratic usefulness. It also makes it possible to avoid substantive arguments about what teachers, students, and administrators should actually be doing. Everyone's task is to strive for excellence, however that might be defined. What is the relationship between the comparability of comparative literature and the comparability instituted by excellence, which, to sum up, has the following characteristics: (1) it purports to have content but actually does not; (2) it grants groups considerable freedom (it does not matter what you do so long as you do it excellently), which is crucial to bureaucratic efficiency; but (3) ultimately it is a mechanism for the reduction or exclusion of activities that do not succeed by this measure. How does the comparability of comparative literature compare with this?

The intertextual nature of meaning—the fact that meaning lies in

9. When Readings was working on this book, I was able to provide him with the example of Cornell's Department of Transportation Services (responsible for campus buses and parking), which had received an award for excellence from its professional organization, whatever that is—apparently for its success in discouraging parking on campus (success in "demand reduction," they called it), by increasing fees for parking permits and progressively eliminating convenient parking spaces. But it is not utterly impossible to imagine that excellence in this realm might have been assigned precisely the opposite content: excellence might consist of making it easier for faculty to park on campus, though I agree that this is not very likely.

10. Readings, *The University in Ruins*, 24.

the differences between one text or one discourse and another—makes literary study essentially, fundamentally comparative, but it also produces a situation in which comparability depends on a cultural system, a general field that underwrites comparison. The meaning of a text depends on its relations to others within a cultural space, such as that of Western European culture, which is in part why comparative literature has been so much inclined to remain Western and European in its focus. The more sophisticated one's understanding of discourse, the harder it is to compare Western and non-Western texts, for each depends for its meaning and identity on its place within a discursive system—disparate systems that seem to make the putative comparability of texts either illusory or, at the very least, misleading. What has made possible much recent work in comparative literature has been the identification, largely by postcolonial theory, of a general postcolonial context within which comparabilities can be generated.

What sort of comparability, then, could guide the transformation of comparative literature from a Eurocentric discipline to a more global one? There is a difficult problem here. On the one hand, as Natalie Melas argues, comparison such as justifies a discipline consolidates a standard or norm, which then functions to give value to works that match up to it and to exclude those that do not, so that comparison—the principle of comparability—rather than opening new possibilities for cultural value, more often than not restricts and totalizes it.[11] But, on the other hand, as we try to avoid this imposition of particular norms, we may risk falling into the alternative practice, which Readings's account of excellence describes, where the standard is kept nonreferential—vacuous—so that it is not imposing particular requirements but where in the end it provides a bureaucratic rather than an intellectual mechanism for regulation and control; and indeed the danger of world literature is that it will select what is regarded as excellent, without regard for the particular standards and ideological factors that might have come into play in the processes of selection.[12]

11. Natalie Melas, "Versions of Incommensurability," *World Literature Today* 69, no. 2 (spring 1995): 331.

12. In his superb book *Within the Context of No Context*, which deserves to be better known as a guide to our condition, George W. S. Trow identifies as a crucial though unrecognized watershed in the history of American modernity "the moment when a man named Richard Dawson, the 'host' of a program called *Family Feud*, asked contestants to guess what a poll of a hundred people had guessed

The problem of comparison is that it is likely to generate a standard, or ideal type, of which the texts compared come to function as variants. Comparatists today are eager to avoid this implicit result of measuring one culture's texts by some standard extrinsic to that culture. Yet the more we try to deploy a comparability that has no implicit content, the more we risk falling into a situation like that of the University of Excellence, where an apparent lack of concern for content—your department can do what it likes provided it does it excellently—is in the end only the alibi for a control based on bureaucratic rather than academic and intellectual principles.

The virtue of a comparability based on specific intellectual norms or models—generic, thematic, historical—is that they are subject to investigation and argument in ways that the vacuous bureaucratic norms are not. One solution, then, is to attempt to spell out the assumptions and norms that seem to underwrite one's comparisons so that they do not become implicit terms. A model here might be Erich Auerbach's conception of the *Ansatzpunkt*: a specific point of departure, conceived not as an external position of mastery but as a "handle" or partial vantage point that enables the critic to bring together a variety of cultural objects. "The characteristic of a good point of departure," writes Auerbach, "is its concreteness and its precision on the one hand, and on the other, its potential for centrifugal radiation."[13] This might be a theme, a metaphor, a detail, a structural problem, or a well-defined cultural function. One could imagine basing cross-cultural comparison on linking principles whose very arbitrariness or contingency will prevent them from giving rise to a standard or ideal type, such as comparing works by authors whose last name begins with *B* or works whose numerical place in a bibliography is divisible by thirteen. I confess, though, that this is scarcely the sort of thing Auerbach had in mind and not a general or principled solution to the problem of comparability. A

---

would be the height of the average American woman. Guess what they've guessed. Guess what they've guessed the *average* is" (George W. S. Trow, *Within the Context of No Context* [Boston: Little, Brown, 1981], 58).

13. Erich Auerbach, "Philology and *Weltliteratur*," *Centennial Review* 13, no. 1 (winter 1969): 15. I owe this reference to David Chioni Moore's stimulating discussion in "Comparative Literature to *Weltkulturwissenschaft*: Remedying a Failed Transition" (Southern Comparative Literature Association meeting, October 1994).

further possibility is to attempt to locate the comparative perspective geo-graphically and historically: instead of imagining the comparative perspective as a global overview, one might stress the value, for instance, of com-paring European literatures *from* Africa, for their relations to the cultural productions of a particular African moment. Better such points of depar-ture that impose criteria and norms than the fear that comparisons will be odious. The danger is that comparatists' fear—that their comparisons will impose implicit norms and standards—may give rise to a vacuousness that is as difficult to combat as is the notion of excellence that administrators are using to organize and reorganize the American university.

The 2004 report makes world literature a central problem of com-parative literature. The virtues and the difficulties of teaching what Djelal Kadir calls the "master construct" of world literature are vigorously de-bated by a series of contributors and respondents.[14] The charge, of course, is that world literature is constructed from the perspective of a hegemon-ic power, which admits representatives on the terms that it establishes in order to compose and compare, and that this is a McDonaldization, in which globalizing America colonizes various cultures, representing them by a bit of local flavor. Kadir cites the "risk of instrumentalizing the litera-ture of the world as objects of neocolonial usurpation and imperial sub-sumption."[15] Katie Trumpener, though, describing a Yale world literature course to which a lot of thought and a lot of faculty expertise has obviously been devoted, argues that one can avoid "a thematically driven, aestheti-cally and culturally flattened view of global texts" by focusing in a well-constructed course on, for instance, "questions of foundational violence, of the logic of feud, massacre, terror, and genocide, as well as the quasi-theological role of literature in mediating ideological shifts and historical

14.   Djelal Kadir in "Comparative Literature in an Age of Terrorism," in Saussy, *Comparative Literature in an Age of Globalization*, 75. The teaching of world literature is ably championed in the 2004 report by David Damrosch in "World Literature in a Postcanonical, Hypercanonical Age"; and by Katie Trumpener in her "World Music, World Literature: A Geopolitical View." Damrosch is editor of the leading anthology of world literature and author of *What Is World Literature?* (Princeton, NJ: Princeton University Press, 2003). The reservations expressed in the report by Haun Saussy and by Emily Apter in "Je ne crois pas beaucoup à la littérature comparée: Universal Poetics and Geopolitical Comparatism" are pur-sued most vigorously by Kadir.

15.   Kadir, "Comparative Literature in an Age of Terrorism," 75.

crisis, enacting conversions and convergence."[16] Concentrating on a number of major narratives, one can also focus on questions of genre, temporality, and narrative technique, consciousness, and perspective to prevent such a course from becoming an imperialistic sampling of national thematic flavors.

One can add that world literature is not just a construct of comparative literature departments, important though our role may be in articulating for a public of students and former students a world literature. Pascale Casanova's *La république mondiale des lettres*, recently translated as *The World Republic of Letters*, describes a world literary system as a set of discursive practices, a system of power/knowledge, in which literary works from around the world come to engage—with reviews, translation, prizes, cinematic adaptation—a system in which innovation has frequently come from the periphery and recognition emanates from various centers (especially, in her view, Paris).[17] So before we comparatists spend too much time and effort castigating ourselves for imperfectly and imperialistically homogenizing the literatures of the world into world literature, we should recall that such processes already take place in the world of literature and have done for a long time. If we prefer, we can think of ourselves as engaging critically, as Casanova thinks of herself as doing, with the world system of literature. Undertaking a critique of "world literature" may suit some more than constructing it. I have not been a partisan of the construction and teaching of world literature, but I do find Katie Trumpener's geopolitical view compelling—especially her concluding questions: "In some respects World Literature remains a daunting, perhaps impossible project. But if not us, who? If not now, when?"[18]

Why not now? If America has forfeited any possibility of claiming to survey judiciously the riches of world culture, our horrific role in the world gives us all the more reason to try to see to it that new generations of students have some knowledge of the complexity of the products of some foreign cultures. This is a teaching project more than a research project, though research in comparative literature can focus on theoretical questions about possible approaches to world literature, their dangers and vir-

16. Trumpener, "World Music, World Literature," 195–96.

17. Pascale Casanova, *The World Republic of Letters* (Cambridge, MA: Harvard University Press, 2004).

18. Trumpener, "World Music, World Literature," 198.

tues. But if it looks as though the field of comparative literature may in the coming years be in part defined by the problem of world literature, comparative literature should also be defined by those features that draw people to the field. And I imagine that this is not "world literature."

The attraction of the field for students and teachers has been tied, I believe, either to a polyglot experience or to an idea of cosmopolitanism. Some people who have lived multilingual, multicultural lives become comparatists because other choices would foreclose possibilities already available to them. American comparatists without a polyglot experience have been driven by a desire to avoid American parochialism, by an interest in other languages and cultures, especially European, both in relation to our own and in relation to the theoretical questions that arise in transnational literary or cultural study.

It is possible to take an interest in the literature of the world as a repertoire of possibilities, forms, themes, discursive practices: comparative literature, I have argued, is the right place, especially today, for the study of literature as a discursive practice, a set of formal possibilities, thus a poetics. But it is scarcely possible to take an interest in all the literatures *and* cultures of the world, so comparative projects are likely to remain driven by particular interests, animated on the one hand by singular knowledge, commitments, languages, and on the other by the general theoretical questions that arise when one reflects on one's interest in multiple kinds of texts. In an essay in the 2004 report entitled "Indiscipline" David Ferris remarks that comparative literature always seeks to incorporate what remains other to it; that inclination may be the force responsible for much of its peculiar history.[19] It is the combination of that comparative, lateral move with the *meta* move that is most distinctive of the discipline and that makes comparative literature, as Haun Saussy puts it, the "test bed for reconceiving of the order of knowledge."[20] As such reconceiving occurs, this should count as the triumph of comparative literature, though of course it will scarcely allow comparative literature to feel triumphant. As with theory, so with comparative literature: our triumphs seem destined to be triumphs without triumph.

19. David Ferris, "Indiscipline," in *Comparative Literature in the Age of Globalization*, 91–94.

20. Saussy, "Exquisite Corpses," 34.

Abbreviations and Short Titles

Atlas	*Atlas of the European Novel, 1800–1900*
AR	*Allegories of Reading: Figural Language in Rousseau, Nietzsche, Rilke, and Proust*
Bodies	*Bodies That Matter: On the Discursive Limits of "Sex"*
Claim	*The Claim of Reason: Wittgenstein, Skepticism, Morality, and Tragedy*
FD	*The Feminist Difference: Literature, Psychoanalysis, Race, and Gender*
Garden	*The Garden of Eden*
How	*How to Do Things with Words*
IC	*Imagined Communities: Reflections on the Origins and Spread of Nationalism*
IO	*Interpretation and Overinterpretation*
LI	*Literary Interest: The Limits of Anti-Formalism*
PD	*Playing in the Dark: Whiteness and the Literary Imagination*
PJ	*Poetic Justice: The Literary Imagination and Public Life*
RR	*The Rhetoric of Romanticism*
RT	*The Resistance to Theory*
Spectre	*The Spectre of Comparisons: Nationalism, Southeast Asia, and the World*
SCEP	*Seventeenth Century English Poetry: Modern Essays in Criticism*

Sources

The author would like to thank the following publishers for permission to reuse, often in substantially revised form, materials that have been published elsewhere:

Amsterdam School for Cultural Analysis, for "Text and Textuality," *Travelling Concepts: Text, Hybridity, Subjectivity*, ed. Joyce Goggin and Sonja Neef (Amsterdam: ASCA Press, 2001).

Cardozo Law Review, for "Resisting Theory," *Cardozo Law Review* 11 (July/August 1990).

Cornell University Press, for "Writing Criticism," from *Writing and Revising the Disciplines*, ed. Jonathan Monroe (Ithaca, NY: Cornell University Press, 2002).

Editions de l'Herne, for "L'Essential de l'arbitraire," from *Saussure*, ed. Simon Bouquet, *Cahiers de l'Herne* 76 (2003).

Duke University Press, for "Philosophy and Literature: The Fortunes of the Performative," from *Poetics Today* 21, no. 3 (fall 2000): 503–19.

The Johns Hopkins University Press, for "Anderson and the Novel," from *Diacritics* 29, no. 4 (1999): 20–39.

The Johns Hopkins University Press, for "Comparative Literature, at Last!" from *Comparative Literature in the Age of Multiculturalism*, ed. Charles Bernheimer (Baltimore: Johns Hopkins University Press, 1995).

Routledge/Taylor and Francis Group, LLC, for "The Literary in Theory," from *What's Left of Theory*, ed. Judith Butler, John Guillory, and Kendall Thomas (New York: Routledge, 2000).

The Board of Trustees of the Leland Stanford Junior University, for "Bad Writing and Good Philosophy," from *Just Being Difficult? Academic Writing and the Public Arena*, ed. Jonathan Culler and Kevin Lamb (Stanford, CA: Stanford University Press, 2003).

The Board of Trustees of the Leland Stanford Junior University, for "What Is Cultural Studies?" from *The Practice of Cultural Analysis*, ed. Mieke Bal (Stanford, CA: Stanford University Press, 1999).

Cambridge University Press, for "In Praise of Overinterpretation," from Umberto Eco, *Interpretation and Overinterpretation* (Cambridge, UK: Cambridge University Press, 1992).

Ohio State University Press, for "Omniscience," *Narrative* (January 2004).

Index

Cultural Memory | in the Present

Cecilia Sjöholm, *The Antigone Complex: Ethics and the Invention of Feminine Desire*

Jacques Derrida and Elisabeth Roudinesco, *For What Tomorrow . . . : A Dialogue*

Elisabeth Weber, *Questioning Judaism: Interviews by Elisabeth Weber*

Jacques Derrida and Catherine Malabou, *Counterpath: Traveling with Jacques Derrida*

Martin Seel, *Aesthetics of Appearing*

Nanette Salomon, *Shifting Priorities: Gender and Genre in Seventeenth-Century Dutch Painting*

Jacob Taubes, *The Political Theology of Paul*

Jean-Luc Marion, *The Crossing of the Visible*

Eric Michaud, *The Cult of Art in Nazi Germany*

Anne Freadman, *The Machinery of Talk: Charles Peirce and the Sign Hypothesis*

Stanley Cavell, *Emerson's Transcendental Etudes*

Stuart McLean, *The Event and its Terrors: Ireland, Famine, Modernity*

Beate Rössler, ed., *Privacies: Philosophical Evaluations*

Bernard Faure, *Double Exposure: Cutting Across Buddhist and Western Discourses*

Alessia Ricciardi, *The Ends Of Mourning: Psychoanalysis, Literature, Film*

Alain Badiou, *Saint Paul: The Foundation of Universalism*

Gil Anidjar, *The Jew, the Arab: A History of the Enemy*

Jonathan Culler and Kevin Lamb, eds., *Just Being Difficult? Academic Writing in the Public Arena*

Jean-Luc Nancy, *A Finite Thinking*, edited by Simon Sparks

Theodor W. Adorno, *Can One Live after Auschwitz? A Philosophical Reader*, edited by Rolf Tiedemann

Patricia Pisters, *The Matrix of Visual Culture: Working with Deleuze in Film Theory*

Andreas Huyssen, *Present Pasts: Urban Palimpsests and the Politics of Memory*

Talal Asad, *Formations of the Secular: Christianity, Islam, Modernity*

Dorothea von Mücke, *The Rise of the Fantastic Tale*

Marc Redfield, *The Politics of Aesthetics: Nationalism, Gender, Romanticism*

Emmanuel Levinas, *On Escape*

Dan Zahavi, *Husserl's Phenomenology*

Rodolphe Gasché, *The Idea of Form: Rethinking Kant's Aesthetics*

Michael Naas, *Taking on the Tradition: Jacques Derrida and the Legacies of Deconstruction*